MAKING THINGS HAPPEN

The Power of Christian Leadership

Bob Russell

 STANDARD PUBLISHING
Cincinnati, Ohio

Sections quoted from *Who Speaks for God* by Charles Colson are copyright 1985 by Charles Colson and used with the permission of Good News Publishers (Crossway Books).

Scripture quotations are from the HOLY BIBLE: NEW INTERNATIONAL VERSION, Copyright ©1973, 1978, 1984 International Bible Society. Used by permission of Zondervan Bible Publishers.

Library of Congress Cataloging-in-Publication Data

Russell, Bob, 1943-

  Making things happen.

  1. Bible. N.T. Acts—Sermons. 2. Christian Churches and Churches of Christ—Sermons. 3. Sermons, American. 4. Christian Leadership—Sermons. I. Title.
BS2625.4.R87   1987   253   87-13909
ISBN 0-87403-267-9

Copyright ©1987, The STANDARD PUBLISHING Company,
  Cincinnati, Ohio.
A division of STANDEX INTERNATIONAL Corporation.
Printed in U.S.A.

to the elders of
Southeast Christian Church,
who have exerted positive leadership.
Thanks for demonstrating
that the church can be a place
where exciting things can happen

Contents

Saul of Tarsus—Drafted for Service (Acts 9:1-19) 7
How to Treat a New Christian (Acts 9:19-31) 18
The Making of a Leader (Acts 11:19-30; 12:25—13:3) . . 28
When You Share Your Faith (Acts 13:1-13) 39
Keep Off the Pedestal (Acts 14:1-20) 52
When Christians Disagree (Acts 15:1-12, 36-41) 63
Understanding God's Will (Acts 16:1-10) 75
A Strategy for Battle, Part 1 (Acts 16:11-15) 87
A Strategy for Battle, Part 2 (Acts 16:16-34) 99
Coping With Jealousy (Acts 17:1-15) 112
Communicating Christ Effectively (Acts 17:16-34) 123
Dealing With Discouragement (Acts 18:1-11) 134
Revival in the Church (Acts 19:1-20) 146
What's Worship? (Acts 20:7-12) 158
Distinctives of Christian Love (Acts 20:17-38) 169
When God's Will Is Perplexing (Acts 21:1—23:11) 181
Responding to Anger (Acts 22:30—23:35) 193
Courage to Stand Alone (Acts 24:1-21) 205
A Profile of Procrastination (Acts 24:22-27) 216
A Reasonable Faith (Acts 25, 26) 223
Confidence That Inspires (Acts 27:13-26) 235
Faithful Unto Death (Acts 28:1-10) 246

Saul of Tarsus— Drafted for Service

Acts 9:1-19

IF YOU HAD met Saul of Tarsus in the first century, you would not have been impressed with his spiritual potential. Saul was absolutely hostile to Jesus Christ. He did everything he could to stamp out Christianity. Yet Saul became what A.W. Tozer calls "the world's most successful Christian." The apostle Paul carried the gospel to Asia Minor, Greece, and Rome. He established churches that became hubs of influence. He wrote 25% of the New Testament. His letters have had a profound effect on the world ever since the first century. This persecutor became a preacher of the gospel. This murderer became the most dynamic missionary the world had ever seen.

Paul Rees has said, "What Socrates is to philosophy and what Shakespeare is to literature, the apostle Paul is to the Christian faith." This book is about how Paul became a Christian and how he developed into the most outstanding leader the church has ever known. It will focus on the qualities that made Paul a real leader and let him serve as a model for us.

Luke repeats the account of Paul's conversion experience three times in the book of Acts, in chapters 9, 16, and 22. No other incident in the Bible has that kind of exposure, other than the crucifixion and resurrection of Jesus Christ. While most of us volunteer for Christian service, Paul was drafted into service because God needed him as a very special vessel. He went through a process that each of us needs to experience if we are going to be used by God, even though our experiences may not be as dramatic as that of Saul.

A Proud Man

If you were a Christian in the first century, it would have been difficult for you to love Saul. He was arrogant, ruthless, and mean-spirited.

He was proud of his *heritage*. I think Paul grew up in a rich, aristocratic family. In Philippians 4:12 he said, "I know what it is to be in need, and I know what it is to have plenty." His parents were evidently well off. Though they were Jewish, they were Roman citizens. They owned enough property to qualify for citizenship in Tarsus. Being a Roman citizen was a real status symbol and a cultural advantage in that day. Being Jewish, they named their son after King Saul of the tribe of Benjamin, but they also gave him a Roman name, Paulus.

In Acts 22, Paul gave a detailed biographical sketch of his life. "I am a Jew, born in Tarsus of Cilicia," he said. Tarsus was one of the three great university cities in that day—Athens, Alexandria, and Tarsus. That was like saying, "I grew up in Boston" or "I grew up in Berkeley"—one of the university centers of our day. Tarsus, Paul wrote, was no ordinary city. It was a special place.

Paul was also proud of his *education*. His parents could afford to send him away for the best of education in Jerusalem when he was just 15 years of age. Much later he would tell a crowd of hostile Jews, "[I was] brought up in this city [Jerusalem]. Under Gamaliel I was thoroughly trained in the law" (Acts 22:3). The school of Gamaliel was a respected school of that day.

Of all the apostles, only Paul was an intellectual. He was brilliant. He could speak several languages fluently. He was a prolific writer. Paul could go to Athens and debate the intellectuals; he could go to Corinth and speak the language of the Hedonists. He could go to Jerusalem and debate with theologians. He could get on board a ship and discuss weather and navigation procedures with the captain.

Once John Wesley received a note from a self-appointed evangelist: "The Lord has told me to tell you that He doesn't need your book learning, your Greek and your Hebrew."

Wesley replied, not too tactfully, "Thank you, Sir. Your letter was superfluous, however, as I already knew the Lord had no need of my 'book learning' as you put it. However, although the Lord has not directed me to say so, on my own responsibility I would like to say to you that the Lord doesn't need your ignorance either."

Saul of Tarsus was proud of his *intelligence*, and it blinded him to the truth. He was a brilliant man. The Lord needed an intellectual like Saul to advance the gospel. But there is a tremendous danger with intelligence—it may make us proud.

One insightful writer contributed this paragraph: "The greatest mistake of education has been to assume that intelligent people are automatically good thinkers. High intelligence does not insure effective thinking. It may actually make a person a poor thinker. For example, a highly intelligent person can take any view of a subject, then use his intelligence to defend that view. The more perfect the defense, the less chance the person has of exploring the subject. Other aspects of the intelligence trip include the need to be right; the need to show oneself to be more clever than others—critical rather than constructive thinking."

I think Saul was also proud of his *religion*. "If anyone else thinks he has reasons to put confidence in the flesh, I have more: circumcised on the eighth day, of the people of Israel, of the tribe of Benjamin, a Hebrew of Hebrews; in regard to the law, a Pharisee; as for zeal, persecuting the church; as for legalistic righteousness, faultless" (Philippians 3:4-6). Saul of Tarsus felt as if he was God's gift to the synagogue. He kept the law, he was a Pharisee, he was religious, and he was proud of his achievements.

Saul was an ambitious young man. He was one of those people who never does anything halfway. His goal was undoubtedly to become a member of the Sanhedrin, the 71-member Jewish court that ruled the nation. Gamaliel, his teacher, was a member of that elite group. Saul was determined to gain that kind of recognition and status, and that may be what drove him in this inquisition against the Christians.

We first read of Saul at the stoning of Stephen, the first Christian martyr. "The witnesses laid their clothes at the feet of a young man named Saul." When Stephen died, he said, "Lord Jesus, receive my spirit.... Lord, do not hold this sin against them" (Acts 7:58-60). I don't think Saul ever forgot how Stephen died. That death goaded his conscience and he kept trying to wipe it out by persecuting the church.

The Bible says Paul was breathing out murderous threats against the Christians. He gained permission to go to Damascus to chase them down. "I persecuted the followers of this Way to their death," Paul later said (Acts 22:4). He killed and tortured Christians. In Acts 26:11 he said, "Many a time I went from one synagogue to another to have them punished, and I tried to force them to blaspheme."

Most scholars believe that Saul's zeal would have achieved for him a position in the Sanhedrin. In Galatians 1:13, 14 Paul wrote, "I persecuted the church of God and tried to destroy it. I was advancing in Judaism beyond many Jews of my own age." To be a member of the Sanhedrin, you had to be 30 years of age and you had to be married. Chrysostom, an early writer, says that Saul was born in 2 B.C. and died around 66 A.D. He was just about the same age as Jesus. Many scholars believe that Paul was either a widower or that his wife left him when he became a Christian.

Saul was brought up proud and arrogant. We Americans are also a proud people. Our pride sometimes gets in the way of our faith.

Jess Moody says it goes all the way back to the frontier days. A swaggering cowboy wandered into a crowded blacksmith shop and picked a horseshoe up off the floor, not realizing that it was red hot. Immediately he dropped it, but he didn't rub his hand because he was too proud to admit that it had burned him.

Somebody said, "What's wrong, Zeke, too hot for you to handle?"

He said, "Nope, just doesn't take me long to look at a horseshoe!"

We are proud people. But the Bible says there are seven things God hates (Proverbs 6:16), and the very first one is "haughty eyes." You see, pride is concerned about sophistication and dignity, while God wants us to be submissive and teachable. Pride has a difficult time submitting. American Christians have a difficult time kneeling, or carrying a Bible, or taking notes in sermons, or being baptized, or singing enthusiastically, or doing hand motions to a song, because we are concerned about our dignity—our pride. But the Bible says that whoever exalts himself will be abased and whoever humbles himself will be exalted. "Before his downfall a man's heart is proud, but humility comes before honor" (Proverbs 18:12).

A Humbled Man

On the road to Damascus God humbled Saul abruptly. A.W. Tozer said, "It's doubtful that God uses anybody greatly before He hurts him deeply." Before God could use Saul He had to break his pride.

A bright light from Heaven flashed. This light was not lightning—it was Jesus appearing in His glory. When Jesus was on the mountain of transfiguration, His clothing became so dazzlingly bright that His disciples couldn't look at Him. When He rose from the dead, a bright light struck the soldiers to the ground. This same light knocked Saul to the ground.

There aren't many more humiliating experiences than to fall down or to be knocked down in front of people. God knocked Saul right down to the ground and buckled his pride. Sometimes you don't look up until you've been knocked down.

Then a voice thundered, "Saul, Saul, why do you persecute me?" Now this was not a word of conscience, but an audible voice. Paul said the men with him heard the voice, but they couldn't distinguish the words. Suddenly Saul has a submissive spirit. "Who are you, Lord?" (or 'sir' or 'your honor') he said. It is amazing how quickly a man can be humbled. Saul groveled on the ground—"Who are you?" he asked. The voice responded, "I am Jesus, whom you are persecuting." Can you imagine how Saul of Tarsus was taken aback? It's hard to admit that you're wrong. Saul had dedicated his life to wiping out Christianity, and now he had to admit that he was wrong.

My wife and I were once in Williamsburg, Virginia and we wanted to go to the ocean. I got on the interstate. She said, "You're going the wrong way."

I said, "We're going east, toward the ocean."

She said, "No, you are going west."

I said, "I know I'm going east."

"No, you're going west," she said.

We discussed that for a little bit until finally she gave up and said, "I'm just going to wait until you admit I told you so."

In another mile or so I saw a sign (she didn't see it) that said I was going west. I drove on another two or three miles thinking about how I could leave the expressway, buy gasoline, and get back on going in the opposite direction and lie about it so I wouldn't have to admit that I was wrong. But I finally had to say, "Well, you're right."

It's hard to admit it when you are wrong, but think how hard it would have been for Saul. He had been so outspoken. He had been vehement against Christianity. He had insisted there was no way Jesus of Nazareth was alive, and suddenly he heard, "I am Jesus, whom you are persecuting." Saul had to admit he was wrong.

God wasn't finished yet. Saul asked, "What do you want me to do?"

Jesus said, "Get up and go into the city, and you will be told what you must do."

When Saul got up and opened his eyes, he could not see. A physical handicap can humble you, and this blindness rendered Paul helpless—the Bible says he had to be led by the hand. This man who had come to Damascus so arrogantly, marching into Damascus to arrest the Christians, now had to grope for his way around. "For three days he was blind, and did not eat or drink anything" (Acts 9:9).

George Matheson suggests that Paul's "thorn in the flesh" he would write about later may have been partial blindness, poor eyesight. God reminded Saul throughout the rest of his life of this humbling experience. God has a way of breaking down our defenses. He can crush our pride in an instant.

When the Titanic was built, the builders boasted that even God couldn't sink it. But in April of 1912, on its maiden voyage, an iceberg cut a 300-foot gash in the side of that ship. It went down with 1500 people. The last song the orchestra played was, "Nearer, My God To Thee."

God can humble us like that too. The Bible says, "If you think you are standing firm, be careful that you don't fall!" (1 Corinthians 10:12). The death of a loved one, the loss of a job, the disappointment of a relative, the breaking of our health—just when we think we have it all together and we have really arrived—boom, He can wrench us to our knees. As we mature in the Christian life we shouldn't need a catastrophe to take us to our knees. The Christian ought to be a humble person all the time, submissive to the spirit of God.

Three things should keep us constantly humble. The first is exposure to other people. If you never travel, you can have a "backyard" mentality, but when you are exposed to other people, you realize that somebody always has more, somebody is always better, somebody is always bigger. My wife bought me a book called "The Twenty Largest Churches in the World," and it is humbling to realize that one church in Hammond, Indiana has 15,000 for Sunday school every Sunday. The largest church in the world is in Seoul, Korea. They have 500,000 members—a Christian church. When you hear about churches like these you realize your own church is pretty small.

One man was always boasting that he had been through the Johnstown flood. Every place he went he dominated conversations because he had survived the Johnstown flood. He died and went to Heaven and there he met Peter. He said, "Peter, I went through the Johnstown flood. I'd like you to get everyone together, because these people ought to hear about that."

Peter said, "That's fine, but just remember Noah will be in the audience." Exposure to other people ought to keep us humble.

The second thing that ought to keep us humble is the memory of past failures. How can we be proud when we remember the dumb things we have done in life? I have a habit of sticking my napkin under my belt when I eat. One afternoon I made four or five hospital calls and came back into the office. The secretary pointed to me and laughed. I looked down and read "Wendy's Hamburgers" right across my lap. But we have all done stupid things. When you remember the stupid things you have done, how can you be arrogant?

The third thing that keeps us humble is constantly comparing ourselves to Jesus Christ. That is the thing we do least and ought to do the most. When we open up God's Word and see how perfect Jesus was in attitude, word, and teaching, we can't help but say, "I am a wretched man, O Lord."

A guide was showing a tour through a famous art gallery. He pointed to a wastebasket in the corner and said, "That wastebasket is where aspiring young artists discard their paintings after they have looked at the works of the masters." When we look at the Master as He is portrayed in the Word of God, it is a humbling experience. We realize how short we fall.

Paul said in Philippians 3:8, 9, "I consider [all other things] rubbish, that I may gain Christ and be found in him." When we humble ourselves before Christ, it is not necessary for Him to strike us to the ground every day to be used by Him.

A New Man

God appeared to a Christian man named Ananias in Damascus. This must have been a startling conversation. The Lord called, "Ananias."

Yes, Lord.

"I want you to go ..."

Surely, Lord.

"to Straight Street ..."

I know where that is.

"the home of Judas ..."

All right ...

"and I want you to meet a man there who is praying."

Certainly.

"His name is Saul."

Wait a minute. Lord, I want to tell you about that man!

That's kind of presumptuous of Ananias, isn't it? Did he think the Lord didn't know? This guy has come to Damascus to persecute us. We are hiding from him!

The Lord simply said, "Go! This man is my chosen instrument to carry my name before the Gentiles" (Acts 9:15).

Since Paul was such a staunch Jew, you might think God would use him to be a missionary to the Jewish people, but God's ways are not our ways. God selected Saul to be a missionary to the Gentiles. God said he would appear before kings. God needed somebody with Saul's sophistication and intellect who could appear before Agrippa and Festus and Caesar. (One of them said on one occasion, "Paul, your great learning is driving you insane!")

"I will show him how much he must suffer for my name," God said (v. 16). We measure success in terms of accomplishments and status. God measures success in terms of sacrifices and crosses and scars. Ananias went as the Lord directed, and he found Saul blind and humbled. He said, "Saul, I have come first that you might have your sight restored, and second that you might receive the Holy Spirit."

He laid his hands on Saul, and the Bible says, "Something like scales fell from Saul's eyes." Then Saul got up and was baptized and began to eat and be strengthened.

Some people have overemphasized baptism to the place where if you can just get a person dunked, he's a Christian. Others have isolated baptism completely from the conversion process. Baptism was Saul's initial response to Christ. It was the point in time when his sins were washed away. Ananias said, "You will be his witness to all men of what you have seen and heard. And now what are you waiting for? Get up, be baptized and wash your sins away, calling on his name" (Acts 22:15, 16). Paul had already met Jesus on the Damascus Road. He had already submitted to Him as Lord, but Ananias said, "I want you to get up and be baptized to wash your sins away."

The Bible compares becoming a Christian to a new birth. When a mother conceives and says, "I am expecting," there is a time of rejoicing (most of the time) that a new life has begun in the womb. But later there is another time of great rejoicing when the baby is born. When we receive the word of Jesus Christ in our hearts, the Bible says we are "born again, not of perishable seed, but of imperishable, through the living and enduring word of God" (1 Peter 1:23). When a person says, "I believe in Christ; I am going to receive Him in my life," we rejoice that a new life has begun, but that person still needs to experience that birth process when he is born of water and of the Spirit, when he is baptized and washes his sins away. Baptism is not to be something that is tacked on later. It should be our initial response to Jesus Christ.

Jesus Christ made Paul a new man in a lot of ways. First He gave Paul a new *personality*. Paul had been proud and arrogant. Now he became a humble, submissive individual. He said things like, "I am the least of all the apostles" and "What a wretched man I am!" When you come to know Jesus Christ, He will give you a humble spirit in the place of pride.

If you are mature in the faith, you shouldn't be demanding center stage all the time. You won't get upset when somebody doesn't remember your name. You don't get all up tight if they don't know who you are and if you are not put in a place of prominence, because you have that humble, submissive spirit.

Second, He gave Paul a new *ambition*. Paul wrote, "Whatever was to my profit, I now consider loss for the sake of Christ.... I want to know Christ and the power of his resurrection and the fellowship of sharing in his sufferings, becoming like him in his death, and so, somehow, to attain to the resurrection from the dead" (Philippians 3:7, 10, 11). Paul was once concerned about status, prestige, and power in the Sanhedrin. Now he's just concerned about service, about going to Heaven when he dies and taking as many people as he can with him.

When you mature in Christ, He gives you a new goal. The accumulation of possessions and prestige isn't so important any more. You're concerned about the church and about going to Heaven.

Your friends will be dumbfounded. They will say, "You mean you gave your money away to build a new church building? You mean you're going to church rather than that party?" They will think you've lost it. But you have become new in Christ. The Bible says, "If anyone is in Christ, he is a new creation; the old has gone, the new has come!" (2 Corinthians 5:17).

Dale Evans, the wife of Roy Rogers, said, "All my life I searched for the pot of gold at the end of the rainbow, but I found what I really needed at the foot of the cross." Jesus Christ makes us new—He gives us a new personality and a new ambition.

These three questions are the most important questions you can ask in life. First, *Who are you, Lord?* Who is Jesus really? Is He the Son of God or is He an impostor? If you conclude that He's the Son of God, that question of identification becomes a question of *submission*. Second, *What do You want me to do?* That is the all important question of *obedience*. I will do what you want me to do. And the third question is a question of *action*. It was asked by Ananias. "*What are you waiting for?* Get up, be baptized and wash your sins away, calling on his name."

How to Treat a New Christian

Acts 9:19-31

IN MY SENIOR year at Bible college I met a tall, gangly basketball player from the University of Cincinnati. Neil stood 6' 11" tall and weighed only 190 pounds. He had been a high school All-American from New York state. We struck up an unusual friendship, not only because of the contrast in our height, but also the contrast in our moral values. I'd grown up in a Christian home and was studying for the ministry, but Neil had almost no Christian training or understanding. In fact he was one of the most foul-mouthed persons I had ever met. When we would meet to go to a basketball game, for the first ten minutes he would just spew out profanity until he would remember whom he was with.

About the only common interest we had was basketball, and we went to each other's games. But as that friendship grew, I invited Neil to go with me to the country church where I was preaching on weekends. He was an instant hit with the people because of his stature and they were an instant hit with him because they fed him every Sunday afternoon. He came with me several times and finally the basics of the Christian life began to sink in. I had opportunities to study the Bible with him seriously on several occasions. Then one Sunday morning in that country church,

Neil walked forward and gave his life to Jesus Christ.

His baptism was one of the most unusual I had ever participated in. The baptistery was right under the pulpit area—they moved the pulpit and opened the trap door. The candidate had to walk across the platform from the changing room. When Neil came out of the changing room, I could hardly keep from giggling. He had put on the longest robe we had and it still looked like a miniskirt. It came down to the middle of his thighs. He got into the baptistery and I baptized him in sections. I thought that I would never get him under the water. He probably thought I would never get him back up! But it was a great day of rejoicing as Neil gave his life to Christ.

About two weeks later, a group of us from the seminary were playing basketball at the local "Y." Neil was playing with us. He took an elbow to the ribs and winced with pain and let fly a four-letter word. He shouldn't have done that, but I was kind of proud of him because I had heard him use a lot worse than the one he selected! But one of the preacher boys stopped the game and put the ball under his arm and precisely intoned, "Well, is that any way for a Christian to talk?"

No, it wasn't. But it wasn't any way for a new Christian to be treated either.

That young preacher failed to understand where Neil was coming from. He failed to be sensitive to his needs at that moment. Henry Drummond wrote, "How many prodigals are kept out of the Kingdom of God by the unlovely character of those who profess to be on the inside?"

The Importance of Discipling New Christians

We can call it discipling, shepherding, nurturing, assimilating—it goes by a lot of different "buzz words" in Christian circles, but I am concerned that Christians be sensitive to the needs of new believers to help them mature in the faith. This is an important subject for a couple of reasons.

The first has to do with retention. We lose many Christian

people because they do not receive the proper nurturing. The average church loses 50% of its people after a five-year period. Some people just fall through the cracks. Others come and just remain on the fringe forever. Just about all of us who have been church members for some time can think of people who were once active in their fellowship but who drifted back into the same lifestyle that they had before. That's tragic.

Now that's not always the church's fault. Jesus compared teaching the Word of God to planting seed. He said some seed would fall into soil and would grow, but it would be choked out by thorns that represented the cares, the riches, and the pleasures of this life. Some people will be lost, and it is not the Lord's fault or the church's fault. They are just foolish, drawn away by the pleasures of this world. The church shouldn't incriminate itself because it doesn't have 100% retention. But some of the defections can be avoided if we do a better job of ministering to new Christians.

The good shepherd in Luke 15 counted the number of sheep in the fold. Ninety-nine out of one hundred were present. He didn't say that was a great percentage—he was concerned about the one that wasn't there. He risked his life to save the stray. We are not in the percentage business. People are important. Every new Christian needs to be nurtured.

The second reason has to do with opportunity. Jesus said, "Open your eyes and look at the fields! They are ripe for harvest." We need to be ready to nurture the new believers who come. It is not much value to bring in 100 new people a month if 100 leave out the back door. Christians need to get involved in the discipling of new people. I don't think we need an elaborate shepherding organization. Those are sometimes artificial and sometimes ineffective. The need is just for Christian people, individually, who will take it upon themselves to properly greet and treat new Christians.

Jesus' Great Commission says to every one of us, "Go and make disciples of all nations, baptizing them in the name of the Father and of the Son and of the Holy Spirit, and teaching them to obey everything I have commanded you." You will never grow as a Christian the way you will if you just gather a few new believers around you periodically and help to nurture them in the faith.

A Biblical Example of Typical Needs

Saul of Tarsus had not believed in the resurrected Christ until he met Christ on the Damascus road. He submitted himself to the Lord. He humbled himself, he was baptized, and Barnabas taught him about Christ, but he was not ready to become a missionary yet. He had a long way to grow.

As a new Christian, Saul had four basic needs. These needs are also evident in the lives of new Christians today, even though their conversions may not be as dramatic.

First, Christian people have a need for *acceptance*. "Saul spent several days with the disciples in Damascus" (Acts 9:19). It was good that the disciples were there to include Saul, because his former friends were now so threatened by him that they wanted to kill him. Saul became a man without friends. He needed the fellowship of people in Damascus who cared.

If a person becomes a Christian from a worldly background, they often need an extra amount of love and acceptance. One young man who became a Christian recently came from a wild background, but he was transparent, humorous, and fun to be around—you couldn't help but love him immediately. He wasn't in the church very long when a man from his Bible school class called him and said, "Just wondering how you're doing tonight."

He said, "Well, I'm just sitting here all by myself realizing I can't have any women and can't go out with my old drinking buddies, just thinking about the joy of the Christian life!"

At times the new Christian feels alone and bored, and he wonders, "What in the world have I gotten myself into?" The sacrifice of worldly pleasure and the defection of former friends are not easy to accept. Christians need to reach out and care. Take time to reach out and include a new Christian in your circle of fellowship.

Paul experienced that in Damascus, but when he came to Jerusalem he had a bigger problem. "He tried to join the disciples, but they were all afraid of him, not believing that he really was a disciple" (v. 26). Evidently the news of his conversion had not traveled back to Jerusalem as fast as news of his persecution had traveled to Damascus. Bad news usually travels faster. The Christians in Jerusalem weren't convinced that this Saul of Tarsus, who had once persecuted them, was now so drastically different, so they kept him at arm's distance for fear he would infiltrate their group and then turn on them.

But a man named Barnabas (the name means "Son of Encouragement") befriended Saul. Barnabas said, "This man's conversion is legit. He's for real. He's been preaching in Damascus. We need to welcome him." Then the disciples in Jerusalem received Saul.

The church needs more encouragers like Barnabas, so we can establish a spirit of acceptance. Some people who become Christians have come from the most moral of backgrounds, but we have also been blessed in the Lord with people who have come to us totally ignorant of the Word. We have had people come who have been in prison. We have had people come who have been dishonest in business, people who have been on drugs, people from multiple divorces, people with all kinds of problems in their backgrounds. These people do not need us keeping them at arm's distance, making them prove the legitimacy of their conversion. They need people to meet them on the steps of the baptistery, saying, "Hey, we're glad to have you! How about coming over to my house tonight for supper?" or, "I'll meet you next week for Sunday school," or "Here's a book that's really been helpful to me." That takes time and the sacrifice of selfish interest, but I'll guarantee that the new Christian will never forget you. He or she will be forever grateful.

Saul's second need was the need for *protection* from his enemies. "After many days had gone by, the Jews conspired to kill him" (v. 23). They were so threatened that they were going to eliminate him. The Christians protected him. They kept him in their homes, and then one night they stuffed Saul of Tarsus in a basket and lowered him over the wall so he could escape from the city. Later Paul wrote that this was one of the most humiliating things that ever happened to him. You can imagine—he had ridden to town with pride and arrogance, and now he had to scoot down in a little basket and be lowered over the wall. That's not exactly a sophisticated position.

New Christians need protection. In a hospital nursery the nurses sterilize everything and wear masks to protect the infants from germs. Babies are fragile and need protection from the diseases that later they will be able to ward off on their own. So it is with babies in Christ. They need protection from the adversary. People will come to them with false doctrine and seek to lead them astray. Former friends will want to renew their relationships. Satan will be like a roaring lion seeking to devour them. The new Christian needs additional protection by the church family.

That doesn't mean we can knock off the enemy, but it does mean we must provide some alternatives to fill the vacuum the enemy wants to fill. Jesus told about a man who had a demon in his house. The man swept the demon out, but he failed to fill the house with anything else. Seven demons worse than the first came in and occupied the vacuum left behind. Christianity has to be more than just removing sin from a person's life. It's got to be the active participation of the Holy Spirit and fellowship in the Christian life.

Years ago in my home church I was working with a man who had an alcohol problem. He had been off the bottle for a number of weeks when New Year's Eve came. I was worried about him. That was the time he was accustomed to having a wild party with friends, so I invited him to come to church. We had a Watch Night Service at the church and he came, but it was a drag for him. He just didn't get into the choruses and the prayer circle, and at 12:15 he left. He stayed out until 4:00 a.m. in bars and got drunk.

It is wise for the church to provide not only Christian teaching, but opportunity for fellowship in an enjoyable atmosphere, whether it's the women's retreat, the men's golf scramble, or the young people's attendance at a Christian concert. Those dynamic opportunities for fun and fellowship together can help us provide protection from the adversary.

The third need Saul had was the need for *patience*—patience in his enthusiasm. Paul Harvey wrote an article entitled "Love in Three Stages." He says the first stage of love is usually romance, when everybody is excited and infatuated and the electricity is flowing—it's a time of enthusiasm. But the romance always fades. The second stage is tolerance. Now each partner has found out that the other partner has faults and they will have to put up with each other. But then there is love in the third degree—mature love, in which they have mutual experiences and mutual commitment and they develop a deep relationship with each other.

Those same three stages can be seen in young people growing up. A 7-year-old is infatuated with his father—Dad can do no wrong. At 17, Dad is the dumbest guy he has ever met. But then he gets to be 27 and he respects his father again, and it's, "My dad used to say . . ."

New Christians go through those stages, too. When they first come to the Lord they are infatuated with the church and the Lord and eager to tell everybody what they have discovered. Actually, new Christians are usually our best evangelists because they have a wide circle of unchurched friends and they are so enthusiastic. That's great, but the new Christian can also be obnoxious and dogmatic sometimes. Enthusiasm out of control can be counterproductive—like a little boy who plants a garden, then goes out every day and digs up the seeds to see how they are growing!

One man got so excited about coming to the church and studying the Bible he was a joy to be around. But he also got bitter about his former denomination. When someone came to the church from that particular background, he was dangerous. He drove people away by grabbing them and saying, "Do you know what the Bible says about purgatory? Don't you know what the Bible says about praying to the saints? It doesn't say what you have been taught." We had to keep him away from those people. His enthusiasm was out of control.

I think Saul of Tarsus was a little like that, if you read between the lines. In the synagogue in Damascus, he "baffled the Jews living in Damascus by proving that Jesus is the Christ" (v. 22). Can't you see him being very dogmatic and forceful? He was going to win them over by his infallible argument, and the result was that they tried to kill him.

In Jerusalem he "talked and debated" with the Jews. He was ready to argue—he had all the answers. He knew he'd convert them if they'd just listen. But he wasn't very effective. The Jews in Jerusalem also tried to kill him. "When the brothers learned of this, they took him down to Caesarea and sent him off to Tarsus. Then the church throughout Judea, Galilee and Samaria enjoyed a time of peace" (v. 30). Loosely translated, that means, "Thank the Lord Saul is finally out of town. He gave us problems as a persecutor and he gave us problems as a preacher." That's enthusiasm out of control.

Be patient with enthusiastic new Christians, but don't try to dampen that enthusiasm. Carl Ketcherside tells of a dead church he worked with. A prostitute was converted to Christianity, and she was so excited about her new faith she began to tell everybody and bring her former friends to church! The elders had a meeting. They said, "We appreciate the apparent conversion of this woman, but we need to be careful that her enthusiasm does not get out of control." Ketcherside was really irritated. He said, "Don't worry, if she's around you guys long enough she'll lose it." Sure enough, she did. Don't dampen that enthusiasm. Dwight L. Moody said, "I'd rather try to restrain a fanatic than resurrect a corpse any day." Understand that enthusiasm. Catch it and be patient with it.

The fourth need of new Christians is *instruction in the Word*. Following his conversion, Saul immediately began to preach in the synagogue. He was doing the right thing because he had a dynamic testimony to share, but he needed further study. Paul said that after he was called by God, "I did not consult any man, nor did I go up to Jerusalem to see those who were apostles before I was, but I went immediately into Arabia and later returned to Damascus. Then after three years, I went up to Jerusalem" (Galatians 1:16-18). After he was converted he went into Arabia, into the wilderness, and he spent some time alone. He was rethinking what the Old Testament prophets had to say about the Messiah, studying the Scripture on his own. Then after many days, up to three years, Paul felt that he had an adequate grasp of the Scripture and he came back.

A new Christian, like a new baby, needs instruction in the Word. We give them that in two ways. First we teach them the Word. When you bring a five-day-old baby home from the hospital you don't tell him, "Now there's the refrigerator and your formula is in there and there's your bottle on the shelf and there's the stove and there's the pan. Good luck." You have to feed that baby yourself. New Christians need somebody to help them learn the basic principles of the Word. They need to be brought to church and the "What We Believe" class and the Sunday school, so they can feed on the basics.

The second way to feed them is to teach them to study the Bible on their own. Children do need to reach the point where we say, "There's the peanut butter and jelly and there's the milk. When you come home from school you can feed yourself." In order to help new Christians grow, we need to teach them to dig into the Word of God on their own. Introduce them to study guides or other books in the library that will help them study. Encourage them to memorize Scripture on their own. Do your best to get them off the spiritual milk bottle.

Unless we learn to feed ourselves, we will depend upon other people the rest of our lives. God wants us to reach the point of maturity where we can grow on our own and, in turn, meet the needs of other people. Hebrews 5:11-14 says,

"... you are slow to learn. In fact, though by this time you ought to be teachers, you need someone to teach you the elementary truths of God's word all over again. You need milk, not solid food! Anyone who lives on milk, being still an infant, is not acquainted with the teaching about righteousness. But solid food is for the mature, who by constant use have trained themselves to distinguish good from evil." Let's leave the elementary truth, he says, and go on to the mature truths. You have to learn to feed yourself, to train yourself as you study the Word of God.

I have a friend who told me that when his youngest son would go out to a restaurant he would always order a hamburger, french fries, and a coke. On his son's twelfth birthday, he took him to a nice restaurant and he ordered a hamburger, french fries, and a coke. My friend said, "Son, just this once let me order for you. If you don't like what I get then you can order a hamburger." He ordered a filet mignon. When the filet came to the table, his son took a bite and said, "Dad, why didn't somebody tell me about this a long time ago?" My friend said later he wished he hadn't because he couldn't get him back on hamburger again.

There is something better than just coming to church on Sunday morning and studying the Bible for an hour in Sunday school, and that is learning to take God's Word on your own and feed daily on it and grow in the Lord.

The Lesson for the Church

Every Christian should become a disciple maker. Don't be content to get wrapped up with a small group of four or five with whom you are secure. Remember when you were a new member of the church, or when you first became a Christian. You needed acceptance, you needed protection, you needed patience, and you needed somebody who would instruct you. Be alert to new Christians you can help. Maybe you can't help everybody, but you can help a few.

The Making of a Leader

Acts 11:19-30; 12:25-13:3

THE OLD MOVIE, "Viva Zapata," has a dramatic deathbed scene. The elderly Zapata is speaking his last words to his son. "Trouble is coming," he says. "Find a leader. If you cannot find a leader, be a leader." That challenge motivated the son to become one of Mexico's greatest and most colorful military figures.

Be a leader—a lot more of us should respond to that challenge, because of a critical leadership void both in the secular world and in the church today. *Time* magazine recently ran a feature article about America's search for leadership. It profiled scores of potential political figures—none of whom seem capable of immediately inspiring the country. The Standard Publishing company has analyzed the needs of Christian churches across America and concluded that our greatest need right now is for the development of leadership in our ranks.

A leader is simply someone who knows where he is going and is able to persuade others to go along. Not everyone can lead, but I'm convinced that a lot more should lead than do. While "the idea of leadership is exciting, the act of leading is costly," said Nelson Price in his book, *Shadows We Run From*. Everybody wants to inspire others to do good things, but few want more responsibility, worries, long hours, and heartaches. Most people cannot stand the pace and the pressure that leadership demands.

Many of you are already leaders. Some of you are administrators, executives, foremen, schoolteachers, or parents. Others of you are leaders in the church. All of you would admit that there is always the need for more insight into your leadership responsibilities. But others of you may be sitting on the sidelines, observing. You need a challenge to leadership.

The apostle Paul will serve as our example. He's the most dynamic Christian leader the world has ever seen. If we look at how he achieved that, we can seek to emulate his approach.

God's Part–Preparation

God had a large part in preparing Saul of Tarsus. Jesus struck Saul down when he was on his way to Damascus to persecute the Christians. A bright light blinded Saul and he had to admit that he was dead wrong. Saul was humbled by God, and suddenly he had a submissive, teachable spirit.

God further prepared Saul by allowing him to experience failure. Robert Coleman has said, "If you can learn from your failures there is no end to what you can learn." Saul began to preach in the synagogue of Damascus with great fervor, but he was overzealous and didn't realize much success. He had to escape from Damascus at night. When he went to Jerusalem he repeated the same mistake. He went into the synagogues and argued with such great fervor with the Jewish people there that they tried to kill him. The believers took Saul down to Caesarea and sent him home to Tarsus. Finally the church enjoyed a time of peace.

For over a decade Saul lived in obscurity. We are not sure exactly what he did. In Galatians 2:1 Paul wrote, "Fourteen years later I went up again to Jerusalem, this time with Barnabas." For over a decade, Saul didn't lead anybody. He was being prepared in relative obscurity for his job. You see, before Saul could achieve maximum usefulness, God needed to develop a new spirit in him. Out of the public eye, his fiery spirit had to be tempered. He had to develop a sensitivity for people. J. Oswald Sanders wrote, "Spiritual leadership does not develop best in the glare of publicity. Further, since God aims at quality in his chosen instruments, time is no object with him. We are always in a hurry but God isn't."

This had to be a frustrating decade for Saul of Tarsus. He knew he had leadership ability. He knew he had been called to lead. Why wasn't he leading? But God, slowly and quietly, was preparing Saul for the task He had in mind.

Often God prepares leaders by putting them either in the crucible of suffering or some place of insignificance. Moses was a shepherd in the wilderness for 40 years before God said, "Let's go. Let's lead the children of Israel out of Egypt." Joseph was in a dungeon for two years—a nothing. Then God tapped him on the shoulder and said, "I want you to be Prime Minister." After David was anointed to be king he spent months living in caves, hiding from the jealous King Saul. Jesus lived in obscurity for 30 years. Then He wandered in the wilderness for 40 days before He began His three-year ministry.

Sometimes I talk to young preachers who are frustrated because they feel they are stuck in an insignificant place. They want a greater role. They say, "Here I am in Gravel Switch, Kentucky and nobody knows I'm here." But sometimes the Lord forges His servants in unnoticed, quiet places.

Occasionally a noted community leader will join a congregation, and the church is tempted to thrust that person into a place of leadership too quickly for fear they will lose him. But usually a person needs a quiet time of getting to know the people of the church before he can assume a leadership role. When Paul outlined the qualifications of an elder, he said, "He must not be a recent convert, or he may become conceited and fall under the same judgment as the devil" (1 Timothy 3:6).

Maybe you're a little frustrated with your role right now.

You feel like you want to be calling the plays and you are standing on the sidelines. It may be that God is tempering you, preparing you for the limelight of leadership later. It's been said, "Character is what a man is in the dark." God may be testing you in obscurity to develop the kind of character He needs that can withstand the spotlight. God will more than compensate for those barren years, if you are faithful and wait patiently for Him. "I will repay you for the years the locusts have eaten," He says (Joel 2:25).

The Church's Part — Encouragement

After God had prepared Saul, the church had a role to play—one of encouragement. In Antioch there lived a special person by the name of Barnabas. Barnabas didn't have the fame that Peter and James and John had, but when you read the few references to Barnabas you find out he really was a special servant. We first meet him in the book of Acts when the young church at Jerusalem was undergoing financial stress. A man by the name of Joseph stepped forward and sold his field and gave all the money to the church. The apostles nicknamed him Barnabas, which means "Son of Encouragement." His generosity encouraged the church.

When Saul of Tarsus was converted, the church kept him at arm's distance because they weren't convinced about him. But Barnabas put his arm around Saul and brought him into the church, introduced him to the people, and said, "Hey, this guy's for real." In Acts 11, Barnabas is at it again. When the Jerusalem church heard the church at Antioch was growing, they sent Barnabas to help the church and encourage them to remain true to the Lord. He was a good man, full of the Holy Spirit and faith.

Antioch was the third largest city in the Roman Empire, with about 500,000 people. When the Christians in Jerusalem were persecuted, they scattered, and many of them went to Antioch. So the church there started to expand rapidly. Acts 11:21 says, "The Lord's hand was with them, and a great number of people believed and turned to the Lord." When Barnabas saw what was going on in this church—this rapid expansion—he thought, "This church needs more leadership. They need to have an expanded staff. I know just the man, Saul of Tarsus. We haven't heard from him in ten years, but he's the man for the job."

Barnabas didn't ask for volunteers. He selected the right man. Too many times in the church we ask for volunteers, when what we need to do is to find the right person and ask that person to serve. It's easier to ask for volunteers, but it's wiser to select someone who can do the job.

One church had the same minister for about ten years, and they had a successful ministry during that time. But when the minister resigned, the Chairman of the Board flippantly said, "Well, I need a Pulpit Committee. Do I have any volunteers?" Some enthusiastic but unperceptive people volunteered, and that church has never recovered from the shallow selection that committee made. Important appointments ought to be the result of prayer and careful selection.

Barnabas went to Tarsus himself and looked for Saul. Barnabas wasn't one to say, "It's my job to come up with the ideas. You guys implement them." He put shoe leather into his faith. He went to Tarsus himself. The Greek word implies that he had to look a long time to find Saul. Saul wasn't in a place of prominence. When Barnabas found him he said, "I want you to come to Antioch, Saul." This had to be an exciting encounter. Barnabas was an encourager. He said, "You're just the man they need, and you can do a good job, Saul." Saul was ready and the two of them came to Antioch.

The most impressive thing about Barnabas can be seen by contrasting two verses of Scripture. Acts 13:2 says, "Set apart for me Barnabas and Saul." Notice the order. Up to this point it was always Barnabas and Saul. But in Acts 13:42 we read, "As Paul and Barnabas were leaving the synagogue." From this time on it was always Paul and Barnabas—Paul's personality was so strong he took over. He became the dominant force, and Barnabas had to take a secondary role.

Maybe you cannot be a leader, but you can be an encourager to leadership like Barnabas was.

The church encouraged Saul too. "For a whole year Barnabas and Saul met with the church and taught great numbers of people" (Acts 11:26). Saul served as an associate minister in this Antioch church for a year. The people responded well to his teaching. Nothing encourages a teacher or a preacher more than responsive people. You can see how God was easing Saul into this role of leadership. He gave Saul a year in a positive situation. (That's why some churches always have interns serving. The interns have a year to serve in a positive situation before they get their feet wet in the real world.)

Then a prophet named Agabus predicted a severe famine in Jerusalem, and the Christians in Antioch took up an offering to help. Barnabas and Saul were sent to Jerusalem to deliver the gift to the Jerusalem church. Here again God was easing Saul into being a missionary. He had to go to meet strangers on behalf of Christ. Then, "When Barnabas and Saul had finished their mission, they returned from Jerusalem, taking with them John, also called Mark" (Acts 12:25).

The church at Antioch then sent these three men on a special missionary tour. "After they had fasted and prayed, they placed their hands on them and sent them off" (Acts 13:3). In the New Testament, the laying of hands on a man's head was done for one of three purposes. Sometimes it was for healing. Ananias laid his hands on Saul and his sight was restored. Sometimes it was for imparting a special gift of the Holy Spirit. The apostles could lay their hands on people and grant the Holy Spirit. In this case the laying on of hands was for ordination or encouragement.

The church at Antioch had a missionary outlook. When the Jerusalem church was in trouble they took up an offering. When the Holy Spirit said, "I want you to send leaders out," they sent the best they had. The church should be a growing body, but it also needs to reach beyond its own boundaries to the world. Warren Wiersbe tells of a church that had a neon sign that kept flashing "Jesus Only." But the first three letters burned out and it kept flashing "us only, us only, us only." When the church gets introverted, it ceases to have the blessings of God. If we are the church of Jesus Christ there needs to be that constant outreach.

I spent an evening in a home recently, and stayed in the room of a grade-school child. In that room was a huge globe. I measured the size of that globe with my hands; it took five double hand spans to reach around it. Then I took the tip of my finger and placed it on Louisville, Kentucky. Not only did the tip of my finger cover Louisville, it covered almost the entire state! We are only a small part of God's world. We need to have a missionary vision. Paul was encouraged by the local church to reach out, and they made him a leader.

Saul's Part—Consecration

God had prepared Saul and the church had encouraged him, but now the rest was up to Saul himself. If he was going to be a leader he had to have some personal consecration. Saul developed five characteristics in himself. They are five essential characteristics of anybody who wants to be a leader.

The first is *sincerity*. It's been said that the number one ingredient for leadership is sincerity. You can't fake sincerity for very long. Perceptive people begin to see through. They will not follow you if there is an inconsistency in your life, no matter how gifted you are.

Saul was always sincere. Even when he persecuted the church, he was for real. Nobody doubted that he was legitimate—he was not a hypocrite. When he became a Christian, he was 100% a Christian. A sincere leader doesn't just mouth the words. He or she demonstrates the desired goal by living it out.

General Patton was once leading his troops across Europe. They were tired when they came to a deep, icy cold river, and the men began to grumble. No way were they going to swim across that stiff stream with backpacks. Patton didn't say a word. He waded into the water with his backpack and swam across to the other side. He turned around and looked at the men and swam back. Then he said, "Men, are you ready to go?" They all swam across. People don't need to be told as much as they need to be shown. The Christian leader must be sincere enough to model the Christian life.

The second characteristic of a consecrated leader is *decisiveness*. You cannot be a leader and be wishy-washy. You've got to make up your mind. A lot of people just cannot decide—they keep putting it off. As Charles Swindoll suggests, their favorite color is plaid. But Saul was a decisive person. When Barnabas said "I want you to come to Antioch," Saul was ready to go. He once said, "But one thing I do: Forgetting what is behind and straining toward what is ahead, I press on toward the goal . . ." (Philippians 3:13, 14).

In the book, *In Search of Excellence,* Peters and Waterman list the number one principle for success as a bias for action—a preference for doing something, anything, rather than sending a question through cycles and cycles of analysis and committee reports. In other words, there comes that time when somebody has to bite the bullet and say, "Let's go, I'll take that responsibility on myself."

The problem is that we want everyone's support so we delay the decision to avoid criticism. Bill Cosby said, "I don't know what the secret of success is but I am going to tell you the key to failure. The key to failure is trying to please everybody." If you try to please everybody, you are going to be a weak leader. A leader has to be decisive. The one essential quality for a successful leader is the ability to make decisions and not look back.

The third quality of a consecrated leader is *vision*. A good leader has to be able to dream—to stimulate followers into seeing what can be. Paul always had a vision. He could see beyond Antioch, to Macedonia and Asia Minor, to Rome and Spain—into the world for Christ. He had spiritual claustrophobia. A good leader is somewhat of a dreamer. People don't respond to security, they respond to a challenge. They want to stretch and become something more than they are. A good leader is able to inspire people to stretch and believe something can be done and then do it.

Marvin Rickard preaches at the Los Gatos Christian Church near San Francisco. I have always been impressed with that church. They have over 4,000 every Sunday morning, 2,000 on Sunday nights, and they give a million dollars a year to missions. Rickard says there are three types of people in the church—in most organizations, for that matter. The first he calls the catalyst. This is a person who makes things happen. Tell him it can't be done and the catalyst is challenged to prove you are wrong. He may not be well-organized by nature, but he gets things done. He may spend lots of money or leave some loose ends, but you have to admit he causes progress and growth.

Once the church is moving forward and attendance is up, the next kind of person that emerges into prominence is the organizer. He loves to put things in order—in departments, chains of command, orderly schedules, and committees.

After things are better organized and still growing, the third kind of person emerges—the gifted administrator. The administrator sees the need for tighter control on expenditures, the development of policies, purchase orders, job descriptions, and budget procedures.

Rickard says the older an organization gets the more the administrator types seem to take control. They are uncomfortable with those who are visionary, so they tie them up tightly with red tape. The catalysts can't function any more. They either quit or move on to someplace else, and soon people begin to say, "How can we get this church moving again?" For a church to maintain growth over a long period, it is necessary to have all three types of people—but you have to give some space to the dreamer and the catalyst so that you can keep being challenged.

The fourth essential characteristic of a leader is *compassion*. A.W. Tozer said, "Nothing can take the place of affection. Those who have it in generous measure have a magic power over men." This is probably the one ingredient Paul needed to develop. He was already sincere, he was already decisive, he was already visionary, but God took ten years to help him develop a spirit of sensitivity for people. I don't think he had that at first. He wouldn't have persecuted people and tortured them if he loved them. But his association with Barnabas and his in-depth training in the school of obscurity taught him to love people.

Paul was not a rigid legalist the way some people portray him. He met with the elders at Ephesus and wept and embraced them. He called Timothy "My dear son;" he loved him like a son and expressed that love. Paul once said that if it were possible, he would go to Hell if his Jewish friends would just believe. He was willing to compromise his personal preferences in order to advance the gospel. He learned a sensitivity for people.

It is impossible to be an effective leader if you don't care for people. As Cavitt Roberts said so well, "People don't care how much you know if they don't know how much you care." The first step to being a good leader is to let people know that you care about them.

The final characteristic of a consecrated leader is *zeal*. Paul never lost his enthusiasm. He was excited all his life. When he came to the end, he said, "I have fought a good fight." His enthusiasm was contagious. He never quit.

Enthusiasm is essential to leadership. You don't have to be loud. You don't have to be the "rah rah" type. But people ought to sense an intensity about your life. Emerson said, "Every great and commanding movement in the annals of history is the triumph of enthusiasm." Henry David Thoreau said, "None are so old as those who have outlived enthusiasm." If you are not enthusiastic any more, don't say, "It's because I have matured." You have become indifferent.

If any people ought to be excited, it is Christian people. Did you know that the word *enthusiasm* comes from two Greek words, *en theos*, meaning "in God"? Where there is God, there is enthusiasm. It was prophesied about Jesus, "Zeal for your house consumes me" (Psalm 69:9).

I have been preaching for 20 years and I can honestly say I have never been more excited about the need for Christianity and the future of the church than right now. The politicians don't have the answers. The economists don't have the answers. The military doesn't have the answers. Educators don't have the answers. Only in Jesus Christ is there hope.

And as the country preacher says, "If that don't turn you on, you ain't got no switches."

The Cincinnati Reds were at the bottom of their division in most of 1985, but the next year they were pennant contenders. The difference is one word—*leadership*. I am not a fan of Pete Rose's lifestyle, but I am a fan of the way Pete Rose plays baseball. He is sincere. He is consumed by the game. He is decisive. When he took over the helm, he said, "I am going to play myself at first base." He has vision. He began to inspire the players to believe that they could be winners. He has compassion. The players say he understands where they are coming from. He took the players' side during the baseball strike. Who can deny his zeal? At age forty-two he was diving into bases and running to first base on a walk. Somebody said Pete Rose plays every baseball game like it's the final game of the World Series. That zeal is contagious.

If you transfer that kind of leadership to the church, we will have leaders worth following. People who have been prepared by God in the crucible of obscurity. People who have been encouraged by the church to step forward and take charge. People who have the dedication to develop in themselves a sincerity that's constant, a decisiveness that's wise, a vision that's challenging, a compassion that's obvious, and a zeal that's contagious. That's Paul—Paul, who said, "You follow me as I follow Christ." And maybe that's you too.

When You Share Your Faith

Acts 13:1-13

YEARS AGO A builder in the church I serve sold a home to a couple who had just moved into our community. After becoming acquainted with them he invited them to attend church with him the following Sunday. Sensing their reluctance, he added, "I'll tell you what. If you don't like it, I'll buy you a steak dinner next week." That couple was later baptized and the husband became a deacon.

Most of us need to be more aggressive in sharing our faith. I wouldn't suggest we bribe people into attending church or become so obnoxious in evangelism that we turn people off, but I do think most of us need to be bolder in sharing what Christ means to us.

In Matthew 28:19, 20, Jesus gave the marching orders for the church. He said, "Therefore go and make disciples of all nations, baptizing them in the name of the Father and of the Son and of the Holy Spirit, and teaching them to obey everything I have commanded you." Those marching orders are for every soldier of the cross. No one is exempt because of temperament, knowledge, or unique assignment. Every one of us must share our faith.

There are four levels of witnessing, each a little more intense than the previous level. First there is the *silent wit-*

ness. This is the person who says, "I'm not very vocal about my faith. I just let my light shine before men. I win people by my lifestyle, which speaks for itself." That sounds good and never offends anyone, but the problem is it seldom works. When was the last time someone came up to you and said, "I've been observing your life and I'm so impressed. Can you tell me how to become a Christian?" That's very rare. The Bible says, "faith comes by hearing," not by watching. Jesus said, "Go into all the world and preach," not just demonstrate.

The second level of witness is the *opportunistic witness*. This person will on rare occasions speak a word for Christ if the opportunity is obvious. A relative may be having problems or a neighbor loses a loved one and we timidly respond, "Maybe you could try going to church," or "I believe there is life after death, don't you?" The opportunistic witness is careful not to offend anyone or infringe on anybody's rights, but if he has the perfect chance, he will speak up.

Then there is the *invitational witness*. The woman at the well was so impressed with Jesus that she raced back to her hometown and invited her friends to come see the man who had told her everything about herself. Many people aggressively use the church as an effective tool of evangelism today. They constantly invite people to come to a Christmas program, come to a revival or children's presentation, come hear a guest speaker or musical. If the church is alive and effective it can be a tremendous stimulus to evangelism. When people come they learn about Christ.

It's easier and safer to talk with others about church than it is our personal faith. Probably the majority of evangelism that takes place today occurs at this level.

A fourth level of witnessing is the *personal testimony*. One individual tactfully but aggressively seeks to share with another what Christ and His church have meant to him or her personally. The testimony does not have to be dramatic, but just a realistic appraisal of how Christ has made a difference. The person witnessing should be familiar with the basic Scriptures concerning salvation.

The personal witness is rare. Not many Christians have the courage and the ability to share their faith in a personal way.

One day I overheard three people in a fast food restaurant talk about video cassette recorders. They were sitting at a table right next to me and I couldn't help overhear their conversation. For nearly a half hour they discussed the various types of VCR's available. One man in the party had just purchased a VCR and was sharing what little he knew. The others obviously were no experts either.

When I left I thought about the many VCR-type conversations that go on. We can talk unashamedly about non-risk subjects like electrical gadgets even though we don't know very much. Yet when it comes to crucial topics like our faith in Christ and eternal life, we clam up and excuse ourselves on the basis of ignorance. We don't know enough yet! In reality we don't need more information or additional evangelistic training. We simply need a new boldness and a new compassion for the lost.

In these critical days we Christians need to step up in our level of witnessing. If you have been a silent witness, look for an opportunity to speak up. If you have been overly timid about your faith, become more aggressive and tactfully make invitations or share your personal testimony with others.

Hostile Opposition

Once you become an aggressive inviter or personal witness you will encounter the same kind of experiences along the way that Paul did when he first started. Paul and Barnabas had been commissioned by the early church to begin a missionary tour in Asia Minor. This had to be an exciting venture. They took along John Mark, Barnabas' cousin, and they went to the island of Cyprus, which was the home of Barnabas.

The first place to begin sharing your faith is with people you know. That's not always the easiest or the most receptive place, but it's the starting point. Notice the reactions the missionary team received as they traveled and gave their personal testimony. We can anticipate the same reactions today.

First there was *hostile opposition.* On the island of Cyprus the missionaries met a sorcerer named Bar-Jesus. His stage name was Elymas. A sorcerer is one who calls on the powers of darkness to perform magic or supernatural tricks. This sorcerer or false prophet was outspoken in his opposition to Paul and Barnabas. He apparently had influence with the proconsul (mayor) of Paphos. When the proconsul showed interest in Christianity, Elymas was threatened. He could see his influence waning. He was going to lose power and money. So, "Elymas the sorcerer . . . opposed them and tried to turn the proconsul from the faith" (Acts 13:8).

When you evangelize, you can anticipate opposition. The world thinks it's OK to call yourself a Christian and go to church when it's convenient. But when you get so involved that it changes your way of thinking, feeling, and acting, people get uncomfortable. They see your beliefs as a threat to their habits, attitudes, pocketbook, and lifestyle. In all honesty, they are absolutely right. Christianity *does* require a change. We think it's a change that's positive, but it's not an easy one.

People respond in all kinds of ways when threatened. They might begin to withdraw and give you the silent treatment. They might get angry or sarcastically try to cut you down by ridicule. They may attempt to identify you with some "creepy" Christian everybody despises. But there will be opposition. Jesus said, "Woe to you when all men speak well of you."

I have a sister who works in a factory. Everybody knows she's a Christian. She's not obnoxious but she's unashamed. She's an intelligent believer and people respect her. People will come to her for private counsel when they have a problem. Although she is respected she also gets hassled about being a dedicated Christian. She occasionally has to work on Sunday. Recently one man shouted, "Hey Rose, what's a nice girl like you doing working on Sunday? A good girl like you should be in Sunday school giving to the offering, not out here earning money." People laughed. Encouraged, he said, "Let's sing a hymn and make Rose feel better." He proceeded to mockingly sing, "Jesus loves me, this I know." Everybody laughed. Even the nominal Christians laughed nervously because they were afraid not to. It's not easy to tolerate people like that. They aren't easy to love.

Christianity is a threat to a society that is becoming increasingly pagan. We can dilute the message and pretend that Christianity is merely having our name on a church roll and occasionally showing up on Sunday and pose no threat to anyone. But if we share the truth that Christianity is the daily submission to the lordship of Jesus Christ, then people will oppose us. If nothing ever happens as a result of your witness, probably you have not been aggressive enough.

Paul confronted his opponent without apology. He "looked straight at Elymas and said, 'You are a child of the devil and an enemy of everything that is right! ... Now the hand of the Lord is against you. You are going to be blind, and for a time you will be unable to see the light of the sun.' Immediately mist and darkness came over him" (Acts 13:9-11).

It's probably a good thing we Christians don't have that kind of supernatural ability. We might abuse it and try to intimidate people into believing and obeying. The apostles were able to perform miracles for the purpose of confirming the word they spoke. Usually those miracles were positive healing acts, but here is an occasion when the miracle was temporarily crippling. The purpose of the miracle was not for show, but to confirm the message from God.

When you are opposed for standing for the truth, don't cower. Don't be obnoxious, but don't yield. The world is bold in its sin. They are unashamed of abortion, homosexuality, fornication, pornography. This is not a time for the spiritually faint of heart. "Stand firm. Let nothing move you. Always give yourselves fully to the work of the Lord, because you know that your labor in the Lord is not in vain" (1 Corinthians 15:58).

Positive Response

If you aggressively share your faith, you will also encounter a *positive response* from people who are hungry. The proconsul of Paphos invited Paul and Barnabas to share their faith with him. He was an intelligent man. He was hungry to hear the Word of God, and learn answers to the questions of identity and destiny he had not yet resolved. He first heard their teaching and was impressed. Then he saw the miracle that confirmed their word and he believed.

The Bible promises that when we share the Word of God with others it will produce a positive response.

> He who goes out weeping,
>   carrying seed to sow,
> will return with songs of joy,
>   carrying sheaves with him.
>   (Psalm 126:6)

> As the rain and the snow come down from heaven,
>   and do not return to it without watering the earth
> and making it bud and flourish,
>   so that it yields seed for the sower and bread
>   for the eater,
> so is my word that goes out from my mouth:
>   It will not return to me empty,
> but will accomplish what I desire
>   and achieve the purpose for which I sent it.
> You will go out in joy
>   and be led forth in peace.
>   (Isaiah 55:10-12)

Following a Bible study a woman asked to see me. She unfolded a sordid past of four marriages and sinful complications, though she was just in her early 30's. She asked, "Can I come forward and be baptized this Sunday? I'm so thankful for what I'm learning from studying the Bible here. If only I'd known about these principles earlier, it could have saved me from a lot of hurt. But thank you for teaching me the Bible—this is changing my whole perspective!" Nothing boosts me like a positive response to the Word. Sometimes when I get depressed it's not really more Bible study that I need, but more opportunity to share my faith with others. Sometimes we feed on the Word with no exercise and become overindulgent and lethargic.

Don't let the threat of opposition prevent you from experiencing the joy of a positive response. There are few greater thrills than the satisfaction of knowing you've helped win someone to Christ. Don't let a person's intelligence, affluence, or prominence intimidate you. Those people have the same basic emotional and spiritual needs as everyone else. Paul Tillich described three anxieties of modern man that no amount of affluence or prestige can resolve: anxiety about death, anxiety about guilt, and anxiety about a purpose in life. Only Christ resolves those fears. Only Christ can bring peace. Paul shared the gospel with the leading intellectual and political figure on the island of Cyprus, and he responded positively.

I remember being invited to the home of a popular professional athlete. The newspapers featured his story on the front page, complete with the huge salary he had been given by the local pro basketball team. He was a folk hero in the state. I nervously anticipated the difficult questions he might ask. But when I visited him I was almost disappointed to discover that the questions he put forth were the same ones everyone asked—questions I'd answered dozens of times. Everyone's spiritual needs are similar. Some people may have more prestige, but they have the same problems. How can I keep my children from getting destroyed by drugs? How can I keep my marriage together? How can I find hope for life after death? Will there be nuclear war? Only Christ provides a satisfying hope in the context of these basic questions.

In fact, I believe as our world becomes increasingly pagan, the opportunities for evangelism are increased. People are asking, "What's wrong? What's happening to our world?" We've got rock stars blaspheming the cross, sports heroes on drugs, leading Hollywood figures who are homosexuals, an AIDS epidemic sweeping the country, the nuclear threat looming. Something is drastically wrong!

What an opportunity for us to speak up for Christ. What a time to point out that the battle lines are being drawn, it's time to choose sides! People are willing to listen. Many are receptive to the truth. People are searching for the answers that only Christ can give. When the electricity goes out in the deepest recesses of the cave, it's a great time to be selling flashlights!

Jesus said, "Do you not say, 'Four months more and then the harvest'? I tell you, open your eyes and look at the fields! They are ripe for harvest'" (John 4:35).

Disappointing Defection

Some fellow Christian soldiers will disappoint you. A short phrase in Acts 13:13 carries a dramatic story. "In Pamphylia . . . John left them." This was not an amiable separation. John Mark deserted the missionary team without Paul's consent.

Acts 15:36-39 describes an encounter between Paul and Barnabas five years later. "Some time later Paul said to Barnabas, 'Let us go back and visit the brothers in all the towns where we preached the word of the Lord and see how they are doing.' Barnabas wanted to take John, also called Mark, with them, but Paul did not think it wise to take him, because he had deserted them in Pamphylia and had not continued with them in the work. They had such a sharp disagreement that they parted company."

Why Mark bailed out at this point is speculation. Maybe he was afraid. The journey Paul was proposing to Antioch of Pisidia was a difficult mountainous trip with the threat of robbers. Maybe the proposal of a steep, dangerous climb was too much for John Mark. Others speculate that he became homesick. His leaving may have been the result of resentment. Paul's ministry was expanding to the Gentiles; perhaps Mark, who had been reared in a strong Jewish home, was still legalistic in attitude. Paul was pretty patient about most things except the refusal to treat Gentiles as equal before God. Maybe that's why he reacted so harshly later when Barnabas proposed taking Mark again. But whatever the reason, Mark bailed out and disappointed Paul.

If you are a turned-on evangelistic Christian there will be times when other Christians disappoint you. They may not share your enthusiasm. You've discovered the meaning to your life and you're thrilled, but it puzzles and disappoints you to encounter other Christians who are passive and indifferent about their faith—who are just going through the motions.

Some Christians may disappoint you because they don't grow. They became Christians but it seems they've just camped out on the steps of the baptistery. Their attendance at church services is spasmodic. Their daily habits are questionable. They are just as shallow, selfish, petty, critical, and carnal as when they first gave their lives to the Lord. That's disappointing.

But the greatest disappointment is defection. We've all known Christians who at one time were dedicated believers, perhaps leaders in the church, but now they've bailed out. They have left their marriage and chased some temporary fantasy, or they have quit the church and renounced Christ altogether. That's disappointing and disillusioning. We almost get the feeling, "If they can't make it, neither can I." The state of defection is worse than the state of those who have never known the Lord. "They are worse off at the end than they were at the beginning" (2 Peter 2:20-22). They seem hardened and unreachable.

Although there's no evidence that John Mark became entangled again in the world, he did go back home. That disappointed Paul.

Don't put your trust in Christian people; put your trust in Christ. We ought to love fellow Christians, respect their leadership, and put confidence in them to a certain degree, but don't worship them! Don't center your faith on them. People will let you down. People will deceive you. Christian leaders have feet of clay. When you get to know them well you will discern flaws. Only Jesus Christ is worthy of worship. Only Christ never fails. Only Christ is worthy of our complete trust.

> My hope is built on nothing less
>   than Jesus' blood and righteousness.
> I dare not trust the sweetest frame
>   but wholly lean on Jesus name.
> On Christ, the solid rock I stand,
>   all other ground is sinking sand,
>   all other ground is sinking sand.

Personal Struggle

Paul's experience reveals one additional result of sharing our faith aggressively—the possibility of personal struggle.

When Paul was at Pamphylia he became seriously ill. Galatians 4:13 reads, "As you know, it was because of an illness that I first preached the gospel to you." Paul left Pamphylia and went into the hill country of Galatia, Pisidia, and Antioch. It is suspected that Paul contracted malaria in the hot lower region of the Mediterranean and went to the higher altitude for relief and recuperation. Some think that migraine headaches and weakness, aftereffects of malaria, constituted the "thorn in the flesh" that Paul refers to in 2 Corinthians 12:7. Maybe one of the reasons John Mark left was that he saw Paul become ill and was afraid of experiencing the same trauma.

Being an obedient, evangelistic Christian does not exempt you from struggle. Here was Paul, doing exactly what God wanted done, and he became sick. You hear the opposite of that frequently in the media today. Proponents of the health-and-wealth gospel insist that if you walk with God you will be healthy and prosperous. Many Christians are perplexed and resentful when difficulty comes. They interpret it as a sign of God's disapproval. "Why is God punishing me? What have I done wrong?" they ask. But the Bible says, "He ... sends rain on the righteous and the unrighteous" (Matthew 5:45). Paul was sick, possibly with malaria, and all this while perfectly obedient to God. His illness was not God punishing him, but the result of living in a contaminated world.

Being a Christian does not exempt us from trials and temptations. In fact it sometimes intensifies the struggle. Because Job was such a good man, Satan tested him with trials. Satan tempts the dedicated Christian with greater intensity than he does people already in his camp. So being a Christian does not mean exemption from difficulty. It means we are in the line of fire. We are on the front line of battle and have to expect danger, wounds, and hardship. The Bible says, "The Lord disciplines those he loves" (Hebrews 12:6).

The question is, what do you *do* when the difficulty comes? What is your attitude in the midst of the struggle? If you complain, criticize, and demonstrate bitterness, your testimony is negated. People will observe how you react under fire. They want to know if your faith can sustain you. If you maintain a positive spirit, a joyful attitude, and a determined faith, your witness is greatly enhanced. It's the attitude that makes the difference. When Paul got sick, he kept going. He refused to quit. Some people can milk a hangnail forever. Others get knocked flat on their back and bounce back up and keep on going. The difference is not only the degree of difficulty, but also the individual spirit.

President Reagan recently set a good example for the country when following major surgery for colon cancer, he was back at work in about a week. He could have wallowed in self-pity or pleaded for sympathy, but even though he's over 70 years of age, he kept going.

That's not always possible. Some diseases incapacitate people. But even then our attitude should be that of Paul: "If we live, we live to the Lord; and if we die, we die to the Lord" (Romans 14:8).

Art Greer wrote a book entitled *There Are No Grownups in Heaven*. His theory is that some people always find a parking place, while others never find one. One person may say, "When I went downtown today, I prayed the Lord would provide a parking place and I found one just two blocks away. What a good day." Another person says, "Rats! I prayed for a parking spot and three people got closer to the front door than I did." It's a matter of attitude. How close must your parking spot be before you rate it as a positive experience?

What do you think Paul sounded like when he got back from his first missionary journey? Would he say, "It was terrible! I got seasick on that rickety old ship. We got to Cyprus and I anticipated a positive reaction since Barnabas was from that area. But we were opposed by an influential magician. I had to do a terrible thing and strike him blind. It was bad. Then I got deathly ill in Pamphylia, and just when I needed him, John Mark bailed out. Then we took this awful mountain road to Galatia and Barnabas and I bickered over John Mark. It was the most frightening trip I've ever taken. Then we got to Lystra and I was stoned and left for dead. Not many people believed. Brother, am I glad to be back home!"

I don't think that was his attitude. I think Paul said, "Let me tell you how God blessed our journey. We had safe travel. The proconsul of Paphos believed the gospel. We established churches. God spared me from opposition. Great signs and miracles were performed and we have been blessed by God. I'm looking forward to going back." The difference was not in circumstances, but in the attitude toward them.

Hebrews 12:7, 11-13 says, "Endure hardship as discipline; God is treating you as sons. For what son is not disciplined by his father? ... No discipline seems pleasant at the time, but painful. Later on, however, it produces a harvest of righteousness and peace for those who have been trained by it. Therefore, strengthen your feeble arms and weak knees. 'Make level paths for your feet,' so that the lame may not be disabled, but rather healed." If we can be strong under discipline, those who are lame can be healed. Our faith encourages others. Our faithfulness enhances the credibility of our testimony.

"Go into all the world and preach the good news to all

creation" (Mark 16:15). Those are marching orders to us all. That's not advice from a friend, but an order from our Commander. It's a command that requires courage and conviction. There's going to be opposition from the enemy. Stand firm. Let nothing move you. There will be positive response from the spiritually hungry. Rejoice in those victories. There will be defection from some fellow soldiers. That's disappointing, but put your trust wholly in the Lord. There may be personal struggles, but don't lose heart. Maintain a positive spirit and a cheerful countenance, so that others may see Christ is sufficient.

A burly man stopped in my office unannounced some time ago. I knew from several sources that he had lived a worldly life. He'd been attending church for three or four months and said, "Well, preacher, I've decided it's about time I become a Christian." I rejoiced with him in the decision and began to share the Scriptures about how to become a follower of Jesus. I pointed out our need to surrender our will to the lordship of Christ and then be baptized into His name. "That's what I want to do," he said. He was joyful and so was I.

I shook his hand as he left and said, "Thanks for coming. You've made my day."

I'll always remember his response: "Well, thanks to you and this church, you've made my life!"

There's no greater challenge than to share the gospel. There's no greater thrill than to see people respond. There's no greater opportunity than right now!

Keep Off the Pedestal

Acts 14:1-20

THE MORE I study the life of Paul the more impressed I am with his balanced personality. He had incredible influence and power in the Christian world, yet he demonstrated a constant spirit of humility in relationships with people. This balance is evident in Acts 14, when after an impressive miracle, some people in the crowd attempted to treat Paul as a god.

This is an important point for a lot of us who have leadership positions in the church. Some people will want to put us on a pedestal. I was hurrying to a funeral the other day, and I passed a family from my church. I beeped and waved and smiled, and then pulled into the funeral home. Later the mother in the car told me her young son said, "Mom, was Brother Bob going over the speed limit? And if he was going to the funeral home, how come he was smiling?"

Some people, not just children, will want to put you on a pedestal if you are a leader. Others idolize television preachers or Christian entertainers. It can be devastating to them when they discover those leaders have feet of clay. But leaders in nearly every field—medicine, politics, education, business, parents—encounter those who insist on putting them on a pedestal of admiration.

Doctors, teachers, and others who work to counsel people, know that the counselee can develop an unhealthy emotional dependency on them. Weak counselors will try to encourage that because it is an ego boost, but it is still an unhealthy relationship. The more success you achieve in your life, the greater the tendency to mount the pedestal of pride and look for people's applause.

In "Peanuts," Linus once said to Charlie Brown, "When I get big I am going to be a humble country doctor. I will live in the city, you see, and every morning I will get up, climb in my sports car and zoom into the country. Then I will start healing people. I will heal everybody from miles around. I will be a world famous humble country doctor." A lot of people begin with noble ideals, but it is not long before they are climbing onto the pedestal, looking for power and admiration.

Let's examine this incident in the life of Paul and see how he refused to let people put him on the pedestal that belongs only to Jesus Christ.

An Opportunity for Rank Egotism

Paul could easily have developed an ego problem. For one thing, big crowds came to hear him preach. Paul was invited to speak at the synagogue of Antioch of Pisidia. Acts 13:16-41 records his sermon. It was an impressive one, and afterward, "As Paul and Barnabas were leaving the synagogue, the people invited them to speak further about these things on the next Sabbath.... On the next Sabbath almost the whole city gathered to hear the word of the Lord. When the Jews saw the crowds, they were filled with jealousy" (Acts 13:42-45).

It's an ego boost to be asked to speak, and it's an even bigger ego boost to speak to big crowds. I spoke at an on-campus revival at Great Lakes Bible College some time ago in Lansing, Michigan. The young people were responsive and I was gratified. But on the morning I was to leave, I awakened to see two feet of snow on the ground. They canceled school that day and I couldn't leave. In mid-morning one of the students walked on snowshoes to the house where I was staying. He said, "Mr. Russell, the students wondered if you would come over and preach again since you can't go home."

Well, what could I say? I didn't want to let those poor students down! So I went back to preach—but this time only about a third of the kids showed up. It was a real downer.

The attention of people, the applause of the crowd, people taking pictures—all that can inflate the ego.

Paul could have lost perspective not just because of his popularity with the crowd, but because of his awesome power. Paul had the ability to perform impressive miracles. He and Barnabas were "speaking boldly for the Lord, who confirmed the message of his grace by enabling them to do miraculous signs and wonders" (Acts 14:3).

At Lystra while Paul was preaching he noticed a man who had been crippled from birth. He had some kind of birth defect in his feet. He had never walked. As Paul preached he saw that this man had faith to be healed. Certain faces stand out in a crowd when you are speaking—not necessarily those who are really paying attention. This man's faith captivated Paul, so he stopped his sermon and called out, "Stand up on your feet!" The man jumped up and started walking. You can imagine the ecstasy this brought the man who had been healed, but you can also imagine how gratifying it was to Paul to know that he had the awesome power to heal.

Power corrupts almost any person. Think of all the politicians who began with noble motives. They were not going to be bought, they were not going to be bribed, they were not going to sell out to special interests, and then a few years later that's the very thing they have done. Senator Strom Thurmond was asked why Congress could not do something about the awesome federal deficit. He said that it's awful hard to get a hog to butcher itself. Power gets hungry and it's hard to cut it off.

Paul had power. But the most serious temptation came for Paul when people idolized him. "When the crowds saw this miracle they shouted, 'the gods have come down to us in human form!'" (v. 11)

An old legend in that area said that Zeus and Hermes, two Greek gods, had visited the region disguised as mere mortals, but no one had accepted them except an old couple. They sent a flood in retaliation and all the people were drowned, the legend says, except for that couple. Familiar with that story, the people of Lystra were taking no chances. They welcomed Paul and Barnabas into their city and watched them carefully. When they saw this incredible miracle they were convinced that Zeus and Hermes had come to visit them again.

Paul and Barnabas didn't recognize their language and they didn't know what was going on. Barnabas, who was evidently massive in stature, they called Zeus, the head of the Greek gods. They called Paul Hermes, because Hermes was the god distinguished for eloquence. The people spared nothing. They brought out bulls to sacrifice. Garlands of flowers were draped over the bulls and spread before the people. They were prepared to worship Paul and Barnabas.

You see, they were impressed with Paul's eloquence, but they didn't pay much attention to what he had to say. That still happens today. Lloyd Ogilvie in his book, *Drumbeats of Love*, wrote, "We put the communicator on a pedestal and evade the communication. We have a seemingly limitless capacity to give honor that belongs to Christ to the people who seek to introduce us to Him; parents, pastors, friends, and teachers who have brought us the good news and often made them the source of our security. We elevate them to super sainthood and miss for ourselves the dynamic that has made them admirable. We make matinee idols out of Christian leaders."

They were trying to make a matinee idol out of Paul, but he refused to accept their worship.

A Refusal to Accept Adulation

It finally dawned on Paul and Barnabas what was happening and they immediately tore their clothing. That was not a godlike thing to do. That was the radical Hebrew way of expressing consternation at sacrilege. Paul interrupted them and said, "Men, why are you doing this? We too are only men, human like you. We are bringing you good news, telling you to turn from these worthless things to the living God, who made heaven and earth and sea and everything in them. In the past, he let all nations go their own way. Yet he has not left himself without testimony: He has shown kindness by giving you rain from heaven and crops in their seasons; he provides you with plenty of food and fills your hearts with joy" (vv. 15-17). Paul made every effort to prevent the people from putting him on the pedestal. But still the Bible says, "Even with these words, they had difficulty keeping the crowd from sacrificing to them" (v.18).

Paul reacted in horror. His humility was not mock humility. He didn't say, "Aw shucks, fellows, you really shouldn't do this but go ahead anyway." Paul was authentic. He was not out to impress people with his own piety and power. He was out to exalt Jesus Christ.

One of the true tests of leadership is how you react when people put you on the pedestal of false pride. There are four steps up that pedestal and every one of them has to be rejected.

First is the tendency to be sucked in by flattery. There is a difference between a compliment and flattery. A compliment is genuine praise intended to encourage. That's good. But flattery is exaggerated praise intended to manipulate. Proverbs 29:5 says, "Whoever flatters his neighbor is spreading a net for his feet." When you get into a position of leadership, people will flatter you. It's nice to have people think more of us then we deserve and to say nice things, but if we are not careful, we begin to believe those things are true and develop an inflated view of our own importance. Or we attempt to live up to that inflated view, and we become phony. Proverbs 25:16 says, "If you find honey, eat just enough—too much of it, and you will vomit." Too much flattery, if you swallow it all, will make you sick, too.

The second step up the pedestal of pride is to expect "VIP

treatment." There are certain perks in every position—a key to the executive washroom, use of the company car, a special parking place, VIP treatment every place you go. When you have influence, people can treat you very special. It is incredible how nice they can be. Those things are okay if they are not abused, but it's easy to begin to feel superior, to act smug and assume everybody is supposed to treat you as though you are somebody special.

J. Wallace Hamilton tells of a time when John D. Rockfeller entered the New York City Riverside Church late. He whispered to the usher, "Don't take me to my regular seat. That will be too disruptive. I'll just sneak into the balcony." But a couple behind him were just the opposite. They said, "Show us to our regular pew. *We're* not the balcony type." You can begin to feel that everybody is supposed to treat you like somebody important.

The third step up to false pride is to insist on titles and status symbols. Jesus said of the Pharisees, "Everything they do is done for men to see: They make their phylacteries wide and the tassels of their prayer shawls long; they love the place of honor at banquets and the most important seats in the synagogues; they love to be greeted in the marketplaces and to have men call them 'Rabbi.' But you are not to be called 'Rabbi,' for you have only one Master and you are all brothers" (Matthew 23:5-8). In spite of this Scripture passage, some are still offended if they are not addressed as "Professor," "Doctor," "Reverend," or "Coach." That's false pride. That's dangerous self-promotion!

The fourth step up to false pride is the acceptance of expressions of worship without objection. We begin to feel like people should adore us, worship us. Some people from Tyre and Sidon came to King Herod requesting foreign aid. "On the appointed day Herod, wearing his royal robes, sat on his throne and delivered a public address to the people. They shouted, 'This is a voice of a god, not of a man.' Immediately, because Herod did not give praise to God, an angel of the Lord struck him down, and he was eaten by worms and died" (Acts 12:21-23). The nasty death of Herod is a reminder that it is dangerous when you begin to feel that people ought to idolize you. God will knock you off your pedestal one way or another.

Contrast that with Simon Peter when he went to the home of Cornelius, a devout Gentile. "As Peter entered the house, Cornelius met him and fell at his feet in reverence. But Peter made him get up. 'Stand up,' he said, 'I am only a man myself'" (Acts 10:25, 26). Simon Peter, a great leader in the church, refused to let somebody even kneel before him. Something is wrong when Christian people accept adoration from others, like groupies at a rock concert. Christ *alone* is worthy of worship. We are not out to impress people with our piety or our power, but to impress people that Christ alone should be exalted.

Some Reasons for Paul's Response

How did Paul maintain this spirit of humility? What enabled him to keep his equilibrium even though he was smelling the incense of power and influence? Three reasons here apply to us all.

First, he realized that people are fickle. The adulation in Lystra didn't last long. Soon some enemies from Antioch and Iconium came to Lystra and won the crowd over. The same people that wanted to put Paul on a pedestal one day were stoning him the next. Jesus experienced the same fickleness. He rode into Jerusalem on a donkey, and people said, "Hosanna!" A few days later they crucified Him. One reason to stay off the pedestal is that the same people who put you there will knock you off. They will be disappointed when you don't meet their expectations and they'll want to enthrone somebody else. The people who stood for six minutes and applauded Pete Rose when he got his record-breaking 4,192nd hit were the same people that booed him the day before because he went 0 for 4. People are fickle. It is stupid to let their applause go to your head.

Second, Paul's knowledge of his own mortality kept him humble. Look at what these barbarians did to Paul—"they stoned Paul and dragged him outside the city, thinking he was dead." Paul had participated in the stoning of Stephen, the first Christian martyr, and now he was the victim. These people were out for blood. There were no restrictions on the size of the rocks or how many they could throw or how hard they could hit—they wanted to kill him.

I personally think that Paul died here and God resurrected him. In 2 Corinthians 12 I believe Paul wrote about what happened to him after he had been stoned. He says, "I know a man in Christ who fourteen years ago was caught up to the third heaven. Whether it was in the body or out of the body I do not know—God knows. And I know that this man—whether in the body or apart from the body I do not know, but God knows—was caught up to Paradise. He heard inexpressable things, things that man is not permitted to tell" (2 Corinthians 12:2-4). I think Paul died; he had an out-of-the-body experience where his spirit went to be with the Lord and he was able to see Heaven, and he never forgot that experience. He never forgot that he was mortal, he was going to die.

Paul had a physical ailment that constantly reminded him that he was mortal. "To keep me from becoming conceited because of these surpassingly great revelations, there was given me a thorn in my flesh, a messenger of Satan, to torment me. Three times I pleaded with the Lord to take it away from me. But he said to me, 'My grace is sufficient for you, for my power is made perfect in weakness'" (2 Corinthians 12:7-9). His physical ailment kept him humble, reminding him constantly that he was going to die someday.

Wayne Smith, a friend of mine who ministers to a church in Lexington, Kentucky, was in a horrible automobile accident last year. He was cut in the face, gashed in the arm, crushed in the chest, and he shattered a knee. He was hit head-on by a car that swerved across the center line. The first two people on the scene were ministers. One of them knew Wayne, but didn't recognize him because he was so banged up. They hunted for a pulse and found none. "All we can do for this fellow is pray," they said, and they placed their hands on his shoulder and prayed. Wayne attributes his life to their prayer. I rejoice that he is back preaching and doing well.

Wayne has been—and still is—the most popular after-dinner speaker in Kentucky because he is so funny. He spoke three years straight at the Kentucky Annual Mayors' Convention. When they invited him back this year, he explained he had just been in an automobile accident, but they insisted that he come.

Over 800 people attended the Mayors' Convention. Wayne told just two jokes at the beginning and then said, "Men, I really don't feel like joking with you. I am a new man. I have just survived an automobile accident.

"I see that the theme of your Mayors' Conference is 'Changing Our Cities.' I want you to know you cannot change our cities until you are changed. And there is only one way you can be changed, and that is to let God change you." Then he preached a sermon to them.

When he was finished a number of them were weeping. They gave him a five-minute standing ovation. Several came up to him and said, "I haven't been to church in years, but I am going to. I know that you're absolutely right."

But Wayne said it didn't matter what they thought. With that experience, he was reminded that he had been called to preach the gospel. People's opinions don't matter. We need to remember constantly that we are mortal. All the applause of people will one day go for naught.

The final reason Paul kept his equilibrium was that he focused on Jesus Christ and not himself. I love these little phrases in the Bible that tell whole stories in just a few sentences. Verses 20 and 21 say that he went to Derbe and preached the good news. You know what I would have done? I would have gone to Derbe and said, "Find me a place where I can have a little R&R." But Paul went to the next city and he exalted Jesus Christ again.

To Paul the voice of man was faint because his ear was tuned to the more compelling voice of God. "I care very little if I am judged by you or by any human court, . . . it is the Lord who judges me" (1 Corinthians 4:3, 4). He wrote,

"We make it our goal to please him," (2 Corinthians 5:9) and, "If I were still trying to please men, I would not be a servant of Christ" (Galatians 1:10). When Paul went to Corinth, he said, "I resolved to know nothing while I was with you except Jesus Christ and him crucified" (1 Corinthians 2:2). Paul never forgot that only Jesus Christ belonged on the pedestal. All of his popularity and power was only for the glory of God.

Dan Issel was a member of our church when he was playing professional basketball with the Kentucky Colonels in Louisville. He has since moved away, but recently I had an occasion to renew our friendship. It was good to see that Dan was still growing with the Lord.

I asked, "It seems to me that with all the athletes abusing drugs and forgetting the Lord that you have kept your balance. Why do you think that is?"

He thought about it for awhile and said, "I think there are two things. First I was brought up by godly parents who took me to church every Sunday and I had those values drilled into me. My dad always said, treat the people nice on the way up because you are going to meet them on the way back down and the shoe may be on the other foot."

But the second thing he said was, "I believe that whatever ability I have been given, I have been given by God, not to glorify myself, but to glorify Him. Right or wrong, people do pay attention to people who have the ability to throw a ball through a hoop. If I act egotistical I would be doing just the opposite of what God would have me do. I realize I've fallen short in a lot of areas, but I do want to show people how a Christian should act in my particular position."

Paul demonstrated that it is possible to be in a position of power and influence and remain true to Jesus Christ. But it takes effort to stay off that pedestal.

> When I survey the wondrous cross,
> On which the Prince of glory died,
> My richest gain I count but loss,
> And pour contempt on all my pride.

Forbid it, Lord, that I should boast,
Save in the death of Christ my God;
All the vain things that charm me most,
I sacrifice them to His blood

See, from His head, His hands, His feet,
Sorrow and love flow mingled down;
Did e'er such love and sorrow meet,
Or thorns compose so rich a crown.

Were the whole realm of nature mine,
That were a present far too small;
Love so amazing, so divine,
Demands my soul, my life, my all.

When Christians Disagree

Acts 15:1-12, 36-41

WE LIVE IN a world of constant conflict. As Jesus said, "Nation rises against nation and kingdom against kingdom." That conflict exists not only internationally but here in our own country. People disagree with each other over foreign policy, defense, abortion, prayer in school, and hundreds of other issues. Even in our families, where we ought to be loving one another, so many times there is disagreement, conflict, and bickering.

What is true of the world is also true of our church. It would be wonderful if Christians in the churches across America never disagreed. What a testimony it would be if Christians lived in total harmony—if the church was an island of peace in the storm of the world. It was said of the early Christians that they were all of one accord in one place. Ideally, that's the way it should be, since Jesus is called the Prince of Peace, and since He prayed that His followers would be one.

But Christians have serious disagreements too. We disagree with each other over issues like inerrancy of the Bible, social drinking, capital punishment, interracial marriage, the meaning of millennium, the frequency of Communion, the meaning of baptism, and worship styles. Often those disagreements have logical arguments on both sides and they are not easily resolved.

This past week I overheard two Christians disagree in a congenial manner. One said, "You know, I think when we worship on Sunday morning, we shouldn't clap because Sunday morning ought to be a time of reverence."

The other said, "No, I think Sunday morning ought to be a time of joy."

"Well," the first man said, "the Bible says God's house is to be a house of prayer."

"Yes," the other said, "but the Bible also says that Sunday is a time of celebrating the resurrection of Jesus Christ from the dead."

'Yes," the first said, "The Bible also says, 'Be still and know that I am God.'"

The other said, "It also says, 'Make a joyful noise unto the Lord.'"

When the discussion was over, the issue had not been resolved and the Christians went their way. I think they will go to the grave disagreeing on that particular issue.

The early Christians had more serious disagreements than whether to clap in church. Disagreements can create hurt feelings, sever relationships, and even split churches. But when we learn that these early Christians had disagreements also, that kind of reassures us.

Let's look at two incidents of disagreement in Acts 15, see how they were handled, and draw some applications for our own lives. If you are not in Paul's shoes right now and you have never been, you will be someday.

Disagreement With the Legalists

The first is a disagreement between Paul and some legalistic Christians over Gentile evangelism. Some men came to Antioch from Jerusalem teaching that unless you were circumcised, you could not be saved. These men were Christians—former Pharisees who had been converted to Christ. But all of their lives it had been drilled into them that the Jews were God's chosen people. When they became Christians they accepted Jesus as the Jews' Messiah, but they thought that if anyone became a Christian he first had to get his life right with God by being circumcised and observing the law from the Old Testament. When they heard that Paul was baptizing Gentiles without requiring that they become Jews, they were appalled. Everything they held dear was being threatened. Paul had gone too far; he had to be opposed. So they made a long trip from Jerusalem to Antioch to confront Paul.

It is easier to get people fired up over a negative cause than a positive one. These people were against Paul, and they became very zealous. Verse 2 says they had a "sharp dispute." I like how the King James reads—"there was no small disagreement between them." I can understand why. The men were saying, "These people have never been saved because they never became Jews." Paul stood his ground. No way was he going to require that these Gentiles first observe the law. Christianity was not a new form of Judaism. It was a whole new system of salvation altogether. This was a pivotal issue to Paul and he would not concede. Some conflicts can be avoided but sometimes you just have to stand your ground.

The church quickly took six steps to resolve this conflict. It wasn't just left up in the air.

First, *they openly discussed it.* Someone had the courage to bring it out in the open. They didn't secretly divide into camps and undermine each other behind the scenes. I think it was Paul who brought the issue out in the open.

Second, *they selected a mediator.* In 1 Corinthians 6, Paul told the Christians at Corinth not to take each other to a pagan court. That would hurt their testimony with the world. He told them if they had a disagreement between them as Christians, to find someone in the church who could be objective and let him settle it.

This is what the church at Antioch did. "Paul and Barnabas were appointed, along with some other believers, to go up to Jerusalem to see the apostles and elders about this question" (Acts 15:2). This does not mean that the Jerusalem church ruled over the other churches, but that the apostles, whom everybody respected, lived in Jerusalem. The church at Antioch could not resolve this issue on their own, so they found people who were objective who could serve as a mediation team.

Third, *the leader made a clear-cut decision*. Both parties had their say: Paul and Barnabas reported everything that had been done through them, and the legalistic Christians said that the Gentiles must be circumcised or they are not saved.

After much discussion, Simon Peter took the floor and said something like this: "I used to feel the same way you do about the Gentiles until God commanded me to preach to a Gentile named Cornelius. While I was preaching to Cornelius, before I was even through telling him the gospel, the Holy Spirit descended on Cornelius like He did on me at Pentecost, and Cornelius began to speak in other languages. It was clear to me that God accepted Cornelius before he was circumcised. So let's not put a yoke around the neck of the Gentiles that God doesn't put on them and that we cannot follow ourselves."

Then Paul and Barnabas spoke up again. "The whole assembly became silent as they listened to Barnabas and Paul telling about the miraculous signs and wonders God had done among the Gentiles through them" (Acts 15:12). They were thinking, "Look, if these people aren't really saved, why is God doing miracles through them?" There probably hadn't been much silence up to this point but now the leaders were emerging. Then James, the half brother of Jesus, stated his decision. James seemed to be the chief spokesman in the Jerusalem church. He quoted a prophecy from the book of Amos that predicted the Gentiles would be included in the plan of God. "It is my judgment, therefore, that we should not make it difficult for the Gentiles who are turning to God" (vv.13-19).

The fourth step is that *they made some concessions*. They made some compromises. Dick Cavett defined a compromise as "An arrangement whereby people who can't get what they want make sure nobody else does either," but sometimes compromises are essential. They ease the tension, they save face, and they make it possible for harmony to prevail.

James decided they would not require the Gentiles to become Jews, but they would ask for some concessions. They required that the Gentiles abstain from meat sacrificed to idols, that they not eat the meat of strangled animals or drink blood, and they not commit sexual immorality. Now there was nothing wrong about eating meat sacrificed to idols, but that was offensive to some of the strict Jews. Sexual immorality is always wrong, so they wrote a letter reminding the Gentile Christians not to indulge in sexual immorality.

At times, Christians need to practice the art of compromise in matters of opinion to keep the peace.

Fifth, *they clearly communicated the decision*. They sent a letter to all the Gentile believers informing them of the decision. Church leaders have a responsibility to make it clear where the church stands. This decision was not arrived at by a popular vote. It was a leadership consensus; the leaders listened and made their decision. They wrote a letter and communicated to all the people what God had required of them. Verse 31 says, "The people read it and were glad for its encouraging message."

The sixth step was probably the most important. *Those who disagreed cooperated*. There is no evidence that the legalistic Christians fought to undermine that decision. Once the decision was arrived at, there was harmony among the people. The apostles and elders, with the whole church, were in agreement.

I've heard men come out of a board meeting and say, "You know, I don't agree with the decision that the majority has just made, but the decision has been made and I am not going to oppose it any more." They not only don't oppose it, but they get behind the project and support it. That takes a big person; it takes restraint of the tongue and a magnanimous spirit. It takes wisdom beyond that of the world.

Christ works through the combined wisdom of the leaders of the church.

Disagreement Between Paul and Barnabas

Barnabas and Paul disagreed over the ministry of John Mark. The first disagreement was a doctrinal one. This was a personal one. The first had to do with principle; this had to do with opinion.

John Mark had deserted Paul in the missionary tour in Pamphylia. He had been a part of the missionary team but for some reason, he left—either he became homesick or afraid or he was prejudiced about the Gentiles. Paul went on to Lystra sick and had all kinds of trouble. To make matters worse, he was shorthanded because John Mark had deserted him.

Now Paul proposed to Barnabas that they make a return visit. The first missionary journey was over and Paul wanted to go back and visit the churches that they had established.

Barnabas responded, "Great idea, Paul. Let's take John Mark with us again. I think he's matured and ready to go."

Paul said, "He's not dependable, Barnabas. He's a loser."

Should a man who has deserted be given a second chance?? Barnabas said yes and Paul said no. Both viewpoints have merit. Many times when Christians disagree it is not a matter of Scripture, but just a matter of opinion. We have different perspectives because of our background, experience, and temperament. Barnabas was a magnanimous, forgiving Christian. He was the first to welcome Paul and tell the Christians his conversion was legitimate. Barnabas, being a forgiving person, wanted to take John Mark with him. But Paul said, "Absolutely not. He deserted us at Pamphylia and he is not dependable."

The Bible says "There arose a sharp disagreement between them." The word there meant a sudden attack—a convulsion-like argument, a violent disagreement. Barnabas probably said, "Paul, how can you be so mean? Loosen up!" And Paul said, "Barnabas, how can you be so naive? Wise up! Your heart is leading, not your head."

Leslie Flynn in his book, *Great Church Fights*, suggests that the conversation went something like this:

PAUL: Mark? We can't take him. He failed us last time.

BARNABAS: But that was last time.

PAUL: He's likely to fail us again. You can't trust him, he's a deserter.

BARNABAS: He's had time to think it over, Paul. We've got to give him a chance again. He's got the makings of a missionary, and a good one.

PAUL: Tell me, Barnabas, is it because he's your cousin you want to take him along?

BARNABAS: That's not fair, Paul. You know I have tried to help many people who weren't my relatives, and you're one of them. I am convinced this lad needs understanding and encouragement.

PAUL: We need someone who can stand up to persecution, angry mobs, beatings, and perhaps imprisonment. Our team has to be close knit, Barnabas, thoroughly reliable. How can we trust a man who failed us like that? No, Barnabas, no. Recall the words of the Master, "No man putting his hand to the plow and looking back is fit for the kingdom of God." [Whenever you argue with another Christian, it's always good to have a little Scripture to throw in.]

BARNABAS: I have talked to him about his failure and I am sure he won't desert us again. To refuse him could do spiritual damage at the moment of his repentance.

Barnabas probably quoted, "Jesus said, 'Forgive one another as I have forgiven you.'" Paul probably quoted Proverbs 25:19, "Like a bad tooth or a lame foot is reliance on the unfaithful in times of trouble."

Lessons for Modern Disagreements

First, *disagreements are inevitable*. Expect them. Sometimes Christian people get panicky if another Christian disagrees with them. They hate conflict so much they fail to speak up when they should speak up and they compromise their principles. Disagreements are inevitable. Even godly people like Barnabas and Paul disagree. Disagreement is not always a sign of spiritual ignorance or carnality. You may both be walking with God—and you both pray about it and you both read your Bibles and you still cannot come to an agreement.

A naive Christian married couple both believed that because they loved each other and they loved the Lord, they were going to live in tranquility and never have an argument in their marriage. They discovered that it really wasn't like that. The longer they were married, the more they disagreed and the more they churned. The young bride was really disturbed. She knew she wasn't supposed to get a divorce, so finally she said, "Honey, let's just pray to the Lord that He will take one of us home. Then I'll go live with my mother!"

Don't be devastated if occasionally you disagree with a fellow Christian. If you are a thinker you will have disagreement. The only people who never have conflict are people who don't think, who drift along with whatever is in vogue at the time. Disagreements are inevitable—expect them.

Second, *disagreements are dangerous*. Avoid them if possible. Some people love controversy. They are antagonistic because they love to argue. They need to understand that conflict has the potential to hurt. Many divorced people I have talked to said, "it just began with a little contention. I never thought it would get to this."

The Jerusalem conference took up a lot of valuable time that could have been spent evangelizing. The disagreement between Paul and Barnabas separated good friends of ten years. We read that ten years later Paul forgave John Mark, but we never read about Barnabas again. He just sails off the pages of history. "An offended brother is more unyielding than a fortified city, and disputes are like the barred gates of a citadel" (Proverbs 18:19).

Don't be too shortsighted to see the far-reaching consequences of conflict. It can hurt. The best way to handle most disagreement is to avoid it. Prevent it.

A little boy wrote an essay about pins. "Pins save thousands of lives every year," he said.

His teacher asked, "How do pins save thousands of lives every year?"

The little boy answered, "By not swallowing them."

Prevention is usually the best solution. When you can see conflict developing, just keep quiet if the issue isn't vital. Swallow your pride and sidestep the issue. When you see people getting red in the face or raising their voices, that's the time to back off. The Bible says, "If it is possible, as far as it depends on you, live at peace with everyone" (Romans 12:18). If it is possible to avoid conflict, do so. "Blessed are the peacemakers" (Matthew 5:9).

The third lesson is, *disagreements can usually be resolved*. Make concessions. Even when a conflict involves a principle like the Jerusalem conference, concessions can be made that will enable the wrong party to save face. You can make concessions in your attitude without compromising the truth. Someone said that the difference between a fundamentalist Christian and an evangelical Christian was that a fundamentalist Christian is an evangelical who is mad at somebody. That doesn't have to be true—we can stand for the truth without being mad at somebody. If you are proud and obstinate and you don't make any concessions, you may end up a lonely person in your older years.

Most of the time, conflict does not involve principle at all. A compromise can be reached. I believe that Paul and Barnabas could have arrived at some kind of compromise. They could have said, "Let's take John Mark part way," or "Let's take an abbreviated tour and see how he does." But neither party made concessions and a ten-year friendship was dissolved.

Often harmony is simply a matter of being willing to compromise. That's so much more important than personal preference. Should we clap in church or should we not? Let's be reverent on Sunday morning and then when the quartet sings, let's clap and not make a big deal of it. Should we sing the old hymns or the new choruses? Let's have a little of both. Is it okay for the church to have an auction? Let's have an auction but have it off the church grounds. Should a 17-year-old boy whose curfew is 12 midnight be permitted to stay out until 1:00 a.m. when it's a special occasion? Well, let's make a concession and make it 12:05!

When my wife and I were first married, she wanted to put up the Christmas tree two weeks before Christmas. To me that was sacrilegious, because in my home you put up the Christmas tree on Christmas Eve! We argued about that and finally we came to a compromise. She put up the Christmas tree two weeks in advance by herself! Compromise is not a matter of weakness. It is a matter of wisdom; a matter of tolerance. "Love does not always demand its own way" (1 Corinthians 13:5, *Living Bible*).

The fourth lesson is most important—*disagreements can leave deep wounds.* Be forgiving. When we disagree we can use harsh words, we can be vindictive. We can inflict wounds, sever friendships, and hurt people, and in our pride, continue to harbor resentment. Somebody said, "Anger gets you into trouble and pride keeps you there."

Make an effort at reconciliation. Don't insist on your opinion at the cost of a friendship or harmony in the family or in the church. If you are absolutely right, be big enough to forgive and reestablish trust without having to prove you were right all along or without making them say "I'm sorry." If you were partially at fault, swallow your pride and apologize. At least make some gesture of reconciliation if the offense was years ago and you don't want to bring it up again.

A woman came into my office just elated. "I hadn't talked to my father in years because of a disagreement," she began. "But he's just had open heart surgery. He's in a hospital in Florida. I broke down and telephoned him just to say, 'Dad, I'm really concerned. How are you doing?' He was glad that I called and we had a great conversation. We didn't bring up the past issue, but it is so good to know that we have reestablished communication. We are building a bridge."

Do you need to rebuild some bridges that you've blown away? Bruce Larson tells of a man who was convicted in a church service that he had mistreated his wife. He prayed, "Oh, Lord, I admit to you that I have neglected my wife. I've ignored her, I've been sarcastic to her, I've hurt her. I am sorry." Then it was though he heard the voice of the Lord say, "Don't tell me, tell her." Larson said, "Brokenness is going to the people we've hurt and being humble before them."

Jesus said, "If you are offering your gift at the altar and there remember that your brother has something against you, leave your gift there in front of the altar [don't even worship]. First go and be reconciled to your brother; then come and offer your gift" (Matthew 5:23, 24). In other words, your life will not be right with the Lord until you have made that effort toward reconciliation with your brother.

Cliff Barrows said, "There are twelve words that hold a family together [these twelve words hold all relationships together]: "I was wrong," "I am sorry," "Please forgive me," "I love you."

When ten years had gone by and Paul was in prison, he wrote to Timothy, "Only Luke is with me. Get Mark and bring him with you, because he is helpful to me in my ministry." Paul discovered that John Mark had become a faithful Christian. His reasoning might have gone like this: "Maybe I made a mistake in not taking him along, maybe not. Maybe he was just too young for such a responsible position. But whatever the reason, it's in the past. There is no use crying over spilt milk. There's no sense proving who was right, no 'I told you so.'" Paul was too big a man for that. Mark had matured. Big people know what it is to forgive. They know what it is to give a second chance. If anybody had been given a second chance, it was Paul.

John Mark made a comeback, thanks to God, who gives us all a second chance. I guess that's what the poet had in mind when he wrote "Beginning Again."

> He came to my desk with a quivering lip;
>   the lesson was done.
> "Have you a new sheet for me, teacher?

I've spoiled this one."
I took his leaf all soiled and blotted
   and gave him a new one, all unspotted.
And into his tired heart I cried,
   "Do better now, my child."

I went to God's throne with a trembling heart;
   the day was done.
"Have you a new day for me, dear Master?
   I've spoiled this one."
He took my day all soiled and blotted
   and gave me a new one, all unspotted,
And into my heart He sighed,
   "Do better now, my child."

If God were to place all our iniquity upon our own shoulders, which of us could stand? Since God has given us a second chance and a third chance and a tenth chance, shouldn't we do the same to those who offend us?

Understanding God's Will

Acts 16:1-10

A FEW YEARS ago I was contacted by another church and asked if I would consider becoming their preacher. From the beginning of my ministry I determined that I would need two signs before I would relocate. First, I would need to be convinced that my effectiveness where I am was nearing an end. I would like to stay at my present ministry the rest of my life, but most leaders become so common to people that they lose their influence. Second, I would need to be challenged by another ministry. I have always wanted to preach in a growing church and did not want to have a maintenance kind of ministry, so there had to be a special potential somewhere else to excite me.

This particular contact was impressive. The men who contacted me were skilled communicators—business executives and administrators in education--and they knew how to win friends and influence people. They said, "Bob, we've decided that you are the number one choice to be our minister. We know everything about you; we have investigated you; we were in your church service twice last month, even though you didn't know we were here. We know you've had a good ministry here but we think we have more potential at our church. We have 26 acres of ground. We have excellent leadership, a good financial base, and one worship service. We don't want you to decide now. We want you to pray about it and consider coming to our city to look our situation over."

They came at a frustrating time for me. We were having three worship services at that time and all three were filled. I could not envision four services, and all our efforts to purchase adjacent property were fruitless. It seemed to me we were coming to the end of our potential. A number of thoughts raced through my mind for the next few days. I did not want to leave. If it were the Lord's will, would I be willing to leave behind people I love, the home I love, and the Louisville Cardinals (it was basketball season, not football season).

The only answer to that question had to be "yes." If I am really a servant of the Lord, I've got to be willing to go. But it made me ill even to think about it. This was only the second occasion in all of my ministry when I have seriously considered going somewhere else. I remember standing in the shower with tears streaming down my face and saying, "Lord, if that is Your will, I will go."

But how did I determine what God's will was? That is a question we all wrestle with at times.

I have often thought if the Lord would just send us a special delivery letter or make a long distance phone call that we would all respond affirmatively. But most of the time it is not that easy to determine what God wants for our lives. In this particular case, I prayed, I counseled with family and Christian friends, and I listened as some of our church leaders began to talk about relocation, even though they were not aware of the dilemma I was going through at that time. And I watched as doors began to open in a miraculous way. I decided to stay and I believe that God has blessed that decision.

God's Guidance

God promises repeatedly in His Word that He will direct the Christian who seeks guidance.

> Trust in the Lord with all your heart
>   and lean not on your own understanding;
> in all your ways acknowledge him,
>   and he will make your paths straight.
>   (Proverbs 3:5, 6)

"Are not two sparrows sold for a penny? Yet not one of them will fall to the ground apart from the will of your Father. And even the very hairs of your head are all numbered," Jesus said. "So don't be afraid; you are worth more than many sparrows" (Matthew 10:29-31). Paul wrote, "It is God who works in you to will and to act according to his good purpose" (Philippians 2:13). Probably everyone here has prayed with the psalmist,

> Show me your ways, O Lord,
>   teach me your paths;
> guide me in your truth and teach me,
>   for you are God, my Savior,
>   and my hope is in you all day long.
>   (Psalm 25:4, 5)

What does God want me to do? Where does He want me to go to college? What should be my vocation? Whom does He want me to marry? "Show me your ways, O Lord." Should I stay home with the children or should I go to work? Should I change jobs or stay with this one that is secure? Should I accept the leadership role or just remain in the background? Should I confront the problem or should I hope that it goes away? "Teach me your paths." If you are a growing Christian, you have sought and prayed for God's guidance in your daily life.

Let me mention two misconceptions about God's will that I think are the most prevalent. First, there is a popular misconception that God has every detail of our life prearranged. The doctrine of Calvinism is almost a sacred cow in Christian circles. Many believe that God has caused everything that happens to you. If that is true, you don't ever have to worry about searching for God's will because He's already got a program and He will cause it to happen. I don't think Paul believed that way. If he had, he would have never gotten into an argument with Barnabas whether John Mark ought to go along with them or not. He would have just said, "Well, it was God's will that John Mark leave."

We need to acknowledge the sovereignty of God, but we also need to respect the biblical teaching about man's free will. I believe we face many decisions in life in which God has no preference, or decisions between what is good and what is best. I can choose to go to my home by two or three different routes. I don't think God has a preference—they are all equally slow. I don't think that God has our lives programmed like a road map where every detail is outlined for us. I think rather it's like a compass guiding us in the right direction.

A second common misconception is that God's will is always unpleasant. Some Christians are afraid to totally surrender to God's will because they are afraid He will make them miserable—He will immediately send them as a missionary to Iran or make them give 50% of their income, or something tragic. I have a friend who was single for a long time. He said he had a hard time praying that God would show him the woman he wanted him to marry, because he just knew that God's choice would be spiritual but very plain—and he wanted a knockout.

But God's will is not usually unpleasant. It is fulfilling. Romans 12:1, 2 urges us to surrender to God so we can prove what is "his good, pleasing and perfect will." God's will isn't unpleasant, it is pleasing. It is disobedience that makes us miserable. "Delight yourself in the Lord and he will give you the desires of your heart" (Psalm 37:4). I don't think that means if you surrender to the Lord he will give you everything you want, but when you surrender to the Lord, he changes the desires of your heart to coincide with His.

Consider Paul's experience as he began his second missionary journey. He began after a five-year interval to visit churches that he had established on his first trip. From his experience on this journey I want to point out three facts about God's guidance.

God Usually Leads Through Common Sense

As Paul revisited the churches he had established, he came to the town of Lystra. Lystra was the place where he had been stoned and left for dead. To go back into that city required courage. There he met an impressive young Christian man named Timothy.

Timothy was between the ages of 16 and 25. Fifteen years later Paul wrote to Timothy and said, "Don't let anybody despise your youth." It is generally agreed that they didn't call somebody youthful in that day if they were older than 40, so when they first met he had to be younger than 25. Timothy had a good reputation among the believers of that area. He had come to know Christ through the testimony of his mother and his grandmother. His father was a Greek; his mother had been a nominal Jew who had been converted to Christ.

Paul was impressed with Timothy, and he asked Timothy to accompany him on the missionary tour. He wanted to train able young men as interns. When Timothy agreed to go, Paul circumcised him because of the Jews living in the area. Now some critics accused Paul of an inconsistency because he had just insisted at the Jerusalem conference that one did not have to become a Jew before becoming a Christian, and now he was having Timothy circumcised. He did it simply because it made good common sense.

Timothy was the son of a Jewish woman. Not to circumcise him would have limited his usefulness. The Jews would have refused to listen to Timothy, so Paul made it possible for him to minister to everybody, according to a principle he set forth himself: "I have become all things to all men so that by all possible means I might win some" (1 Corinthians 9:22). This had nothing to do with Timothy's salvation; Paul was just exercising wisdom to eliminate argument and barriers to the gospel.

God usually leads through plain common sense. Leslie Weatherhead told about a man who prayed for God's guidance. "I prayed and prayed but nothing divine came," the man said, "so I just used my common sense and it worked out fine." Weatherhead said, "It didn't seem to occur to the man that God had given him a mind specifically for that purpose."

"'Come now, let us reason together,' says the Lord" (Isaiah 1:18). God has given you the capacity to reason with Him. Why is it that we think discerning God's will is something miraculous or spectacular?

One fellow lived in a low-lying area. A man in a jeep drove up one day and said, "This area is about to be flooded—you need to evacuate." He replied, "I'll just stay here and trust the Lord." Pretty soon the waters were swirling around his front porch and he sat in his rocker. A man arrived in a boat and said, "You need to get out of here." He said, "I'm just trusting the Lord." Finally he was on the rooftop, water swirling around the house, and a helicopter came and lowered a life ring. He said, "No, thanks, I'm going to trust the Lord. The Lord will take care of me."

The man drowned, and he stood before the Lord complaining that He hadn't taken care of him. The Lord answered, "I sent a jeep, a boat, and a helicopter. What did you want me to do?"

God's will is not always miraculous. He has not created us as helpless infants. He has given us sound minds and He expects us to use them. There is no excuse for a Christian to go through life as a space-head. First of all, God has given His Word, which communicates His mind. We need to saturate ourselves with the mind of God. Second, He said if we pray for wisdom, He will give it. Third, we associate with Christian friends. "He who walks with the wise grows wise, but a companion of fools suffers harm" (Proverbs 13:20). As you read the Word, pray, and associate with Christian people, you ought to gain wisdom and know the mind of God. God reveals His will through common sense.

God Sometimes Leads Through Circumstances

Paul was "kept by the Holy Spirit from preaching the word in the province of Asia" (Acts 16:6). Up to this point, Paul evidently just chose where he would go. He did what seemed best to him. He decided that he would go to Ephesus, but the Holy Spirit hindered him. Some people think the Holy Spirit spoke in an audible voice—"Don't go that way." I think Paul encountered a series of closed doors. Maybe he got sick and couldn't go, or the boat trip got canceled, or the Jews opposed him. One time after another he tried to go in the direction of Ephesus and the Holy Spirit prevented him. Whether it was inner feeling or outer frustration, the result was the same; Paul couldn't do what he intended to do.

He went in another direction. "They tried to enter Bithynia, but the Spirit of Jesus would not allow them to" (v. 7). This had to be frustrating to Paul. Nobody likes ambiguity. God wasn't telling Paul where He wanted him to go; He was just telling him where He didn't want him to go. But sometimes the Lord's "no" becomes a part of His ultimate "yes."

A young woman prays for God's guidance in selecting a mate. She dates a man who is not a Christian. She loves him, but she knows the Bible says "don't be unequally yoked together," so she breaks it off. Then she dates another man who is a Christian but there is not the right chemistry, so she breaks it off. She dates somebody she really likes, but he breaks it off. One door after another seems to be closed, and she is frustrated—but God's immediate "no" can be a part of His ultimate "yes." There may be somebody else down the road.

A man told me last week that he lost an excellent job in sales because a local company went out of business. So he prayed for God's guidance and looked for another job, but nothing opened up. Finally came the ideal job. He knew it was God's will for him. He prayed and prayed. Out of 300 applicants he got down to the final two—and then he didn't get the job. And nothing else opened up. He said, "Finally I took a job in insurance, the one field that I said I would never go into, and it's just now that I am beginning to see that God's hand was in it."

God's will is often delayed. Sometimes He just says "no." Paul had to do two things that are unpleasant for the modern American Christian. The first is *wait;* doors kept closing and Paul had to wait. We are an instant society and we want God's will right now, but the Bible over and over emphasizes that God's timetable is usually slower than ours. God is never in a hurry, but He's never late. "They that wait upon the Lord shall renew their strength."

A man asked, "Lord, is it true that with You a thousand years is like a day?"

The Lord said, "Yes it is. A thousand years is just like a second."

The man asked, "Lord, is it true that a million dollars to You is like a penny?"

"Yes, it is, a million dollars is just like a penny."

He said, "Well, can I have a million dollars?"

The Lord said, "Sure, just a second!"

God's will comes to those who patiently seek it. A lot of times we have to wait and endure a series of closed doors.

The second unpleasant thing that Paul had to do was *work.* He didn't just sit back and fold his arms when one door closed. He went to another door. He kept moving. He kept pushing on doors to see which one would open up. The secret of patience is doing something else in the meantime. To determine God's will takes effort. He wants us to study His Word, to pray hard, to talk with other people, and to try to find out what His will is.

In the garden of Gethsemane Jesus prayed for three hours, and the Bible said "his sweat was like great drops of blood." Understanding the Father's will did not come easily or quickly for Jesus or for Paul; nor will it come easily for us. But God guides us through circumstances even when we are not aware of it. Paul may have been frustrated, feeling a sense of futility, but God had him just where He wanted him.

If you acknowledge God, He will direct your paths. He may not show you why you are on that path or where that path is going. We just have to rest assured we are right where He wants us to be.

J. Wallace Hamilton tells of a traffic policeman at 42nd and Broadway in New York City who saw a cat come up to the curb holding a baby kitten in her mouth. "She wanted to cross the street but the roar of the traffic frightened her. She would start across and then draw back. She would make a second attempt and then retreat. It was too dangerous to go. But the policeman, who had a sensitive heart, stopped all the traffic and the cat darted across to safety. The policeman's hand came down and the traffic resumed. Hamilton said, "That cat never knew that she was the object of public care and that the authority of a New York City policeman was called upon at that moment to guide her through the danger spot." Nor do we know how often the strong hand of God goes up to get us across, open the way, and guide us to safety.

That closed door, that aborted job opportunity, that sickness, that terminated relationship, may be the providence of God to protect us from something that we are not even aware of and though we can't see it, we have to trust that as we acknowledge Him, He is directing our paths.

God Occasionally Leads Us Through Dramatic Revelation

In the city of Troas Paul had a dramatic vision. A man from Macedonia was standing and begging him, "Come over to Macedonia and help us." Commentaries speculate about who this man from Macedonia was. Maybe it was Alexander the Great, the Greek conquerer, who envisioned a one-world government. I think it was Luke. Luke was the doctor who became Paul's travel companion and the author of the book of Acts. Verse 10 is the first time that Luke uses the term "we" in the book—"We got ready at once to leave for Macedonia." Whoever the man was in the vision, it was God speaking directly to Paul, and Paul obeyed at once.

When God's will becomes evident, don't delay in obeying. Thomas Carlisle said, "Our grand business is not to see what lies dimly at a distance but to do what lies clearly ahead." God isn't playing guessing games with us. He doesn't say, "If you acknowledge me, I will direct your paths" and then laugh up His sleeve when we honestly make the wrong choice and say, "Well, they blew it." He says, "If you will acknowledge me, I will direct your paths."

Sometimes God does that dramatically. My sister Roseanne was working at her post several months ago. During a thunderstorm she thought she heard an unusual noise about 25 or 30 feet away, and she went to investigate it. After she moved, a lightning bolt hit right on the spot where she had been sitting. People came rushing from everywhere to see if she was all right. To this day she doesn't know what the noise was or why she went to investigate. I think that God comes dramatically at times in our lives—maybe to move us or to give us a particular direction.

But let me add that I think He does that very rarely. Be careful that you don't too quickly attribute impressions, dreams, or the advice of others to God's will. People do that flippantly all the time. Some people even make decisions by closing their eyes, opening their Bible, and pointing down to a verse—and that's their answer. One Christian who relied on impressions went out to buy a used car. He prayed the Lord would help him to find the right one. That night he had a dream in which everything was yellow. So the next day he went out and bought the first yellow car he could find. Sure enough, it was a lemon!

I heard of a lady who wondered if she ought to go overseas to the Holy Land. She was afraid because of all the airplane crashes. She awakened in the morning and her digital clock read 7:47. So she said, "Well, I'm supposed to take a 747." That was her sign! I think we need to be careful about those impressions. Paul Little once wrote, "I get nervous when people imply a private pipeline to God. The words 'God led me' are often merely the squirting of spiritual preference on our own self centeredness."

If you feel God is speaking to you, make sure you confirm that. John Wesley wrote, "Do not hastily ascribe things to God. Do not easily suppose that dreams, voices, or impressions are revelations from God. They may be from him; they may be from nature; they may be from the devil. Therefore, believe not every spirit but try the spirits whether they be from God."

Paul was given a vision to go to Macedonia. He went and God blessed. He met a woman named Lydia who became a Christian. She opened up her large home to his missionary team. The church of Philippi was one of the best churches that Paul ever established. In fact, by going that direction, Christianity moved through Europe and to England and to America. If it had gone the other direction it would have gone to Asia and the Orient. But even when he was in Philippi, Paul was beaten and thrown in prison. Just because you work within the will of God doesn't mean that there won't be difficulty. Jesus did God's will, and it led Him to a cross. There may be burdens and thorns and crosses for us, but we have His assurance that if in all our ways we acknowledge Him, He will direct our paths. It is better to walk in the darkness with God than in the light without him.

An old sea captain was asked, "How is it that you can navigate this dangerous channel at night without ever going aground?"

The captain said, "You see those buoys out there in the water? When those three buoys merge into one ahead of me I know that I am in the mainstream of the channel."

There are three signs that we can use to know that we are in the channel of God's will. First, is it scriptural? God will never never violate His Word. He doesn't contradict himself. If you are dating somebody who is not a Christian, don't ask, "Is it God's will for me to marry that person?" He has already said in His Word, "Do not be unequally yoked together." If you are thinking about taking a job that requires you to be absent from church every Sunday, don't even think about whether it's God's will. He says, "Don't neglect the assembling of yourselves together." Is it scriptural?

Second, are the doors opening up? Do you have to hammer them down? I like A. W. Tozer's phrase, "If the Lord's in it it flows—if it is forced, it is of the flesh." Now we have to work and we have to turn doorknobs, but if the doors don't open up with a reasonable amount of effort, we need to back off.

Third, is it what you want? If you are really seeking God's will and it is scriptural and doors are opened up, I think He wants you to do what you enjoy doing. He respects your desires. So many people think that in order to obey God's will they have to do the opposite of what they want. But if you will surrender to God, He will show you "his good, pleasing and perfect will" (Romans 12:2).

A Strategy for Battle (Part 1)

Acts 16:11-15

"ONWARD CHRISTIAN SOLDIERS, marching as to war." Most of us have sung that phrase dozens of times, but it probably doesn't represent our attitude toward the Christian life.

We don't think of ourselves as soldiers involved in a war. We think of becoming a Christian as a kind of life insurance policy to be cashed in at the end. We think of going to church as a kind of spiritual boost to help us through the pressure of the real world. The idea of being a soldier in a war sounds a little extreme and exaggerated.

A Spiritual War

But God's Word frequently uses that imagery of a soldier involved in a conflict to describe the Christian. "Finally, be strong in the Lord and in his mighty power. Put on the full armor of God so that you can take your stand against the devil's schemes. For our struggle is not against flesh and blood, but against the rulers, against the authorities, against the powers of this dark world and against the spiritual forces of evil in the heavenly realms" (Ephesians 6:10-12). Paul goes on to tell Christians to put on the breastplate of righteousness, the helmet of salvation, and the shield of faith, and take the sword of the spirit, which is the Word of God, and go forth to war.

We are involved in a spiritual conflict. We're on the front line of the battle between the forces of God and forces of Satan; the Prince of Peace versus the prince of darkness. Now some people might snicker at a mystical sounding statement like that, but it is the biblical truth. The contest is being waged in the hearts and minds of people—that's the battlefield. Our struggle is not against flesh and blood. We are not battling the Communists in Russia. We are not trying to see if we can have higher attendance than the church down the street. Our battle is in the minds of people, to persuade more to surrender to the lordship of Jesus Christ.

In 1 Corinthians 15, Paul underscores that Satan's destiny is death. Then he says, "Thanks be to God! He gives us the victory through our Lord Jesus Christ." The Christian life is not a playground, it is a battlefield. We are not offering people an alternative lifestyle. We are not adding a new dynamic to their lives. We are at war with the world! The stakes could not be higher! God promises eternal life to those who are on the side of victory and eternal death to those who are on the side of Satan.

Tragically, at the present time we're losing the battle. A recent survey in *Christianity Today* revealed that only 26% of the general public in America believe that Jesus is fully God and fully man. In a recent survey by George Gallup, 81% of the people in America considered themselves to be Christians, but only 12% could be classified as committed. Another poll reveals that over the last two decades, Americans who believe the Bible to be the infallible Word of God has dropped from 65% to 37%.

Christian values are in a retreat across America. We've been driven back by moral perversion, the breakdown of the family, and a soaring crime rate. Charles Colson tells about a letter that appeared in Ann Landers' newspaper column "from a young man brimming with indignation. His girlfriend, after discontinuing her birth control pills without his knowledge, had gotten pregnant. 'Some women cannot be trusted,' he concluded angrily.

"As I read his letter I shook my head," Colson writes. "Sadly, so many consider sex outside of marriage an unquestioned right. Maybe, I thought, Ann's response would set him straight.

"But her answer virtually endorsed his attitude: 'Your letter should be discussed in all high school classrooms in America.... [It] makes abundantly clear that a conniving (or careless) girl can make a tremendous difference in a man's life.'

"I almost crumpled the paper. No mention of moral right or wrong, just commiseration and the shocking proposal that all high schoolers be taught how to be promiscuous safely."

Let's face the fact that right now we Christians are losing the struggle for the hearts and minds of people. Can we reverse the trend? Can we yet prevail in our struggle for people to be saved? That answer lies in the question of whether or not there will be enough Christian people who have the courage to begin to do battle, to be a Christian soldier of the cross.

A Successful Battle Strategy

When the apostle Paul went to the city of Philippi, he experienced a great victory. His message was well received and the church was on the advance. Acts 16 records three conversions in that city from an amazing cross section of the population. It begins with the conversion of Lydia, a wealthy woman, then a slave girl who was in rank poverty, and then a man from the sturdy middle class, a Philippian jailer.

The church Paul established here was one of the strongest he had ever started. Later Paul wrote a letter to the Philippians that talks about their joy. Paul had such success in Philippi that the people in the next town said, "These people who have turned the world upside down have come here." What did Paul do to make his evangelistic advance so successful? From his experience, we can learn some hints about how we can reverse the retreat of our day.

Paul took the gospel out of the synagogue and into the marketplace. Apparently when Paul went to Philippi there was no synagogue there. His usual practice was to go right to the Jewish synagogue, because the people there believed in one God and looked for the coming of the Messiah. There Paul would have a ready audience. But a city had to have ten family units to qualify for a synagogue and Philippi was apparently a strongly anti-Semitic city. When some men wanted to oppose Paul they said, "These men are Jews" (Acts 16:20). The Jewish population in this city was small and there was no synagogue there. When Paul arrived he could have been discouraged; instead he searched the city to find somebody with spiritual sensitivity.

He found a group of women who worshiped God every Sabbath day down by the river. Verse 13 says, "We sat down and began to speak to the women who had gathered there." Women in that day were regarded as second-class citizens, but the gospel of Christ consistently elevated the status of women. The church in Philippi, one of the strongest that Paul ever started, was founded by a group of women.

It seems to me that generally speaking, women have a greater degree of spiritual sensitivity than men. For example, in almost every church you'll find more women in the choir. I don't think I've ever seen a choir that had more men than women. I think the male ego is so weak that we have a hard time humbling ourselves before the Lord.

As Paul taught these women he noticed one in particular who was responsive. Her name was Lydia. The text says she was a businesswoman, a dealer in purple cloth. Barclay points out that the purple dye she used was gathered drop by drop from shellfish—a tedious process—and this made the garments she sold very expensive; these garments were worn primarily by royalty. So Lydia was a dealer in expensive clothing and she was apparently successful. She had a house large enough to accommodate the whole missionary team.

"The Lord opened her heart to respond to Paul's message" (v. 14). She and the members of her household were baptized. Notice that Luke selects her submission to baptism as the tangible sign that she had surrendered to Christ. Jesus had told the disciples, "Go into all the world and preach the good news to all creation. Whoever believes and is baptized will be saved" (Mark 16:16). When Lydia opened her heart to the gospel, Paul instructed her to be baptized even though she was a woman of prayer and a woman of means.

I love the symbol of baptism. It symbolizes the death, burial and resurrection of Christ, but it also symbolizes our humble spirit of submission to Christ. I've seen people come forward wearing expensive jewelry, tailor-made clothing, and $100 hairdos. But soon, when they are ready to get baptized, all their jewelry is off. The expensive clothing is exchanged for the simple white robe everyone wears. That $100 hairdo is about to be destroyed. It's as if they are saying with the hymn writer, "Lord, nothing in my hand I bring, simply to the cross I cling." They are lowered briefly into the water, just as Jesus was buried in the grave, and they are brought back up just as Jesus arose from the dead. In the eyes of the world they probably look terrible when they're drenched, but in the eyes of the Christian family, they are a beautiful picture of humility.

Baptism is not humiliating, but it is humbling. Jesus said if you don't humble yourself and become like a little child, you cannot expect to enter the kingdom of God. I think that baptism reveals the wisdom of God, as that person humbles himself before the Lord. Lydia responded to Christ and she was baptized.

She invited Paul and the others to her home. She must have been the kind of person that insisted they come. "'If you consider me a believer in the Lord,' she said, 'come and stay at my house,'" and Luke says, "She persuaded us" (Acts 16:15). In that day there were few hotels and few restaurants. Hospitality was an important virtue. The first thing Lydia did upon becoming a Christian was open up her home. If God has blessed you with a decent house or apartment, don't turn it into a museum. Open it up. The Christian home should be the home of the open door. Bring home Christian friends and visitors to the church, like missionaries or singing groups, and practice hospitality.

I grew up in a modest home, but I'm thankful that my mother was constantly inviting people to visit or to have dinner with us. I met evangelists, missionary teams, and Bible college personnel. To this day, I will meet those people at a convention and they will say, "I remember being in your home. We went out and played basketball together and we went down with you when you milked the cows." I never had one person say, "I was in your home once, and I remember your mother's glasses didn't match and that frayed part in the carpet." It's the fellowship that's important.

At 11:30 one Friday night, there was a knock on my front door. Ten or twelve people from the church who were returning home from a basketball game were standing in my front yard. They sang a Christmas carol, though it was the first of November. I said, "Come on in, you're embarrassing me in front of the whole neighborhood!" We had some chocolate chip cookies, and it was after midnight before we could get them to leave! We had a good time together. I think the Christian home ought to be the home of the open door, even at midnight. Open your home. Lydia did, and that's evidence of Christianity.

Paul took his message down by the riverbank. There wasn't any synagogue, but he didn't give up. He went out into the marketplace. If we are going to make an advance in our war against evil, we've got to take the message out of the church building into the street. Jesus told His people, "You are the salt of the earth." The salt isn't doing the job if it's just in the salt shaker. It's got to permeate the food. He said, "You are the light of the world." The light is no value if you put it under a bushel. It is to be put on the lampstand, so it gives light to all who are in the house so everybody can see. Jesus told His followers to go into all the world with the gospel, not just the church.

We are not going to make a significant impact in our community by sitting in the church building talking to ourselves. An army doesn't win a battle sitting in the barracks polishing its weapons. It has to march into the battlefield. We need to come to church to be instructed and to receive inspiration, but the church building is not the battlefield—it is the ammunition dump.

In his excellent book, *Who Speaks For God?*, Charles Colson emphasizes getting the message into the secular marketplace. He writes, "Our best writers shouldn't all compete for spots with *Christianity Today* or CBN, but should infiltrate the newsrooms of the *New York Times* and CBS. Christian scholars should debate their secular counterparts and shatter the myth that Christian faith is intellectually inferior. Christian business people need to apply biblical principles to everyday office decisions."

Christian people across the country have been picketing the Seven-Eleven food chain because it is one of the leading peddlers of pornography in America. But one Christian businessman in Cincinnati, Carl Linder (Linder is the founder of the United Dairy Farmer stores in Cincinnati), resolved the situation in one day. He bought all 63 of the Seven-Eleven stores in southern Ohio and the next day he removed Playboy and Penthouse from the shelves. He said, "Adult magazines don't fit into our marketing scheme." That's the Christian businessman going into the marketplace with the gospel.

One young man I know is studying to be a religion professor. "My goal is not to be a professor in a Bible college or seminary," he says. "I want to be a religion professor in a state university, because many times when our young people take religion courses at the university they are taught by people who don't believe the Bible and their faith is undermined. I want to go as a person who believes the Bible is the Word of God and to undergird their faith instead of destroying it."

What We Need

All of us have the responsibility to go and to take the message into the marketplace, wherever that may be. If we are going to do that, Colson suggests several steps.

We must *discern the false values of our culture.* We've got to know the enemy. I am told by people who fought in Vietnam that one of the toughest things about fighting there was that many times you didn't know who the enemy was. Tragically, so many of us in the church have become so comfortable with our culture that we are not able to discern the false values that come at us again and again. We have heard them so often that we've come to accept them as true. We don't know who the enemy is.

We worry about sex and violence and vulgarity on television, but sometimes it's the more subtle messages that are destructive. The media suggests all the time that to enjoy yourself, you've got to have liquor. We are told, in a subtle way, that if you stand for traditional values you are an uncompassionate hypocrite. The impression is left that in order to be happy you must have material possessions. We need to discern those false values that come at us constantly.

My family was sitting around the breakfast table one morning when we began to study the back of a Wheaties box. The company was trying to get consumers to send in money to buy Wheaties T-shirts. Pictured on the box was a family of four people dressed in Wheaties T-shirts. They all looked so happy. The more we looked at that the sillier it seemed, and we began to comment, "You know, if we want to have real happiness in this home, we'd better send away for those Wheaties T-shirts because look how happy those people are." If you are a little perceptive, you will see that materialistic philosophy coming at you again and again. It's so ludicrous it's funny.

We saw a TV commercial in which a father had just purchased a fireplace for his family. He put the log in the fireplace and the scene was so cozy as the mother and father and two children sat down and smiled as they looked into the fire. My 14-year-old said, "Oh, sure, they're going to sit there and smile at the fire all night long. That's so dumb. Ten seconds later they will say, 'Boy, this is boring. What are we going to do now?'"

We absorb this stuff so much that some of us come to believe it's true. You can't be happy without possessions. You can't stand for traditional values without being uncompassionate. You can't have a good time without drinking. Be alert to discern the false values that are coming at you.

Second, we must *know the Bible.* "We must study and know the holy infallible Word of God." An army has to have ammunition. Our sword, our only offensive weapon, is the Word of God. Surveys today reveal a terrible ignorance of the Bible in the average church. While 81% of those surveyed consider themselves Christian, only 42% know who it was that delivered the Sermon on the Mount—Jesus Christ. Only 46%, George Gallup says, could name the four Gospels—Matthew, Mark, Luke, and John.

I heard about a little boy who was asked by his Sunday school teacher, "Who knocked down the walls of Jericho?"

"I don't know, but I didn't do it!" he said.

The teacher was furious. She grabbed him by the ear and marched him to the Chairman of the Board. "I asked this young man who knocked down the walls of Jericho and he said he didn't do it," she told him.

The Chairman of the Board said, "We'll take care of him." He called a meeting of the whole board. An hour later they reached a decision: "This young man comes from an outstanding family. If he said he didn't do it, we believe he didn't do it. We vote that we just pay for the damages and forget it."

If we don't have a solid biblical foundation, we are not going to be able to defend our faith. We will be easy prey for the philosophies of hedonism and materialism and humanism that are attacking. In these critical days we've got to know the Bible. We've got to study it in class and study it personally.

Colson says that the world has heard enough puffy testimonies all having the same happy endings. They need something of substance. They need to hear a reason for the hope that we have.

Third, if we are going to take the gospel to the marketplace, we've got to *crown Jesus Christ as Lord* of our lives. "The *New York Times* asked the founder of McDonald's what he believed in. 'God, my family, and McDonald's hamburgers,' he replied, but then added, 'and when I get to the office I reverse the order.'

"His apparently facetious remark masks an ironic truth: for many Christians, God has first priority—on Sunday mornings—but life goes on as usual the rest of the week."

"Being a Christian is more than mouthing pious hymns or believing in a vague deity," Charles Colson writes. "To follow the Christ of the Scriptures inevitably—and radically—alters one's opinions and values on everything from lifestyle, to the dignity of life, to justice, to art, to intellectual perceptions. It involves the totality of our lives—and only as we grasp that truth and make Christ Lord of all can we ever hope to make an impact on the totality of our culture."

Colson tells of sitting at a banquet one night with the president of CBS. A tremendous opportunity, he thought. So he told the TV executive that millions of Christians were offended by the kind of programming the networks provided.

"Knowing TV executives are keenly interested in profit and loss statements, I suggested it would be good business to air wholesome family entertainment. 'After all,' I said, 'there are fifty million born-again Christians out there.'

"He looked at me quizzically. I assured him that was Gallup's latest figure.

"'What you're suggesting, Mr. Colson, is that we run more programs like, say, *Chariots of Fire?*'

"'Yes!' I exclaimed, 'That's a great movie with a marvelous Christian message.'

"'Well,' he said, 'CBS ran it as a prime-time movie just a few months ago. Are you aware of the ratings?'

"All at once I knew I was in trouble.

"He then explained: That night NBC showed *On Golden Pond;* it was #1 with 25.2 percent of all TV sets in America tuned in. Close behind was *My Mother's Secret Life,* a show about a mother hiding her past as a prostitute. It was #2 with 25.1 percent.

"And a distant third—a big money loser—was CBS with *Chariots of Fire*—11.8 percent. In fact, of the sixty-five shows rated that week, 'Dallas' was #1, *Chariots of Fire,* #57.

"'So,' my companion concluded, 'where are your fifty million born-again Christians, Mr. Colson?'

"Good question. Where are we?

"If even half of Gallup's fifty million born-again Christians had watched the show with the Christian message, *Chariots of Fire* would have topped the ratings."

The disturbing truth, Colson concludes, as studies by both the secular and Christian networks show, is that the viewing habits of Christian people are not much different from those of the world. Television is just a medium that gives people what they want. We have no right to boycott or complain if we're watching, along with the crowd, the very things that we are protesting.

If we are going to affect our world, Christ must be Lord of all. He must have priority over everything from Monday morning's business decisions to Saturday night's television viewing—not just Sunday morning. C. S. Lewis said that there is one thing Christianity cannot be—moderately important. "No one serving as a soldier gets involved in civilian affairs" (2 Timothy 2:4).

Somebody asked Billy Graham how, with so much evil in the world, he could still be optimistic about the future. Graham said, "I've read the final chapter in the Book, and the final chapter in the Book assures us that Jesus Christ is going to win, that He's going to come in triumph." There will be eternal life for those who give Him their allegiance, but eternal death for those who have rejected Him.

At the sign of triumph, Satan's host doth flee;

On, then, Christian soldiers, on to victory!
Hell's foundations quiver at the shout of praise;
Brothers, lift your voices, Loud your anthems raise!"

By the seashore, in the schoolroom, at your place of business, loud your anthems raise.

A Strategy for Battle (Part 2)

Acts 16:16-34

WHEN PRESIDENT REAGAN and Soviet leader Gorbachev hold a summit conference, the attention of the whole world is focused on that meeting. Everyone hopes for some reassurance that the two superpowers can avoid nuclear war. But as crucial as the conflict is between Russia and the United States, that is not the most critical confrontation of our time.

A more important spiritual battle is being waged continuously between the forces of God and forces of Satan. No summit conference can resolve that conflict. It will not be resolved until the end of time. The war takes place in the hearts of men and women across this world. It has eternal consequence; it means eternal life to those who surrender to the authority of Jesus Christ, and it means eternal death for those who reject Him. And frankly, right now we Christians are retreating. The traditional family is falling apart; Christian moral values are eroding; abortion and crime rates are skyrocketing. If we are going to reverse the retreat we must develop a new, more aggressive strategy for battle.

The apostle Paul made a significant impact on every cultural level of the city of Philippi. He established such a meaningful work that his enemies later reported that Paul and his friends had turned the world upside down. Paul took the message out of the synagogue and into the marketplace. So the first change of strategy for our modern church is to concentrate more in getting the message out of the church building and into the community. An army doesn't advance by sitting in the barracks polishing its weapons. We've got to encounter the world on their turf. We've got to be the salt of the earth.

That means three things: First, we discern the false values of our culture; we know who the enemy is. Second, we know the Word of God. An army has to use its ammunition. Third, we crown Christ Lord of all of our time; not just Sunday morning, but our business decisions on Monday and our television viewing on Saturday night.

Mark Price, an outstanding basketball player for Georgia Tech, was a preseason all-American in almost every publication. I say *almost* every publication because *Playboy* magazine left him out. Mark Price is a dedicated Christian. He refused to have his picture taken for Playboy because he doesn't want to endorse the magazine's philosophy. That's standing for Christ in the marketplace in a dramatic way. Most of us don't have that kind of opportunity to stand for Christ, but we can let our allegiance be known in our world outside the church building wherever that may be.

Open Confrontation

Paul's second strategy was to confront the opposition when it was necessary. Paul's success in Philippi was not without opposition. "Once when we were going to the place of prayer, we were met by a slave girl who had a spirit by which she predicted the future" (Acts 16:16).

I believe in demon possession. When Satan was cast out of Heaven, a host of other rebellious angels was cast out of Heaven with him. The Bible calls these beings "demons." On rare occasions demons can dominate a person and take control. They have supernatural power.

We've had so many movies in the last decade about demon possession that we've probably overexaggerated the problem. There was "The Omen," "The Amityville Horror," "The Exorcist," "Poltergeist," and many others. Today as soon as somebody gets a headache or some child acts rebellious, some people are quick to say he's demon-possessed.

In Sunday school a little boy acted up until the teacher grabbed that boy by the collar shook him until his teeth rattled. "I believe the devil has a hold of you!" said the teacher.

The boy said, "I believe he has too!"

I believe that demon possession still occurs today, but it is rare. Demon possession is almost always the result of involvement in Satan worship or in the occult, the use of drugs, or some gross sin of the flesh. The Bible assures us "greater is He that is in you than He that is in the world." Demons must be respected for their power, but they need not be feared.

The girl in Acts 16 was possessed by a demon that enabled her to predict the future with supernatural accuracy. She earned a lot of money for her owners with this gift. Insecure people would come groping for some reassurance about the future and pay good money to hear her prediction (after people receive a prediction about the future it only adds to their anxiety because they're not sure if it's reliable or not).

Verse 17 says, "This girl followed Paul and the rest of us, shouting, 'These men are servants of the Most High God, who are telling you the way to be saved.'" She was telling the truth, but it was disturbing to receive the endorsement of a demon. People ridiculed this girl. Her testimony was counterproductive. Paul tolerated it because he didn't want to stir up controversy, but "finally Paul became so troubled [for the condition of the girl and the advancement of the gospel] that he turned around and said to the spirit, 'In the name of Jesus Christ I command you to come out of her!' At that moment the spirit left her'" (v. 18).

Then the slave girl was released from bondage to the demon, but her owners were furious at Paul. They had exploited her misfortune for economic advantage, so it was no joy to them that the girl's sanity was restored. They were angry because their source of revenue was gone. They seized Paul and Silas and dragged them before the authorities and demanded that they be punished. The enemies of the gospel don't mind it as long as it stays in the church building. But when the gospel begins to affect the pocketbooks of those on the outside, whether it is the drug dealer, the pornographer, the television producer, or the liquor store owner—that's when the gospel will be opposed.

At times it is necessary to confront the opposition regardless of the consequences. I am not a crusader. I feel it is my job to sow the seed of the gospel and cultivate its growth. Some Christians feel led by God to picket abortion clinics or X-rated theaters. I thank God for them, but I don't feel that's my job. I could spend all my time fighting various segments of Satan's program and have no time for the sharing of the gospel. I think we need to be on the offensive, and just share the Word and let the devil worry about how to stop us, rather than vice-versa.

I think that was Paul's general strategy. He didn't seek to be controversial. He tried to avoid conflict, but the demon-possessed girl became so disruptive that he had to do something. Sometimes we have to identify and oppose the adversary. It takes a great deal of perception to know when those times occur, because if we're not careful we can get involved in all kinds of minor skirmishes that sap our energy and resources. But if a major battle is disrupting the advance of the gospel, we'd better muster the courage to enter the conflict.

For example, right now a battle is being waged over the inerrancy of the Bible, and it is having a disruptive influence. Over the last 20 years, the number of people in America who believe that the Bible is the inerrant word of God has declined from 65% to 37%. Most people have not read the apologetic arguments for and against, but they are being influenced by some of the so-called scholars who are attacking the integrity of the Bible.

An article appeared on the front page of our newspaper two weeks ago entitled "Scholars Judging the Authenticity of the Sayings Attributed to Jesus." Thirty scholars from various seminaries across the land have gathered in a seminary in Indiana to determine what sayings of Jesus they are going to leave in the new Bible they are going to compile. They voted on which of the Beatitudes are acceptable. Only three Beatitudes survived out of 13. They say that Jesus' promises that He is going to come again probably will not remain in their Bible because those sayings are creating fear in people.

Isn't it silly to think they are going to vote on whether Jesus' sayings are authentic, and change everything that has stood for centuries? That's like us voting on whether Abraham Lincoln really delivered the Gettysburg Address! "Although they knew God, they neither glorified him as God nor gave thanks to him, but their thinking became futile and their foolish hearts were darkened. Although they claimed to be wise, they became fools" (Romans 1:21, 22).

Do you think God would go to all the trouble of sending His Son to die for us and then not bother to preserve His Word accurately for us over the ages? That doesn't make sense. I wonder how those who are going to vote on the Bible are going to vote on John 10:35, which says, "The Scripture cannot be broken."

Dr. Lewis Foster, a professor at Cincinnati Bible Seminary, said twenty years ago that "We are coming to a day when Christianity is going to be divided between those who believe the Bible as the authoritative Word of God and those who reject it." We are at that point today. Those who reject it are no longer in the camp of Christianity. Harold Lindsell, in his book *The Battle for the Bible*, said, "It is a watershed issue. The first generation questions it; the second generation picks it apart and doesn't leave much remaining and the third generation has nothing left to believe."

Some people in Paris, France were taking a guided tour through the Louvre, the famous art gallery, viewing the masterpieces of the great artists that have withstood the test of time. But one aspiring young artist in the group, a sarcastic critic, began to make fun of the masterpieces. He would do this differently, he didn't see what was so great about that, and so on. Finally the guard, who had come to appreciate the works of the masters over the years, turned to the critic and said, "Sir, the paintings are not on trial." To the pseudo-scholars of our day who are attempting to pick apart the sayings of Jesus, I would say, "The Bible is not on trial—you are."

Virtue Under Pressure

Paul and his companion, Silas, went to prison for disturbing the peace. They were stripped of their clothing, severely beaten, and thrown in an inner dungeon. The jailer was told to guard them, so he placed them in stocks. Now the pressure was on Paul. He had gone from complete success one minute to total disaster the next. This would have been an opportune time for him to question, "God, where are You? You gave me that vision of the man from Macedonia to come over and help, and now here I am in jail."

A few years ago it appeared that the St. Louis Cardinals were about to win the World Series. They were just three outs away in the sixth game, but disaster struck. There was a bad call at first base and they lost the game. The Cardinals went into the seventh game and fell apart. They lost by a large margin. Under the pressure of that defeat, some of them lost composure and began to charge the umpire and curse and hit water coolers.

How you react under pressure tells a lot about your character. Paul and Silas maintained their composure under pressure. *They maintained a spirit of joy amidst suffering.* It wasn't a pleasant experience to be beaten and locked up in a stench-filled inner dungeon—a dark hole. They could have really complained. Instead, they spent their time singing and praying. Now that's unusual. I wonder what they were singing—"Rescue the Perishing"? "I Feel Like Something Good Is About to Happen"?

The other prisoners were listening to Paul and Silas. They had heard cursing and groaning and complaining coming from that interior hole, but never had they heard singing and praying. Adversity is a great opportunity to influence others for our faith. I've got a plaque in my office that reads, "Joy is not the absence of suffering, but the presence of God."

They also were forgiving instead of retaliating. Suddenly a violent earthquake shook the prison. The prison doors flew open and everybody's chains fell off. It is remarkable how quickly God can reverse your circumstances. You may be in the pit one minute, and the next everything's turned around. The world calls that a coincidence. Somebody said that a coincidence is when God works a miracle and does it anonymously.

All the prisoners were released. The jailer, seeing that everybody was free, concluded that his life wasn't worth a nickel because he was under orders to guard the prisoners at the expense of his own life. He drew a sword and was about to commit suicide. Now remember this is a man who had beaten and abused Paul just hours before. Paul and Silas could have hidden in the rubble and whispered, "Now he's going to get what he deserves." But Paul shouted, "Don't harm yourself! We are all here!" Paul forgave the jailer even before he asked for forgiveness. There was no grudge, no attempt at revenge.

At the peak of his career, an all-pro linebacker for the New York Giants was traded to the Washington Redskins. Over fifteen years later, he said in an interview that being traded was the most crushing blow he had ever experienced. "I was so angry at the General Manager for trading me that I vowed I would not rest until he was fired. I played with a vengeance every time we played against him," he said. "I will never forget what he did to me and I will never ever forgive him."

That's the world's reaction under pressure. "No one treats me like that--I'm going to get even. I'll make them pay if its the last thing I do." But who gets hurt? Back in the days of Amos and Andy, Amos once said, "Every time I see this friend of mine he hits me on the chest and he hits me hard. I'm going to get even with him. Next time I see him I'm going to tape a stick of dynamite to my chest and it is going to blow his hand off." The retaliator is the one who gets hurt.

A recent story in *Guideposts,* called "Seventy Times Seven," told about a remarkable instance of forgiveness. For more than two years Frank and Elizabeth Morris dedicated their lives to punishing the drunken driver who had killed their only child. Driven by hatred, they monitored every court appearance, called the jail to make sure he was serving his weekend sentences, and watched his apartment trying to catch him violating his probation.

"We wanted him in prison," Mrs. Morris said. "We wanted him dead for killing our boy."

After two years that boy was arrested again for drinking, thus breaking his parole, and Mrs. Morris then realized she needed to visit him in prison. She realized that as a Christian she needed to forgive, to break down her hatred. Eventually the boy was released into their custody for visits to their church and other outings. One day Frank Morris stopped by the Little River Church of Christ, where he served as choir director, and baptized the boy, Tommy Pigage, into Christ. Now the Morrises drive him to church twice a week and often set a place for him at their dinner table. Unable to find satisfaction through revenge, they found satisfaction through forgiveness and helping him rebuild his life along with their own.

"The hate and bitterness I was feeling were destroying me," Mrs. Morris said. "I needed to forgive Tommy to save myself."

Tommy Pigage, age 26, said, "They've given me a better life. They have made it much easier for me to live with myself and to forgive myself."

When someone has done you wrong, you can harbor resentment and bitterness and turn everybody off, or you can respond as the Morrises did and as the apostle Paul did and work through forgiveness. Forgiveness is not just passively saying "I'm not going to punish you." It is acting kindly toward the offender.

Look what happened to the apostle Paul when that occurred. The jailer rushed in and fell trembling at the apostle's feet. Have you ever just missed being killed in an accident? You get out of the car and your knees feel like water. That's the way this man felt. His life had almost ended and he cried out, "What must I do to be saved?" The other prisoners weren't the only ones listening to Paul and Silas sing. The jailer had been listening too, and he asked a spiritual question. Paul responded, "Believe in the Lord Jesus, and you will be saved." There is only one way to be saved, and that is by trusting Jesus Christ for your salvation.

Some Christians quote this verse and stop there. "Just believe in the Lord Jesus Christ," they say. But this is a general truth that needs elaboration. Not all the details are given. I can ask how I can get to Western Kentucky University from Louisville, and you could say, "It's easy—just take I-65 South." That's the general truth. But I need a few more details as to where to get off the interstate and how to get to the university.

To tell people, "Believe in the Lord Jesus Christ and you will be saved" is true, but some details are needed. The Bible says, "You believe that there is one God. Good! Even the demons believe that—and shudder" (James 2:19). People need to be informed about what it *means* to believe—to surrender our will to Jesus Christ, to make a public confession of faith in Christ, to repent of sin, and to be baptized into Christ.

Paul and Silas "spoke the word of the Lord to him and to all the others in his house. At that hour of the night [after midnight] the jailer took them and washed their wounds; then immediately he and all his family were baptized" (Acts 16:32, 33). If you spend an hour teaching a non-Christian how to be saved, and you don't say anything about being baptized, you are not telling it the way Paul told it.

I have some Christian friends that get defensive about the subject of baptism. As soon as it is mentioned they say, "That doesn't have anything to do with salvation, does it?" They are defensive because some Christians leave the impression that all you have to do is get somebody wet and they're saved. But it is kind of like asking, "The marriage license doesn't have anything to do with the wedding, does it?" There had better be a whole lot more than that, but the license does have something to do with it. Baptism was man's commanded response to the grace of God.

When Jesus found a man born blind, He put clay on the man's eyes and told him to wash in the pool of Siloam. The man went and washed and then he could see. Now who healed the man? Jesus did. What healed the man, the water? No, his faith in Christ. When was he healed? When he applied the water. Baptism doesn't save you, Christ does. But baptism is a point at which God reaches down in grace and man reaches up in obedience and the two meet.

Sometimes I hear this objection: "What about a guy who's out in the desert and can't be baptized? Or a person who is on his deathbed and can't be baptized?" We trust the grace of God. God is a perfect judge. The hypothetical case isn't the one that bothers me. What concerns me are the people who know what Christ has commanded and refuse to do it. Can you imagine the man born blind saying, "Jesus, I am not going to wash in the pool of Siloam. You can heal me without that"?

Paul and Silas maintained their composure under pressure. As a result, the jailer and his household were won to the Lord.

Standing for Your Rights

Another point about Paul's strategy was that he stood for his rights when it was an advantage to the church.

The next morning the city authorities ordered Paul to be released and leave town. But Paul was a Roman citizen, even though the authorities didn't know it. Roman citizens had certain rights. It was illegal to beat a Roman citizen without a public hearing. Paul said, "They beat us publicly without a trial, even though we are Roman citizens, and threw us into prison. And now do they want to get rid of us quietly? No! Let them come themselves and escort us out" (Acts 16:37).

That doesn't sound like Paul. You'd think Paul would say, "Oh, that's okay, men. Don't think anything about it." But he stood for his rights as a Roman citizen because he wanted to protect the church. He wanted the church to be exempt from future persecution. He wanted the outsiders to know that the church had some friends who were influential. The authorities ate humble pie. "They came to appease them and escorted them from the prison, requesting them to leave the city" (v. 39), and evidently Paul did. When it is for the good of the church, Christians may have to stand for their rights. The world stands for its rights when it is for a personal advantage. But Christians should stand for their rights if it is an advantage for the kingdom of God.

For example, some cities in California have made it illegal for Christians to meet in homes for Bible study on a regular basis. They say the home groups constitute a church, posing a traffic problem in the subdivisions. It's okay to have a Tupperware party, but they can't have home Bible studies in some sections any more. The Christians are taking that matter to court saying that it violates their freedom of assembly, and freedom of speech, and freedom of religion, and rightfully so. We have certain rights that we can stand on for the advancement of the gospel. Christians don't have to be wimps—if it is for the overall good of the kingdom, we must stand for those rights and privileges that we have.

Marvin Rickard is the preacher at the Los Gatos Christian Church near San Francisco. It is the largest Christian church in the nation, with nearly 5,000 people attending every Sunday morning. By being near San Francisco, their church waged a real battle over homosexuality. The Council of Santa Clara County wanted to vote in a new homosexual law that forbade any kind of discrimination. The bottom line was that homosexuals could teach in the schools and they could manage day care centers without discrimination against them. A thousand Christians jammed the board room when they had the Council meeting. Marvin Rickard was asked to speak representing them. He wrote about this experience in his book, *Let It Grow*.

"The atmosphere was crackling with tension and frustration on the side of the Bible believers," he said. "The chairman of the board of supervisors asked me by name to come to the podium and express once again the reasons for our objections to the proposed ordinance. TV cameras were everywhere, as before. Just as I started to speak on behalf of biblical morality and righteousness, a most unusual thing happened. It took just a moment to realize what it was, but as I was speaking a powerful California earthquake rolled across the Santa Clara Valley, rocking that building and all within it for several minutes.

"Hundreds of Christians stood to their feet and began to applaud! Then they began to laugh and cheer, breaking into song after song. I remember the ashen, sober faces of the supervisors. The drama of it didn't escape them, but they were resolute, except for the chairman, to reject the Bible and the God who controls earthquakes. To them it was coincidence. To us it was Providence.

"When the earthquake ceased and subsided to little aftershocks, I said, 'You supervisors may wonder why we all laughed and cheered when the earthquake hit. We are students of the Bible and we know that many times in scripture God demonstrated His presence and ultimate authority on earth by sending an earthquake. We believe that He wants to show you that His Word is still true regarding homosexual sin.' At that, the place erupted in a great standing ovation to God and the Bible, many people pointed heavenward.

When everyone finally sat down again with the steady rapping of the gavel, I spoke once more. 'We urge you to reject the proposed ordinance, but if you should vote as you indicated you intend to, I guarantee we will solicit the required names on petitions to place the issue on the ballot of a special election for all the people. And we will vote it out!'

As one, the people again rose to their feet cheering and applauding. Again the gavel rapped for order and quiet. Something in me welled up into one more statement. 'Mr. Chairman," I said, 'If you vote for this ordinance, which has the effect of accepting homosexual practices as normal and good, we Christians serve you notice that, one by one, we intend to vote you right out of office!' I can't describe the incredible roar of approval by those hundreds of Christians."

"The churches were fulfilling their proper role as salt and light in the community. Salt to retard the spoilage and light to illuminate the darkness of perversion before the entire community."

The Council voted the ordinance in, but the community voted it down and then they voted those people out of office.

Rickard adds this concluding thought: "Not many of us seek to be controversial or enjoy that role if it should fall our lot. Yet if only one sentry is awake on the wall when the enemy is set to attack, he had better sound the alarm. With the rise of secular humanism and the decline of our former Judaic-Christian heritage in America, we have to face the fact that other battles lie ahead. We don't want to get the church involved in partisan or personal politics, but when a moral matter ends up on the ballot, we can be thankful that we still have political means of responding."

We are at war with the world. The Christian life is not a playground; it's a battleground. That means we've got to get out of the church building and into the fray. That means that we have to confront our enemy when it is necessary. It means that we must maintain our Christian virtues under pressure so others might see Christ living in us. It may mean that we have to stand stubbornly for our rights if it benefits the kingdom. But the purpose of it all is that Christ may be honored, that people may be saved, and that all might share in the ultimate victory of Jesus Christ.

Coping With Jealousy

Acts 17:1-15

A YOUNG MAN was driving through a wealthy section of the city, and he saw a beautiful Mercedes Benz sitting in front of an estate. A sign in the car window read, "For Sale—$100."

The man couldn't believe such an expensive car was selling for $100, but he pulled into the driveway, went up to the door and knocked. He asked the woman who answered if the sign was correct.

"Yes it is," she assured him.

"Is something wrong with the car?" he asked.

"No," she said, "it runs perfectly."

Without asking any further questions, he whipped out his checkbook and bought the car. As he stuck the title into his pocket, he asked, "Lady, why are you selling this car so cheaply?"

The woman replied, "My husband ran off with his secretary a few days ago, and he wired me from Hawaii this morning telling me to sell his car and send him the check."

Is any emotion more dangerous or deadly than jealousy? It is as "unyielding as the grave. It burns like blazing fire" (Song of Solomon 8:6). Cain was jealous of Abel and murdered him. Saul burned with jealousy over David's popularity and sought to kill him. The chief priests and the Pharisees were jealous of Jesus' popularity and they crucified Him. Jealousy is as unyielding as the grave. It burns like blazing fire.

You know that's true from watching soap operas. Have you watched "Die-Nasty" lately? Frequently its theme is jealousy, envy, and discontent at the good fortune of another. That's the motivation for anger, revenge, and all kinds of evil that make for melodrama. "Where you have envy and selfish ambition, there you find disorder and every evil practice" (James 3:16).

You know that's true just by observing life. Jealousy undermines marriages, dissolves romances, creates tension in the office, nullifies unity on a basketball team. Envy can separate members of a church choir, foster competition among church officers, and discourage leaders. When a leader is the target of jealous criticism he is tempted to throw up his hands in despair and quit.

Jealousy may be justifiable. If a wife loves her husband and he runs off with his secretary to Hawaii, she ought to be jealous. The Bible says that God is a jealous God. He loves us and He is jealous when we flirt with the gods of this world because He knows they will disappoint us.

But even justifiable jealousy can lead to all kinds of unreasonable and sinful behavior, and most jealousy is not legitimate. Paul was the victim of jealousy. If you are a leader or an achiever, you will also be a target of jealous attitudes and vicious accusations. How you react reveals a lot about your character and your ability to lead.

The Jealousy of the Jews

Paul had just left Philippi and traveled about a hundred miles through a series of towns until he got to Thessalonica. As he usually did, on Saturday he went to the synagogue. There he would meet Jewish people who believed in God and who were looking for the coming of the Messiah.

Some believers will use a text like this to suggest that we should worship on Saturday because Paul did. But the only reason Paul went on Saturday was because that's when the crowds were there. If he had gone on Sunday, nobody would have been there to preach to except the janitor. Other passages make it clear that the Christians worshiped on the first day of the week.

Paul began with the Old Testament Scripture and proved that the Messiah was going to suffer and die and then rise from the dead. The Jews were looking for a political Messiah who would overthrow Rome. So Paul would probably go back to Isaiah 53 and point out that the Messiah was to be led like a sheep to the slaughter and our sins were going to be laid on His crucified body.

Paul was so persuasive that some of the Jews believed, "as did a large number of God-fearing Greeks and not a few prominent women" (Acts 17:4). The God-fearing Greeks were Gentiles that the Jews had been able to convert to Judaism. They were proud of these converts. But now Paul had come and was proselyting them. Some prominent women, perhaps wives of politicians, businessmen, or entertainers, were also talking about Paul's teachings. So the Jewish leaders felt threatened and were jealous of Paul. They did three things—the three things that jealousy still does today.

First they stirred up opposition. "They rounded up some bad characters from the marketplace" (v. 5). (The *King James Version* says they "took unto them certain lewd fellows of the baser sort.") Loosely translated, they went down to the Friday night wrestling crowd or the local motorcycle gang and said, "Hey, you guys looking for some action?" They got an unruly mob together to make trouble. Jealousy is usually cowardly because it is motivated by insecurity. It seldom confronts the issue head-on.

The second thing they did was to threaten physical abuse. "They rushed to Jason's house [Jason was a Christian who had opened his home to the missionaries] in search of Paul and Silas in order to bring them out to the crowd. But when they did not find them [either they were hiding or they had already escaped], they dragged Jason and some other brothers before the city officials" (vv. 5, 6).

Third, they resorted to slander. "These men who have caused trouble all over the world have now come here," they said (v. 6). They hadn't caused trouble; their opponents had caused trouble. "They are all defying Caesar's decrees, saying that there is another king, one called Jesus" (v. 7).

One of the characteristics of slander is that there is usually a grain of truth in it. There was just enough truth in this accusation to make it believable. Jesus was to be the King of kings and He was to be worshiped. But they made it sound as if Paul was a revolutionary advocating the overthrow of the Roman government. That wasn't true. Everybody got hyper—the crowd, the city officials, and the Jews—and the unruly mob was ready to kill Paul. Finally, "They made Jason and the others post bond and let them go" (v. 9). Jealousy can be unreasonable and destructive.

The Reaction of Paul

Paul was not intimidated by failure. He refused to quit because of jealousy. "As soon as it was night, the brothers sent Paul and Silas away to Berea. On arriving there, they went to the Jewish synagogue" (v. 10). Though he had to leave Thessalonica, he went right to the next town and started over again.

Successful people know how to get back up when they get knocked down. In the book *Leaders—The Strategy for Taking Charge,* Warren Bennis and Burt Nannis say, "For many people the word failure carries with it a sense of finality, but for the successful leader, failure is a beginning; it's a springboard to new efforts." Harry Truman said that whenever he made a bad decision, he just went out and made another one.

William Smithburg, the chairman of Quaker Oats, said that he took responsibility for two big mistakes—first the acquisition of a video game business, which he has since closed down, and second, an accessory business that he bought, then later had to write off. But later he told his employees, "If you want to take risks, there is not one senior member in this company who hasn't been associated with a product that flopped. That includes me.... It is like learning how to ski; if you are not falling down you are not learning."

Thomas J. Watson, Sr., the founder of IBM, called a prominent junior executive into his office. The man had just lost the company several million dollars in a risky business venture.

The young man blurted out, "I guess you want my resignation."

Watson replied, "You can't be serious. We have just spent millions of dollars educating you."

Paul's failure in Thessalonica was not an occasion to quit. It was a springboard for renewed efforts in Berea.

Verse 11 says, "The Bereans were of more noble character than the Thessalonians." It is not true that people are the same wherever you go. People in different sections of the country generally react differently. You get treated differently as a stranger in Atlanta than you do in New York City. I ministered for a couple of years in the suburbs of Cincinnati and found that, generally speaking, there is a warmer response to the gospel in Louisville than there is in Cincinnati, even though the two cities are only 100 miles apart.

The Bereans were more noble than the Thessalonians, though the cities were just 60 miles apart. "They received the message with great eagerness." The Thessalonians had been skeptical, and Paul had to reason and argue with them, but the Bereans were eager and excited about learning. They "examined the Scriptures every day to see if what Paul said was true" (v. 11). Nothing is more gratifying to a preacher than to see people with Bibles open on their laps examining the Scriptures to see if what is being said is true. The Bereans did not take Paul's word at face value. They examined the Word every day. And the response in Berea was greater—"Many of the Jews believed" (v. 12).

But look at the reaction of the jealous people of Thessalonica. "When the Jews in Thessalonica learned that Paul was preaching the word of God at Berea, they went there too, agitating the crowds and stirring them up" (v. 13). Jealousy is a driving emotion. It is not easily put to rest. Frustrated that they hadn't been able to punish Paul in Thessalonica, they traveled 60 miles to try to punish him in Berea.

People get fired up over jealousy. They will go the second mile to invoke revenge. They still do that today. A jealous wife shouted at her husband, "I vow that I will dance on your grave!" So he made arrangements to be buried at sea!

Jealousy and hatred can motivate people to extremes. So when these people from Thessalonica came to Berea, Paul left there and went on to Athens. But he had successfully established churches in both those cities, Thessalonica and Berea.

The Lessons for Us

If you struggle with jealousy, seek to overcome it. Jealousy is a horrible emotion that has the potential to ruin your happiness. It can destroy you emotionally, physically, and spiritually. "A heart at peace gives life to the body, but envy rots the bones" (Proverbs 14:30).

As you struggle with jealousy, keep a couple of things in mind. First, *stop comparing.* I know of a preacher who has had a good, growing ministry but he isn't happy where he is because a friend of his, who has more talent and a larger area in which to minister, has a faster growing church. The first minister can't enjoy his ministry because of comparison.

If you are a competitive person, you may be in the groove of determining your self worth by comparing yourself to others. Maybe it began when you were in grade school, when you brought home a good report card, but your parents said, "That's fine, but how does it compare with the other children in your class?" Maybe you scored ten points in a basketball game, but you weren't satisfied because somebody else scored 16 and got more attention. Or you look at your home, and it's a nice home, but you can't be content with it because a friend of yours has one that is nicer or larger.

If you get your self worth by comparison, if you have to be superior to those around you to be happy, then you constantly fall victim to the pangs of jealousy. But one of the liberating truths of Scripture is that God is not comparing you with anybody. He's not grading on a curve. "Think of yourself with sober judgment, in accordance with the measure of faith God has given you" (Romans 12:2). Just as the body has different members, God has created us differently. Quit comparing yourself to others. That's like comparing apples to oranges. That's immature; it's grade-school stuff! It's a sure formula for discontent.

Second, *start praising*. Jealousy blinds us to our blessings. We need to stop and consider how good God has been. When you start praising God and His goodness, praise crowds out jealousy. When you begin to praise other people for their accomplishments, your encouragement crowds out jealousy too.

Chances are the person you envy probably doesn't have it as good as you think. Tom Mullins, a popular author, said that he and his wife began to get jealous of the teenage son of some friends of theirs. Their own teenage son was a good boy, but he was unkempt and awkward and he lacked all the social graces they had tried to develop in him. Their friends' son, Jeffrey, was always saying "Yes sir," and "No sir," and he made such a good impression around adults that they would find themselves saying, "We wish our boy was more like Jeffrey. Why can't he be more polite like that?"

Then one day Jeffrey's mother said, "We wish our sons were more like your son. Jeffrey is so prissy and effeminate. Your son is so rugged and manly. We wish he were more like him."

Paul said, "I have learned in whatever state I am to be content." Quit comparing; start praising God for the good things He has given you and eliminate jealousy from your life.

But what if you, like Paul, are the victim of jealousy? If you are a leader or an achiever, you will encounter jealous opposition. You've always imagined that if you accomplish something, everybody's going to admire and applaud you, and you will live happily ever after. If you believe that, you probably believe in the tooth fairy too. That's just not true. The more you accomplish, the more leadership you assert, the more the jealous tongues start wagging. Sometimes those jealous tongues come from those who were close to you whom you thought would be supportive.

When that happens, there are two wrong reactions. One is hostility—you begin to flaunt your accomplishment and tell the critics, "Stick it in your ear." You've probably seen ads that encourage you to do that: "Buy this car and you will be the envy of your neighborhood."

I took my boys fishing years ago. The lake had just been stocked, and we could look right down in the water and see some trout swimming around. My youngest son threw in his line, and it wasn't 30 seconds before he had a strike. "I've got one, I've got one!" he said, and he pulled it out. And Rusty, the older son, said, "Way to go, Phil, way to go."

Phil threw the line back in and caught a second fish. "I've got two, I've got two," he said.

Rusty said, "Boy, I hope I get one." He threw his line over near where Phil had thrown his.

Phil caught a third one. "I've got three, I've got three, Russ!" he said. "How many have you got?"

Rusty said, "Dad, tell him to shut up."

But he didn't. He caught five fish in a row. He kept saying, "Boy, this is great. I've got five fish, can you believe that? Five fish. Russ, how many have you got so far?" I told Phil to quit flaunting it because he was making his brother feel terrible, but Phil made up a little song then—"I went fishing and I caught five, I went fishing and I caught five"—and he sang it while sitting on the bank.

"Dad, will you tell him to quit singing?" Rusty said.

"Phil, quit singing that song," I said. But Phil started humming the song. And by then, Rusty knew the words!

"Dad, tell him to quit humming," Rusty said.

Has God blessed you with a little more than your neighbor? If God has blessed you with a beautiful family, don't flaunt that. Don't deliberately try to evoke envy from others. That's childish. If you get your pleasure from parading your plenty, that's immature. Be sensitive to those around you. Be gentle. Don't react in hostility.

The second wrong response is apology. I know people who feel like they have to apologize for their achievement or their leadership. "I'm sorry we moved into this larger house. I hope it doesn't make you feel uncomfortable." "I'm sorry my family is together and happy. I know yours is broken up and you're miserable. I'll pretend to be miserable too."

Paul did not apologize for the fact that he was converting people right and left. He continued to do it. When our church started to grow by leaps and bounds, I was surprised at the critical comments that came from people outside our church. People would say things like, "It's a country club church. They are self-centered. They are focused around one personality." I wanted to respond to those criticisms. I found that I began to apologize, and I didn't even talk about the church lest somebody be offended—until I traveled to other areas of the country. From Seattle to Atlanta, wherever there is a large, growing church, some people criticize and get jealous about it. We need to be careful not to flaunt our success, but we can't pretend that nothing is happening. If God is blessing us He should be praised, and if people feel jealous, then that's their problem.

The right reaction to jealousy is that of the apostle Paul—not hostility, not apology, but continued ministry. He didn't flaunt his blessings, deliberately trying to evoke envy, but neither did he apologize. He just kept on doing what God had called him to do.

Nehemiah was commissioned to rebuild the walls of Jerusalem. When it became obvious that he was going to be successful, some jealous people started criticizing him. Sanballat and Tobiah, two of the critics, tried to ridicule him and get him to stop. They said, "Oh, if a fox leans up against that wall it will fall down." Nehemiah just kept on working. When he was nearly finished, the critics sent him a letter, saying, "Would you come down to the valley and hold a conference with us about what you're doing?"

Nehemiah's answer was classic. He said, "I am carrying on a great project and cannot go down. Why should the work stop while I leave it and go down to you?" (Nehemiah 6:3)

Years ago an article appeared in the Saturday Evening Post called, "The Penalty of Leadership." It said, "In every field of human endeavor he that is first must live in the white light of publicity. Whether the leadership be vested in a man or a manufactured product, emulation and envy are ever at work. In art, in literature, in music, in industry, the reward and punishment is always the same. The reward is widespread recognition, the punishment fierce denial and detraction.

"When a man's work becomes a standard for the whole world, it also becomes a target for the shafts of the envious few. If his work be merely mediocre he will be left severely alone. If he achieves a masterpiece it will set a million tongues a-wagging. Jealousy does not protrude its fork-tongue at the artist who produces a commonplace painting. Whatsoever you write, paint, play, sing, or build, no one will strive to surpass or slander you unless your work be stamped with a seal of genius.

"Long after a great work has been done, those who are disappointed or envious continue to cry out that it cannot be done. Spiteful little voices in the domain of art were raised against our own Whistler as a phony long after the big world had claimed him as an artistic genius. Multitudes flocked to Bayreuth to worship at the musical shrine of Wagner while a little group of those he had dethroned and displaced argued angrily that he was no musician at all. The little world continued to protest that Fulton could never build a steamboat while the big world flocked to the riverbank to see his boat steam by.

"The leader is assailed because he is a leader and the effort to equal him is merely added proof of that leadership. Failing to equal or excel, the follower seeks to depreciate and destroy, but only confirms once more the superiority of that which he strives to supplant.

"There is nothing new in this. This is as old as the world and as old as the human passions of envy, fear, greed, ambition and the desire to surpass; and it all avails nothing. If the leader truly leads, he remains the leader. Master poet, master painter, master workman, each in his turn is assailed and each holds his laurels through the ages. That which is good or great makes itself known no matter how loud the clamor of denial. That which deserves to live, lives."

Paul continued to lead without responding to his critics. We don't remember the names of the jealous critics, but the name of Paul lives on.

Jesus did the same. He didn't flaunt His authority. In fact, when He performed a miracle, He would say, "Don't tell anybody about this." But neither did He apologize for His identity. They asked Him, "Are you the King of kings?" and He said, "Yes, I am." For that stance He evoked envy and jealousy and they crucified Him. And yet He died deliberately for our sins.

Communicating Christ Effectively

Acts 17:16-34

AN AD AGENT in New York City recently performed an interesting experiment. He dressed in ragged clothing, put on sunglasses, carried a tin cup in his hand, and wore a sign around his neck that read, "Blind." He spent the entire day in Central Park, and he collected $44.10. The next day he did the same thing under identical circumstances, only this time the sign around his neck read, "It's Spring, and I Am Blind." That day he collected $161.65!

There's a big difference between communication and effective communication. That's important to anyone who is a leader in a field that requires communications skills. Lawyers, schoolteachers, department heads, sales managers, board chairmen, coaches, committee chairmen, heads of household—all are called upon to convey their thoughts and ideas to others.

Every Christian has the responsibility to communicate to other people what Jesus Christ means to him. We all need to be as effective in that communication as we can be. Certainly one quality that made Paul such an effective leader and motivator was his ability to communicate who Jesus Christ was and what Christ demanded of people.

Some suggest that Paul was not a good speaker because of

what he wrote in 2 Corinthians 10:10: "Some say, 'His letters are weighty and forceful, but in person he is unimpressive and his speaking amounts to nothing.'" Paul probably wasn't impressive physically, but he could not have left the kind of impact he did on the world without being an effective speaker. In the next verse Paul wrote, "Such people should realize that what we are in our letters when we are absent, we will be in our actions when we are present." Paul was an excellent communicator not only in what he wrote, but in what he said. He made this evident during his stay in the city of Athens.

Athens was an intellectual center of its day. Its glory days were past, but it was the cultural center, the university town of Paul's day. Here the philosophers, intellectuals, and students would gather to discuss the latest intellectual fads. Athens was also an architectural city. It was a tourist attraction with a 60,000-seat stadium and impressive structures like the temple of Zeus and the Parthenon, a portion of which stands today. But the sad thing about Athens was that it was a pagan city. As many as 30,000 statues had been erected as idols to various gods in the city.

Paul quietly slipped into Athens alone. He had to leave Thessalonica and Berea in a hurry because of jealous opposition, so he left his companions Timothy and Silas behind to stabilize the churches there. He came to Athens and waited for his companions to join him. What do you do when you're in a large city all by yourself? That reveals a lot about your character. Paul toured this impressive city, but he didn't think as much about the scenery as he did about an opportunity to talk to somebody about Jesus Christ.

Four qualities made Paul an effective communicator of the gospel.

Genuine Conviction

Paul sincerely believed that the people here needed Christ more than anything else in the world. "He was greatly distressed to see that the city was full of idols" (Acts 17:16).

The first ingredient to be a good communicator is intensity. You've got to feel something about what you're saying. The purchasing department in a Kroger warehouse has a sign that reads, "Salesman, before you try to sell your product to us, be so convinced of its superiority that when you're finished, we will be more anxious to buy than you are to sell." If you don't believe that what you're teaching is important, you can't expect your students to pay attention. We Christians must believe that Jesus Christ is really needed in our society. He must be genuine in our lives and in our thinking before we can communicate Him to others.

I talked for over an hour with an ex-narcotics agent recently. He started out as an undercover agent in Miami, and then got so involved in the role that he began buying and selling drugs for his own profit. He was arrested for trafficking in drugs and sent to prison. There he came under the influence of Charles Colson of Prison Fellowship and he became a Christian. Now that he's been released, he's working full-time with Prison Fellowship.

I asked him what he thought could be done about the increase in drug traffic in America. He said, "It won't be stopped through legislation. It's just too easy for two small boats to meet in the ocean a few miles offshore and exchange cargo, or for a private plane loaded with drugs to land on a secluded airstrip. We can't stop it. Our only hope is Jesus Christ. Our only hope is that we can win so many people to Christ that drugs will not be needed any more."

Paul had that kind of intensity when he went to Athens. He saw through the intellectual charade and realized that these people did not have any answers to the ultimate questions about their identity and their destiny. In this supposedly cultural center of Athens, they were bowing down to man-made idols. They needed to hear about Jesus, the only Son of God, who died for their sins and who could give them real hope. That truth was about to burst within Paul. The Bible says, "he was greatly distressed," and the word for *distress* meant "violent emotion." Jeremiah 20:9 says, "His word is in my heart like a burning fire." That's the way it was with Paul.

Broad Awareness

An effective communicator has to have knowledge of people and of his subject. Paul was well-educated. He knew the people in Athens were intellectual; he knew their philosophies, and he wasn't intimidated by them.

Some Christians suggest that Paul made a mistake in Athens because he talked so much about philosophy and not enough about Jesus. While Paul was capable of making a mistake, I don't think he made one here. He was guided by the Holy Spirit and he had to begin where the Athenians were. He had to begin with the familiar. There's a big difference between the way I talk to 100 preachers at a retreat and the way I speak to 100 high-school seniors at a graduation exercise. A communicator has to begin where the people are. Paul reasoned with the Jews in the synagogue on the Sabbath day, but during the week he talked in the marketplace with those who happened to be there. The marketplace in Athens was more than just a place where the farmers and merchants brought their wares to sell. It was the gathering place for people who were looking for something to do, kind of like Fisherman's Wharf in San Francisco. People go there to be entertained or to see what the action is for that day. There Paul would have the opportunity to exchange ideas.

The Epicureans and the Stoic philosophers began to debate with Paul. The *Epicureans* believed that the goal of life was pleasure, and they indulged in every kind of sensual pleasure for selfish gratification. That sounds familiar. The *Stoics,* on the other hand, were fatalists. They believed that the gods caused everything that happened, so they tried not to react with emotion. They prided themselves on their self-sufficiency and self-control. Both groups were hard to reach with the gospel. They ridiculed Paul as a "babbler." They made fun of him when he talked about the resurrection of the dead.

But then they brought Paul to a meeting of the Areopagus. The Areopagus was a 500-foot high hill in the center of Athens, and it was also the name of the council that met on the hill. The council was a group of 20 or 30 men who were supposed to be the foremost intellectuals of the city. Paul was invited to go to the Areopagus because he had created such a stir in the marketplace. Evidently this was not an arrest—Paul was in the limelight, so they invited him to come. That would be like being invited to go on "Nightline" with Ted Koppel or the David Letterman or Phil Donahue shows. "You are bringing some strange ideas to our ears," they said, "and we want to know what they mean" (v. 20). The Athenians loved to talk about the latest fads, Luke tells us. But even though Paul was in the limelight with these intellectuals, he was very much at home because he had such an awareness of what people were thinking.

If we're going to communicate Christ to our generation, we're going to have to know our audience. Every audience is different. But we need to keep in mind two basic facts about the American people today.

The first is that people do not respond well to the authoritarian approach. It used to be effective to communicate as a parent to a child—I'm the teacher, you're the student. But people are more sophisticated these days, more independent; they resist authority. It's the same whether you're preaching from the pulpit or talking with somebody across the table. If I said to you, "I'm going to tell you this one time, and I want you to get it straight!" you would immediately be on the defensive. If we're going to talk to people we need to talk to them as one adult to another—on a peer level. We need to say, "Look, I don't claim to have all the answers, but here are some things I've discovered that I think are true." Or, "I'm not perfect, I'm still trying to grow, but here's where I am in my Christian life." People are much more responsive to that kind of approach.

The second fact about the American audience is that people have a short attention span. It used to be that a lecturer could talk for two hours and people would sit and work through it. But that's not true any more. We read the *Reader's Digest*. We're used to 30-second commercials and ten-minute segments of entertainment on the tube. If we don't like it, if it's not fast enough, we turn the dial. That means as communicators we've got to be alert and make the subject move. We've got to use humor, illustrations, or visual aids and be alert to people when we're talking to them.

One wit defined preaching as, "The art of talking in someone else's sleep." That isn't very encouraging! If we're talking, we've got to make sure somebody is listening.

Besides knowing his audience, Paul also had a broad awareness of his *subject matter*. To know the audience takes observation; to know the subject takes preparation. You cannot be an effective communicator if you don't know the subject well. For example, when I was invited to speak to a group of women about quilting, I knew I was in trouble.

I overheard a woman in our church talking to my wife about quilting, so I interrupted them and said, "That's all you girls ever talk about, quilts!"

She answered, "Well, all you talk about is basketball."

"That's not true," I responded. "I can talk about a lot of things—basketball, football, baseball, quilts—I can talk about anything." We laughed.

Later that day my wife was all excited, telling me about the development of the Amish people. As they moved westward, their theology became more liberal and their quilts became more colorful.

A couple of weeks later the same woman I had been teasing overheard me talking to somebody about basketball. She asked, sarcastically, "Bob, do you prefer the Amish quilts of Pennsylvania or the Amish quilts of Indiana?"

I immediately replied, "Well, I personally prefer the Amish quilts of Indiana because as they moved westward their theology got a little more liberal and they got more colorful in their quilts."

Her mouth dropped open.

A few weeks later I got a request in the mail to come to their Homemakers Club as an expert on quilts, and I foolishly accepted. That week I had to do some fast learning about quilts. There was no question-and-answer period following! When I got finished, I was like the woman who said to her neighbor over the backyard fence, "I've already told you more than I know."

You cannot talk about a subject if you are not thoroughly aware of that subject. Paul knew his subject. He had studied the Scriptures. He knew Jesus Christ personally. He'd also studied the philosophies of his day; so in his speech he was able to quote from two of the Athenian philosophers. He quoted them from memory, and the people stood there very much surprised and impressed. The more knowledge we're able to accumulate, the better prepared we are to communicate on different levels. Knowledge is not an enemy of faith, but its ally. We need Christians with keen minds who will study, accumulate knowledge, and be alert to current events so that they can give the gospel respectability and communicate with every cultural level.

C.S. Lewis, one of the great intellectual Christians of our century, wrote, "If all the world were Christian it might not matter if all the world were uneducated. But as it is, a cultural life will exist outside the church whether it exists or not. To be ignorant, not to be able to meet the enemy on their own ground, would be to throw down our weapons and to betray our uneducated brethren who have, under God, no defense but us against the intellectual attacks of the heathen. Good philosophy must exist, if for no other reason, because bad philosophy needs to be answered. The cool intellect must work not only against cool intellect on the other side, but against the muddy heathen mysticisms which deny intellect altogether. The learned life then is for some a duty."

Profound Simplicity

Paul's sermon was logical and easy to follow. It seems to me that one of our mistakes in communication is that we try to make the message too complex. We get bogged down in detail, or we try to make the simple complicated, thinking that complexity is the mark of genius.

J. Wallace Hamilton tells of two men who came out of a church. "Boy, that was deep, wasn't it?" one said.

The other responded, "Yeah, I didn't understand it either!"

One characteristic of brilliant communicators is the ability to make the profound understandable. That's what was so great about Jesus. No one had anything deeper to say than Christ, but the Bible says that the common people heard it gladly.

Paul's sermon began with a positive approach. "Men of Athens! I see that in every way you are very religious" (Acts 17:22). He didn't condemn them for their idol worship. He didn't alienate them by negativism. He didn't say, "What a bunch of ignorant heathens."

Then he used a current illustration to get their attention. "As I walked around and observed your objects of worship, I even found an altar with this inscription: TO AN UNKNOWN GOD" (v. 23). One commentator says that a terrible disease had swept through Athens years before. They tried to sacrifice to various gods to stop the epidemic, but it continued. Then one of their poets, Epimenides, proposed setting a flock of sheep loose in the city, and wherever the sheep laid down, they would sacrifice the sheep to the nearest idol. If the sheep did not lay down near an idol, they would just create a new one on the spot and add the inscription, "To an Unknown God."

Paul said, "I want to tell you about this unknown God. He's the true God."

Notice six logical steps in his message. First, this God is the creator of the universe. "The God who made the world and everything in it is the Lord of heaven and earth and does not live in temples built by hands" (v. 24). We don't make Him; He made us!

Second, He is the ruler of the nations. "From one man he made every nation of men, that they should inhabit the whole earth; and he determined the times set for them and the exact places where they should live" (v. 26). God ordained that there would be separate countries. But God didn't create the world and just remove himself from it. He is actively involved in the affairs of nations.

Third, He is the sustainer of life. "God did this so that men would seek him and perhaps reach out for him and find him, though he is not far from each one of us" (v. 27). Paul then quotes two of their philosophers, one of whom said, "In him we live and move and have our being," and another who said, "We are his offspring" (v.28).

Fourth, he is the Father of us all. "Since we are God's offspring, we should not think that the divine being is like gold or silver or stone—an image made by man's design and skill" (v. 29).

Fifth, He wants to be the Savior of our souls. "In the past God overlooked such ignorance, but now he commands all people everywhere to repent" (v. 30). To repent comes from two Greek words meaning "change your mind," or "change your thinking." They had thought of God as something they created, but they would need to think of God as someone who created them. That's a vast difference. We have to repent and be His child or else one day we will be answerable to Him.

Sixth, He will be the judge of the universe. "He has set a day when he will judge the world with justice by the man he has appointed" (v. 31). The standard of judgment is not going to be a moral code—it's going to be a man. Are you friend or foe of Jesus Christ? Paul said that God "has given proof of this to all men by raising him from the dead." That is the foundational proof of Christianity.

See how simple Paul's message was to these scholars? This God that you're worshiping as an unknown God is the creator of the universe, the ruler of nations, the sustainer of life, and the Father of us all. He wants to be the Savior of our souls. One day He will be the judge of the universe. Even a small child there could understand what Paul said.

Expectations

Another aspect of Paul's communication was that *he had realistic expectations*. One reaction was ridicule. "When they heard about the resurrection of the dead, some of them sneered" (v. 32). Today if you try to share your convictions about Christ, some people will scoff at you as being archaic, puritanical, fundamentalist, out of touch, or too straight.

Billy Graham was on one of those free-thinking talk shows recently. The brazen host asked him in front of the audience, "Were you a virgin when you got married?" Dr. Graham responded, "Yes, I was." As soon as he said that the audience snickered and ridiculed. Some whistled and hooted. I admired Billy Graham for keeping his composure, but it was sad. No one in the audience had made the kind of contribution to our society that Billy Graham has, and probably a lot of them really don't have their lives together. It's the easiest thing in the world to ridicule the truth. You can attack the truth about as effectively as you can shoot a beebee at a battleship. It doesn't make a whole lot of difference.

Other people who listened to Paul procrastinated. They said, "We want to hear you again on this subject" (v. 32). That sounds like a decent response. No one should make hasty decisions. But the most convenient cop-out in your relationship with Jesus Christ is to say, "I'm going to wait a while. I'll think about it. I'll study more. I'll decide later." Being neutral about Jesus Christ is like a paratrooper jumping out of an airplane being neutral about pulling the ripcord.

A few people believed. "A few men became followers of Paul and believed. Among them was Dionysius, a member of the Areopagus, also a woman named Damaris, and a number of others" (v. 34). Some believed, but most did not.

If you expect an overwhelming response to what you say, you're going to be devastated. A leader must have a tough hide. No matter how good your product, no matter how effective your sales pitch, not everyone is going to buy. No matter how well you communicate your expectations to your employees, not everybody is going to follow instructions. No matter how well you teach your children, they are not always going to be faithful to the Lord. No matter how logical or dynamic your lesson, not all students are going to pass the exam. No matter how well the truth of the gospel is communicated, you'd better anticipate rejection.

Some will ridicule your message and some will ignore it. That's what Jesus taught us in His parable of the sower in Matthew 13. Some of the seed will fall on hard ground, some will fall on shallow ground, some will fall on thorny ground, and some will fall on productive ground. The problem is not with the seed, but with the soil. Jesus concluded His parable by saying, "He who has ears, let him hear."

One of the smartest men I've ever had the privilege of being associated with is Dr. Lewis Foster, until recently a professor at the Cincinnati Bible Seminary. Dr. Foster graduated at the top of his class in both undergraduate and graduate school. He is considered one of the world's leading authorities on Alexander the Great. He was at his best in question-and-answer sessions. People would ask him questions and he would quote dates and names and places. Dr. Foster was a guest lecturer at our church years ago. For about an hour he talked about the period between the Testaments. Everybody paid keen attention, including my oldest son, who was five years old at the time. I noticed him sitting right in the front row, soaking up every word.

On the way home I asked him, "Russ, how did you like that?"

"That was great!" he said. "You know, Dad, maybe you ought to preach more like that. Even a child can understand it."

Shortly after that I sat down and wrote out the gospel in one-syllable words. There's nothing more profound and yet easier to understand:

God made man and loved him. Man sinned and fell from God's grace. But God, in His great love, sent His Son to die for our sins, and He raised Him from the dead. Now if we yield our lives to Him, He will cleanse our sins and give us life and grant us peace.

He who has ears, let him hear.

Dealing With Discouragement

Acts 18:1-11

"I AM NOW the most miserable man alive. Whether I shall ever be better I cannot tell."

Those words were spoken by Abraham Lincoln following a series of failures in his life that had cast him into a pit of despair. They illustrate the fact that nearly everyone gets discouraged on occasion.

You are a rare person if you never get "down in the dumps." You are rare if you never lose your enthusiasm for your job, your schoolwork, your marriage, your Sunday school class, or life in general. In fact, the more successful you are, the more vulnerable you are to discouragement. Ambitious people set high goals for themselves; when they fail to reach those goals, that's discouraging. Discouragement is common in January and February. The holidays are over, winter arrives, and the daily grind resumes.

There's a difference between depression and discouragement. Depression is prolonged melancholy usually brought about by a series of events. Discouragement is the temporary loss of enthusiasm for a particular project. Discouragement focuses on a goal that seems unattainable, and some temperaments are more prone to discouragement than others. Some people hardly ever get discouraged; others have to struggle with discouragement frequently. The important factor is not how often you get discouraged, but how you handle it. Do you persevere? Do you tenaciously work it through to victory, or do you just bail out and quit?

Warren Wiersbe tells of a minister who in 20 years had ministered to ten different churches. He put on his resume that he had 20 years of experience in the ministry, but Wiersbe said, "No—he had two years of experience ten different times." If you don't work through discouragement and stay with your task, you will never mature. First Corinthians 13:7 says, "Love ... always perseveres."

Like Abraham Lincoln, the apostle Paul knew what it was like to be discouraged. "We do not want you to be uninformed, brothers, about the hardships we suffered in the province of Asia. We were under great pressure, far beyond our ability to endure, so that we despaired even of life. Indeed, in our hearts we felt the sentence of death" (2 Corinthians 1:8, 9). We're not sure when that experience of despair hit the apostle Paul, but it seems to fit into this time frame when he came to the city of Corinth on his second missionary journey.

Paul told the Corinthians that he first came to them "in weakness and fear, and with much trembling" (1 Corinthians 2:3). Paul had just been driven out of Macedonia by his opponents. He had been blandly tolerated by the intellectuals in Athens. Now he came timidly to Corinth. His self-esteem may have been low. His confidence may have been shaken. He may have been discouraged at this point in his ministry. God appeared to Paul in a vision to encourage him.

Paul remained in Corinth for 18 months. That's the longest he stayed at any missionary stop on his entire journey up to this point. He established a large church there. Paul was able to work through his discouragement and he emerged victorious.

Reasons for Discouragement

Every leader needs to understand the causes and the cure for discouragement. One of the reasons Paul could have become discouraged at this point is the *wickedness* of Corinth. Sin can be discouraging if you participate in it, or it can be discouraging if you are seeking to overcome it.

Three young men sat down beside me once at a high school basketball game. Each had an earring in one ear—dangling from one of their ears each of them had a cross. With crosses in their ears they sat there making suggestive remarks about the cheerleaders and using some pretty profane language. That was frustrating for me because I couldn't do anything about it. It wasn't a good idea to get into a fight, and it was not a good time to try to convert those young men. If you are in the business of trying to overcome sin in the midst of such a wicked world, it's discouraging at times.

Corinth was an awful city. It was a cosmopolitan city, a seaport town. It was a crossroads between the east and the west. Sailors loved to stop at this port of Corinth because it was noted for its loose morals. They had a temple to the goddess Aphrodite attended by a thousand prostitutes. In fact, the phrase, "to live like a Corinthian" was synonymous with hedonism in that day.

Paul came into this city to preach the gospel of Christ. He wanted to tell these people, "Christ wants to forgive your sin and give you real life." But that would require repentance and a change of lifestyle. It would require control of their appetites. When he saw these pleasure-seeking, indulgent people of Corinth, he could have felt a sense of futility about his mission. Anytime you have a task in which you feel like your responsibilities are greater than your resources, that's a seedbed for the weeds of discouragement.

Another reason Paul may have been discouraged was *loneliness*. Paul was rushed out of Berea because his enemies sought to kill him. He left his traveling companions, Timothy and Silas, behind. He went to Athens alone and now he came to Corinth alone. If you are alone for a period of time, that's fertile soil for discouragement, too. Charles Schulz in *Peanuts* defined loneliness as "being alone when you don't want to be." A widow, a college student away from home, a soldier, a single person who goes home to an apartment alone and fixes a dinner for one, each of them knows what loneliness is all about.

You can feel alone in a crowd. If there's nobody in a crowd of people who knows you or who cares about you, that only intensifies your loneliness. There were plenty of people in Corinth, but no one who could share with Paul.

Dr. Philip Zimbardo, a professor of psychology at Stanford, and author of one of the most widely used textbooks in that field, addressed that issue in a *Psychology Today* article entitled "The Age of Indifference." He wrote: "I know of no more potent killer than isolation. There is no more destructive influence on physical and mental health than the isolation of you from me and us from them. It has been shown to be a central agent in the ideology of depression, paranoia, schizophrenia, rape, suicide, and mass murder." If all we have are surface relationships with people, that can create loneliness and despair.

Every day you can hear people having conversations like this:

"How are you doing?"

"I'm great. How are you doing?"

"I'm great, too. How's your family?"

"They're doing fine. How about yours?"

"They're doing fine, too."

"You enjoy the game last night?"

"Yes, I did. I think we're doing better. Good to see you."

"Good to see you, too."

Sometimes those are best friends! That's about as deep as we get.

If all we have are surface relationships, that's discouraging because we're never able to relax and be ourselves. We never have the assurance, "I'm accepted just as I am." We have so many layers around us to protect ourselves, it takes a while to peel those things away. If we never develop deep enough relationships with other people to relax and let them see ourselves as we really are, if we always have to put on a happy face and be "up" and give good advice, then that intensifies loneliness. Anne Morrow Lindbergh said, "The most exhausting thing in life is being insincere." If you're always insincere, if you always have to pretend with people, no matter how many people you have around you, then you are lonely, and that's a seedbed for discouragement.

A third reason for Paul's discouragement could have been *weariness.* Judging from Paul's itinerary on this second missionary journey, he could well have been emotionally and physically exhausted. Paul traveled 2000 miles, 1500 of which he walked. That would be like walking from Louisville to Jacksonville, Florida and back in a year's time. When you travel, you eat in different places, sleep in different beds, and maintain a different schedule. It's exhausting even when you're on vacation. Paul's health was not the best and he was not on vacation. Every place he went he suffered pressure—the stress of opposition, financial pressure, the pressure of trying to preach the gospel wherever he went.

Dr. Thomas Holmes and his colleagues at the University of Washington developed a famous stress test. They originally did their work for the military to correlate the connection between pressure and disease. They rated the severity of different problems that people experience. For example, the death of a spouse was 100 stress points, divorce was 73 stress points, a jail sentence was 63 stress points. They said if you experience between 200 and 250 stress points in a year, the chances are that you will have a serious illness. But if you experience between 300 and 350 stress points in a year, chances are 80% or better that you will suffer an emotional or physical breakdown.

Translate those figures to the apostle Paul's experience on this missionary journey—his jail sentence, his split with Barnabas, his personal injury when he was persecuted. It's estimated that Paul had 420 stress points during this time! No wonder he was exhausted! No wonder he was a prime candidate for despair. Every person has a limit; once you get run down emotionally or physically, it's easy to lose your vision and become discouraged.

One other reason that Paul may have been discouraged

was *repeated rejection*. From a human perspective, Paul had experienced a lot of failure on this trip. In one city after another he had been ridiculed, arrested, and stoned. He had some dramatic successes, but the opposition was so strong, failure was frequent. In Corinth, "the Jews opposed Paul and became abusive." Now that's an old story, but Paul's reaction was strong. He told them, "Your blood be on your own heads!" (Acts 18:6) Lloyd Ogilvie says "That's about the closest Paul ever came to swearing." He was irritable and under pressure. Had he been in a positive spirit and rested, he may not have been so short. But you get the feeling that Paul had had enough.

Experiences of failure can take us into the pit of despair quickly. That's especially true if you're a perfectionist or an ambitious person. Your emotional state is so closely tied to your accomplishments that when you fail to achieve your self-imposed standards, your confidence is shaken, your self-esteem declines, and discouragement sets in. That's why some of the world's most successful people had periods in their life when they felt like they were total failures. Elijah, Moses, Churchill, Lincoln, Spurgeon, Hemingway, and others felt that they were total failures at points in their lives.

Resources for Keeping On

But even though Paul had all these reasons for quitting, he didn't quit because God gave him the means to keep going. First, God provided Paul with some *solid friendships*. "He met a Jew named Aquila, a native of Pontus, who had recently come from Italy with his wife Priscilla" (v. 2). They had left because in 49 A.D. the emperor Claudius had banished all Jews from Rome. Paul immediately had important things in common with this couple. They were Christians and so was he.

I was on a plane a while back and a man I'd never met sat down beside me. He took a Christian book out of his brief case and started to read it. I introduced myself. He put his book down, and for the next 45 minutes we had a conversation like we had known each other for months. When you have a common commitment to Jesus Christ, there's an instant rapport that you have with people who also share that commitment.

Paul also shared a common trade with these people; "he was a tentmaker as they were" (v. 3). They were strangers in a foreign country; they were looking for companionship. They had come from Rome; Paul had always wanted to go to Rome. They, like Paul, knew what it was like to be persecuted. Claudius had kicked them out of the city. Paul developed a meaningful friendship with this Christian couple.

When you are discouraged, you tend to withdraw from people, to isolate yourself, to say, "I don't want to see anybody, I don't want to have to pretend, I don't want to talk to anybody." But just the opposite is needed. What you need is exposure to people who care, who are sensitive to your needs—friends who will encourage you. "See to it brothers, that none of you has a sinful, unbelieving heart that turns away from the living God. But encourage one another daily, as long as it is called Today, so that none of you may be hardened by sin's deceitfulness" (Hebrews 3:12, 13). When you get discouraged, you need to be with friends who care.

Now you might say, "I don't have any friends like that. All I have are surface relationships." And you can sit back and wail and moan and hope that somebody will come. What you need to do is to be unselfish yourself. Look for other people who need encouragement and boosting up. Then when you need encouragement, they will return the favor.

One of the most popular preachers I know is Wayne Smith of Lexington. Everybody across America who knows Wayne loves him, and whenever he has a problem, everybody is there to boost him up. When he was recovering from an automobile accident, he got hundreds of cards, telegrams, and visits. The reason he has so many friends who care is not that he's a funny man, which he is, nor that he's a great speaker, which he is, but because he's an *encourager*.

Wayne called me yesterday and said, "Bob, I just read your church paper. You had 187 additions in your church

Sunday. I can't believe that. That is great. That's the greatest thing that's happened in our movement since the Cane Ridge Revival." He said, "Do you know how many additions we had in our church Sunday? None. We made our nursery workers happy last Sunday. We didn't have any baptisms so they didn't have to wait around. But I'm just calling to congratulate you. I'm thrilled over what's happened in your church."

That's why Wayne gets encouragement—because he encourages other people. He wasn't envious, he just rejoiced. He didn't wallow around in self-pity saying "Why didn't somebody come minister to me?" He ministered to somebody else.

If you want people to notice when you're down and take the time to encourage you, then you go notice somebody else when they're down. "The man that makes friends must show himself friendly" (Proverbs 18:24). It's that simple. Be an encourager to other people, and then when you're discouraged, others will encourage you.

Second, Paul *worked with his hands*. "Because he was a tentmaker as they were, he stayed and worked with them" (Acts 18:3). In his youth, Paul studied to be a rabbi. According to Jewish practice, every rabbi had to learn a trade so that they wouldn't have to take any money for their teaching and their preaching. The rabbi was less likely to become a detached scholar that way. He knew what it was like to be a working man. Paul's parents had taught him the craft of tentmaking—he was a leather worker. So when he came to Corinth he began to work with his hands again because he was broke. That may seem insignificant at first, but it was probably helpful to Paul in overcoming discouragement.

J. Wallace Hamilton has an interesting article about depression. He says one way to help yourself come out of it is to do something with your hands, because that is not only a diversion, but provides a sense of accomplishment. So many of us have jobs in intangible areas of social work or teaching or technologial areas where we see very little accomplishment. But when you do something with your hands, whether it's baking a cake, weeding a garden, mowing the grass, or finishing furniture, then when you're done you have a sense of accomplishment—you have done something and you can see what you've done.

A preacher friend is an excellent golfer, but he preaches in a stagnant church. He says when he gets discouraged he goes out and plays golf. He plays a lot. He says, "I just get such a sense of satisfaction seeing that ball going out 250 yards right down the middle of the fairway. There's something I can do right."

Do something with your hands. Maybe Paul felt alone, rejected, and emotionally drained, but he could still make tents. People would still buy them; he could still support himself. He didn't have to keep on preaching and taking all that abuse.

Third, Paul *maintained his spiritual priorities.* "Every sabbath he reasoned in the synagogue, trying to persuade Jews and Greeks" (v. 4). He kept on doing it. When Silas and Timothy came with a love offering from the churches in Macedonia, Paul was able to quit making tents and give himself exclusively to preaching. Paul refused to quit in his primary purpose of life, which was evangelism. Even though his mood wasn't good, he kept on doing what God had called him to do. You can call it perseverance, staying power, stick-to-itiveness, tenacity, spunk—it's that quality of character that refuses to quit regardless of how you feel. That's the characteristic that separates the accomplisher from the person who does nothing. The successful person keeps getting back up when he's knocked down. That's what we love about Rocky. When Rocky gets knocked down, a lesser person wouldn't get back up. (A lesser person would be dead, in fact!) But Rocky gets back up and goes at it again, and when he knocks out the opponent, everybody in the theater begins to applaud and cheer.

Paul had taken abuse and persecution, but he kept coming back for more, and he began to realize some successes. He was kicked out of the synagogue, but he went next door and started a church at the home of Justus. That would be galling to the Jews who were opposing him, having a church right next door. Then Crispus, the synagogue ruler, became a Christian. "His entire household believed in the Lord." That had to be gratifying to Paul. Then, "Many of the Corinthians who heard him believed and were baptized" (v. 8).

Paul had momentum going his way. Persistence pays. Spurgeon says, "It was persistence that enabled the snail to make it to the ark." When you are discouraged, it is important to maintain your spiritual routine. When you are discouraged, that's the time you are tempted to stay away from church, to withdraw, to neglect prayer, and to dabble in the pleasures of the world as a diversion, but that only compounds your problem. It adds additional feelings of failure and guilt.

"Let us not become weary in doing good, for at the proper time we will reap a harvest if we do not give up" (Galatians 6:9). If you don't feel like going to church, go anyway. If you don't feel like singing when you come, sing anyway. If you don't feel like being pleasant and kind to people, do it anyway. If you don't feel like going to work tomorrow morning, do it anyway. If you don't feel like working hard, do it anyway. Eventually you'll find out that if you're persistent in doing what is right, your spirits pick up. William James, the psychologist, said, "If you act the way you wish you feel, eventually you'll feel the way you act."

Paul was also *encouraged by God himself.* "One night the Lord spoke to Paul in a vision" (Acts 18:9). What a boost this was for Paul, to get a special message from God. God is probably not going to appear to you or me in a vision, but His message to us would be the same. He said, "Do not be afraid; keep on speaking, do not be silent."

God wants the Christian to be bold, fearless, free to achieve. He said to Paul, "I am with you, and no one is going to attack and harm you, because I have many people in this city" (v. 10). God knows how much we are able to take. He "will not let you be tempted beyond what you can bear" (1 Corinthians 10:13). Paul had reached his limit, so God gave him a year and a half of respite.

So don't be afraid. God is with you. He told Paul, "Don't be silent. Keep on speaking. Don't worry about how people respond—that's My task. You must share the message and I'll take care of the results. I have many people in this city. Don't view Corinth as a foreboding city of hostile, worldly people. It's a city filled with potential converts who will join you in a great church. Keep a positive spirit regardless of the opposition."

Tim Hansel spoke about joy last year at the Praise Gathering at our church. It was a paradox that he would speak on joy. Tim was injured in a fall years ago. Since that time he has had severe headaches every day; he has to take dozens of pills each day just to continue to function. But his topic was *joy*. I've been in very few sessions where there was more laughter. Tim said, "Pain is inevitable; misery is optional." Pain is inevitable in your life. You're going to have difficulty, but misery is optional. It's your attitude that makes the difference.

Dr. Charles Swindoll in his book, *Growing Through The Changing Seasons Of Life*, tells about a time when Paderewski, the famous composer/pianist, had a concert in America. It was a social extravaganza complete with tuxedos and long dresses.

Before the concert began a young mother brought her 9-year-old, fidgety child to their seats near the front. She had brought him there against his will. She wanted him to hear the great pianist and hoped that he would be inspired to practice. But while she turned and talked to a neighbor, the boy slipped out of his seat and was drawn to the platform by the ebony grand piano.

Without being noticed, he sat down, this little 9-year-old boy, on the piano stool. He put his small trembling fingers on the keys and began to pound out "Chopsticks." The murmuring of the crowd subsided as everybody turned angrily to the platform. "Get that young man off there," they said. "Who is that? What kind of mother would bring a child like that in here, anyway?"

But the great pianist behind the curtain could tell what

was going on. Quickly he slipped on his coat and went out unannounced to the platform. He bent over the boy, and with his hands reaching around him, he improvised a counter-melody that harmonized with "Chopsticks" to make it sound like a masterpiece. As Paderewski played with this young man he kept whispering to him, "Don't stop, son, keep going. Don't quit, keep going."

Maybe you are hammering out some task in life that you feel is almost futile. It seems to you about as productive as "Chopsticks" in a concert hall. I hope that you will hear the words of the heavenly Master: "Don't quit. Keep going. Don't be weary in doing good, for in due season you will reap a harvest if you do not give up."

Revival in the Church

Acts 19:1-20

I HAVE LIKED the city of Louisville ever since I first moved here in 1966. We're just far enough south to have an occasional snow but not too much. I like the location, the sports, the warmth of the people, and the size of the city. To me this is a great place to live. But Louisville is not a spiritual town. We're not a bad town, but we're not a spiritual town. We've got some well-known seminaries here and some really fine Christian people, but there seems to be a spiritual lethargy in the city.

A good deal of our economy is dependent upon distilleries and the tobacco industry, two commodities that are harmful to the body. Our primary tourist attraction, the Kentucky Derby, hinges on gambling, and we have almost an open city during the Derby festivities. According to *Time Magazine*, Louisville is a center for Satan worshipers and the occult. The dominant newspapers in our town are nationally known for their liberal editorials, espousing humanistic causes. And Louisville has few great churches. There are a few, but in a community our size there ought to be more churches numbering in the thousands, having dynamic ministries and influence, but that's not the case.

All of this underscores the need for a spiritual awakening

in our city. In this time of rapidly declining moral values, the disintegration of the family, and the attack of the integrity of the Word of God, there is a desperate need for a spiritual renewal in our churches in our community.

Spiritual renewal has happened in the past, in places like Nineveh and Jerusalem, in England, and on the American frontier during the great awakening. God promises, "If my people, who are called by my name, will humble themselves and pray and seek my face and turn from their wicked ways, then will I hear from heaven and will forgive their sin and will heal their land" (2 Chronicles 7:14). In Acts 19 we read about a revival that occurred in the city of Ephesus.

Paul concluded his second missionary journey in Corinth. After spending some time there, he moved on toward his home base of Antioch, stopping briefly in Ephesus and establishing a church there. After staying home at Antioch for a period of time, he began a third trip to revisit many of the churches he had established. One of his first stops was Ephesus.

Ephesus was a rich city. It was a river town. It was known as the treasure house of Asia, because most of the trade to Asia Minor flowed through Ephesus. Ephesus was a sports town. The Pan-Ionian games were held there. That brought recognition and revenue to the city. But Ephesus was also an idolatrous town. The opulent temple to Artemis, the many-breasted goddess of fertility, was there. Many of the tourists who came to the town of Ephesus to visit purchased one of the miniature statues fashioned by the silversmiths of the city. Ephesus was a center of sorcery and witchcraft. It was not as intellectually sophisticated as Athens nor as corrupt as Corinth, but a kind of spiritual lethargy had settled over Ephesus.

When Paul visited the church there he had a tremendous impact on the entire city. He stayed for about three years—that's the longest recorded stay at any of his preaching points. He changed attitudes, he reversed people's lives, and "the word of the Lord spread widely and grew in power" (Acts 19:20). The influence of this church became so great that it affected the entire economy of the city, and the merchants were in an uproar. How did Paul create such a revival there, and how can we duplicate the circumstances in our communities?

Spirit-Filled Leadership

When Paul arrived in Ephesus he found twelve men who were incomplete believers. Evidently they had been influenced by the preaching of Apollos, who knew only the baptism of John. Paul asked them, "Did you receive the Holy Spirit when you believed?" They said, "No, we have not even heard that there is a Holy Spirit." Paul asked, "Then what baptism did you receive?" Paul made a connection between their baptism and their receiving the Holy Spirit. They said, "John's baptism" (Acts 19:2, 3). Then Paul explained the difference. John's baptism was a baptism of repentance, proclaiming the One who was to come, Jesus. But the baptism of Jesus is the baptism of forgiveness through His blood and the reception of the Holy Spirit.

In Acts 2:38 we have the first complete Christian definition of baptism. "Repent and be baptized, every one of you, in the name of Jesus Christ so that your sins may be forgiven. And you will receive the gift of the Holy Spirit." When we repent and surrender our lives to Christ and are baptized into Him, our sins are forgiven and we receive the gift of the Holy Spirit. Some Christians will suggest to you that there are *two* baptisms—a water baptism and a Holy Spirit baptism—that the water baptism was John's baptism and the Holy Spirit baptism was Jesus' baptism. But Ephesians 4:5 says there is "one Lord, one faith, one baptism." The New Testament Christians practiced water baptism.

When we genuinely surrender to Jesus Christ and are baptized into Him, we are promised the indwelling of the Holy Spirit. Jesus told Nicodemus that unless you're born of water and the Spirit you cannot enter the kingdom of God. Titus 3:5, 6 says, "He saved us through the washing of rebirth and renewal by the Holy Spirit, whom he poured out on us." When we become Christians, God doesn't just remove the sin from our lives and leave a vacuum. He fills us with His Spirit to empower us for the Christian life.

Now you might say, "I believed in Christ and I was baptized, but I didn't get any electrical shock of the Holy Spirit. I didn't go into a trance." Receiving the Holy Spirit is not a standardized emotional experience. It is a divine promise. God promises that when you yield your life to Him, when you're baptized into Him, He fills you with the Holy Spirit. You need to understand Him and employ that gift.

Have you ever seen a little baby discover his hands for the first time? He's lying in the crib, maybe three months old, and he looks. "Hey, I've got hands!" He learns to move those things. "I can control them." Pretty soon he does creative things with those hands—he starts sucking his thumb, then he begins to learn to catch a ball, write, type, play the piano. He had hands all along, he only needed to discover them and learn to use them. As a Christian, when you gave your life to Jesus Christ, you were granted the gift of the Holy Spirit, and you need to employ that and begin to rely on it more and more. The Bible says, "Greater is he that is in you, than he that is in the world" (1 John 4:4, *KJV*).

Once these twelve men were baptized into Christ Jesus, Paul gave them an additional blessing. "When Paul placed his hands on them, the Holy Spirit came on them [in a miraculous way], and they spoke in tongues and prophesied" (Acts 19:6). The apostles had a special ability to lay their hands on people and impart supernatural gifts. The purpose of that ability was to confirm the Word that the apostles were speaking (Hebrews 2:3, 4). When Paul laid his hands on these twelve men, they were given the ability to speak in languages they had never studied—that was supernatural. They were able to predict the future.

Only three times in the book of Acts do you read that the people spoke in tongues—Acts 2, Acts 10 and Acts 19. This was a demonstration of the special power of God's Spirit among them. Nowhere in the Scripture does it suggest that every Christian should speak in tongues, or that if you don't speak in tongues you're not filled with the Holy Spirit. In

1 Corinthians 12, Paul said that God gives different gifts to the body, but that speaking in tongues is the least of the gifts and not everybody speaks in tongues.

These 12 men became the nucleus of this Ephesian church. "Paul took the disciples with him and had discussions daily in the lecture hall" (Acts 19:9). Here is the first essential for a spiritual renewal—a Holy Spirit-filled nucleus. The church will rise no higher than its leaders, and if the leaders are relying on human wisdom and human strength, it will be reflected in the church.

That's one of the things that has impressed me from the very beginning about the church I am serving now—the leaders are guided by the Spirit of God. Butch Dabney was an elder and chairman of the pulpit committee who came to visit me in 1966 and talked with me about this church. He said, "We have an opportunity to build a great church in Louisville. We want it to be the very best church it can be." And then he said (I'll never forget it), "We think if we're doing it for the Lord it ought to be done first class."

When I came to visit the leaders of the church, I found that the same spirit permeated all of them. Over the years I've heard them say many times, "Let's do what's right," "Let's do what the Lord would have us to do," and "God has led us in the past; let's be open to His leading at this point." At our last meeting, the Chairman of the Board said, "Men, God is blessing this church in a special way. Let's begin the meeting tonight with a silent prayer and each of us thank God for His leading and ask for His continued blessing." A spirit-filled nucleus is essential for revival.

A Christ-Centered Message

"Paul entered the synagogue and spoke boldly there for three months" (v. 8), and then the Jews became obstinate. So he took the disciples and had discussions daily in the lecture hall of Tyrannus. This was not the first time a church began in a school. He lectured there for two years, and all who lived in Asia heard the Word of the Lord. There was a lot to be preached against in Ephesus. There was that temple and that false god, and there was greed and sensuality, but Paul didn't preach about that. He preached the Word of the Lord. He preached positively. People quit buying the idols, and Paul was accused of upsetting the economy of the city. But Paul wasn't being negative. The city clerk said, "They have neither robbed temples nor blasphemed our goddess" (Acts 19:37). Paul was just lifting up Jesus Christ.

Our message in Sunday school and church has to be a positive, Christ-centered message. There's a lot wrong with our world, but if we spend all of our time ranting against drugs and immorality and abortion and homosexuality, and that's all we talk about, it identifies the problem, but not the cure. When Jesus Christ is honored, when His word is preached, then there is curative power. "The word of God is living and active. Sharper than any double-edged sword, it penetrates even to dividing soul and spirit, joints and marrow; it judges the thoughts and attitudes of the heart" (Hebrews 4:12).

A couple of Saturdays ago I was riding in the car and I was angry at somebody. I felt somebody had mistreated one of my children. When you yourself are mistreated, you can accept that more easily, but if somebody mistreats one of your children, you get angry. My vindictive spirit came out. "I'm going to get even with him!" I thought. "He's not going to get by with this." I was churning inside. Then I looked at the clock in the car. It was 11:30, and I remembered I had a radio program that came on at 11:30, so I turned it on.

I was preaching on the radio about forgiveness; the parable about the unjust steward. "The king had forgiven him of a debt of three million dollars, but he turned around and wouldn't forgive a man who owed him $20.00. If God has forgiven us so much, everything we've done against Him, we ought to be willing to forgive those little things that people do against us—without demanding that they repay, or without them even asking for forgiveness." It made me mad just listening to that! I sank down in the seat and I thought, that's right, I can't get even with this person. I've just got to forgive him. The word of God convicts. It doesn't matter who's preaching; it might even be yourself! It'll convict you.

When the word is shared and Christ is lifted up, we're fed, we're edified, and a spirit of revival begins to work among us. Jesus said, "This is what the kingdom of God is like. A man scatters seed on the ground. Night and day, whether he sleeps or gets up, the seed sprouts and grows, though he does not know how" (Mark 4:26, 27). People ask me, "Would you come and talk to our men's group about what makes a church grow?" One of the first things I say is, "I don't know." In our Sunday school classes and from the pulpit we try to share the seed of the word of God. Jesus went on to say, "All by itself the soil produces grain—first the stalk, then the head, then the full kernel in the head. As soon as the grain is ripe, he puts the sickle to it, because the harvest has come" (Mark 4:28, 29).

It's really not that complicated. We just share the Word of God, it takes root in people's lives, they begin to grow, they get ripe enough, we just put the sickle to them and harvest them. That's it! That's what Paul did in Ephesus—he preached the Word of the Lord for two or three years, and it produced a revival.

Extraordinary Power

"God did extraordinary miracles through Paul" (Acts 19:11). A miracle is an event contrary to the laws of nature as we understand them. A miracle is God intervening with His own laws to perform the supernatural. There is a difference between miracles and answered prayer. If God heals us through natural processes, that may be an answer to prayer, but not necessarily a miracle. A miracle doesn't happen very often. We don't expect to see a lot of them. The Bible says God did *extra-ordinary* —very rare—miracles through Paul. "Handkerchiefs and aprons that had touched him were taken to the sick, and their illnesses were cured" (v. 12). That is very rare. I cringe when I hear radio preachers say, "If you'll just send in your check, we'll send you a pillowcase you can sleep on or a miracle-working cloth you can carry around with you." The spirit of God was flowing in a special way at Ephesus.

The church still ought to be a place where people are healed. I don't know of anybody who can go into a hospital and just touch people one by one and heal them instantly. But the church still needs to be the place where some extraordinary healing processes take place in people's lives. The church where I serve has a variety of ministries. We have an evangelistic ministry, we have an instructional ministry, but we also have a healing ministry—things like the Divorce Recovery Workshop, the ministry to people who have trouble with alcohol or drugs, or the ministry to the people who have family members in prison. Those are ministries that help heal deep emotional wounds.

Occasionally I get letters from people who say, "I was going through a real crisis in my life when I came to your church. The fellowship and the feeding of the Word of God really helped me through. Thank you." God does healing works in the church to bring about revival.

Some of the miracles that God performed were exorcisms; evil spirits left people (v. 12). The New Testament gives some accounts of people who were controlled by demonic forces. They would become suddenly violent without explanation, or cut themselves, or throw themselves into a fire. Jesus would cast out these demons.

Missionaries in pagan countries tell of people who are demon-possessed. All of a sudden the person will speak with another voice or become violent without explanation. As our society becomes increasingly pagan, and as involvement with drugs, the occult, and Satan worship intensifies, demon possession may become more commonplace.

We might not be called upon to release a lot of people from demons, but we do have an opportunity as a church to release people from the grip of evil in their life. When one young man became a Christian here and then decided he was going to study for the ministry, some of his former fraternity brothers nicknamed him "Flip." They thought he had really flipped out, there was such a dramatic change in his life. A couple of weeks ago a man was baptized here. He said to me, "I've lived 32 years of a wild life. That's enough. Boy, what a relief."

Paul released people from the grip of evil in their lives. When he did that, some Jewish leaders were impressed. They had heard Paul say to demon-possessed people, "In the name of the Lord Jesus I command you to come out," and the evil spirit would come out. So they went to a man possessed of an evil spirit and said, "In the name of Jesus, whom Paul preaches, I command you to come out." Verse 15 is interesting. "The evil spirit answered them, 'Jesus I know and Paul I know about, but who are you?'" That had to be embarrassing.

This verse tells me that our faith in Jesus Christ has to be a personal faith. We can't say, "I'm relying on the faith of my mother," or "I'm relying on the God of my preacher." It has to be a personal commitment to Jesus Christ. The man who had the evil spirit pounced on them, beat them up, ripped their clothes off and ran them out of the house humiliated. I bet the Jewish leaders never tried that again!

"When this became known to the Jews and Greeks living in Ephesus, they were all seized with fear, and the name of the Lord Jesus was held in high honor" (v. 17). When things start happening in the church, when people's lives are changed from evil, when people are ministered to and healed of emotional scars, the word gets out, and the name of Jesus Christ is held in high honor.

A Repentant Spirit

"Many of those who believed now came and openly confessed their evil deeds" (v. 18). They began to publicly confess their private sins. When the revival broke out, the Christians were convicted. They realized their Christian lives had been half-hearted. They had been participating in activities they should not have been participating in. "A number who had practiced sorcery brought their scrolls together and burned them publicly" (v. 19). When they calculated the value of the scrolls, the total came to be, in our present currency, over a million dollars worth. They eliminated the source of temptation. They wanted to completely forsake the past, so they burned their books.

When you abandon what is wrong in your life, don't give it to somebody else. Don't sell it. Get rid of it. A man came into my office a while back with a sack of marijuana—he said it was $50.00 worth. "I've been smoking this stuff three times a day and it's destroying me," he said. "I am giving it to you as a pledge, as a pact together, that I'm not going to do it anymore. I want you to get rid of it." When he left I was proud of him. Then I realized, I've got $50.00 worth of marijuana on my person! I didn't think it was a good idea to burn it, so I stuck it under my coat and went down the hallway, praying that I would not have a heart attack, and I got rid of it.

Is there a sack of goodies you need to get rid of? Do you have some bottles or pills, or a collection of magazines, or a subscription to a particular TV service, that you know is blocking the flow of the Holy Spirit in your life? Maybe it's time to get rid of it. Mark Twain said, "Man is the only blushing animal, and the only one that needs to." Jesus said, "Unless you repent, you too will all perish" (Luke 13:3). God cannot bless our lives as Christians, and He cannot bring a revival to the church, if we are all harboring secret sins. David said, "If I regard iniquity in my heart, the Lord will not hear me" (Psalm 66:18, *KJV*). Warren Wiersbe said, "The Christian is not sinless, but he should sin less and less and less." There needs to be a surrender of our lives to the Holy Spirit's power and a repentance from past sins.

Genuine repentance involves three words. The first is *conviction*. We are convicted by our conscience or by the Word that our behavior is wrong. We feel guilty. The second word is *contrition*. When we repent we are sorry. "The Lord is close to the brokenhearted and saves those who are crushed in spirit" (Psalm 34:18). God loves the broken heart, the bent knee, and the tearful eye. We need to be crushed because of our sin.

The third word is the most crucial, and that's the word

change. When we repent, we change. We change our minds, we change our value system, we change our attitudes, we change the direction of our lives. It takes more than admission of guilt, it takes more than tears. It takes genuine repentance, a change of mind and direction, for revival to come. "Godly sorrow brings repentance, ... but there is a worldly sorrow that brings death" (2 Corinthians 7:10). Peter was convicted that he had done wrong, he wept, and he changed his life. Judas Iscariot was convicted and he was sorry that he betrayed Christ, but he was too proud to repent and change.

Charles Colson gave a good example of what happens when Christ is truly Lord. "After Jack Eckerd, founder of the Eckerd drugstore chain, committed his life to Christ, he walked through one of his stores and saw with new eyes the magazine racks full of glossy copies of *Playboy* and *Penthouse*. Though retired from active management, he called his president and urged him to clean out the magazines. Management protested: the sales accounted for substantial profits. Though as the largest stockholder Eckerd himself stood to lose money as well—a lot of money—he persisted.

"And he prevailed. *Playboy, Penthouse* and their ilk were removed from all 1,700 Eckerd drugstores. And Jack Eckerd has since begun a quiet campaign to get other retail stores to do the same.

"When I asked Jack ... what motivated him, he answered simply, 'God wouldn't let me off the hook.' The most learned theologian couldn't give us a more eloquent description of the Lordship of Christ in action."

There is no salvation without individual repentance. There is no spiritual power in the church unless it is a repentant body.

Foy Valentine, in his book, *What Do You Do After You Say Amen,* wrote, "Without a fundamental change of mind about all sin, a stuttering, stumbling, stalling church can never act redemptively in a sinful world." The church acting redemptively in a sinful, fallen world—that's our only hope of survival.

"If my people, who are called by my name, will humble

themselves and pray and seek my face and turn from their wicked ways, then will I hear from heaven and will forgive their sin and will heal their land." The next verse says, "Now my eyes will be open and my ears attentive to the prayers offered in this place" (2 Chronicles 7:15). May there be a spirit of continuous revival in this body, so that the Lord's eyes will be opened and His ears attentive to the prayers that are offered in this place.

What's Worship?

Acts 20:7-12

HAVE YOU WATCHED many church services on television? You don't have to observe many before you are impressed with the tremendous variety in worship styles. On Sunday night there's a church service out of Virginia Beach that really rocks. The music is loud and upbeat, the people dance in the aisles, the choruses are repeated eight or ten times, and the people wave their hands as they sing.

On Christmas Eve, you can tune in to a mass from St. Patrick's Cathedral that is very formal. The participants wear robes and the music is liturgical and everybody is very quiet.

In my own city, Louisville, you can go to a church service on the east end in which the minister will speak in quiet, reverent tones, and the people sit quietly and the music is Bach and Beethoven. Or you can go worship in the west end and the minister may be shouting and the people may be responding back to him, "Amen!" Larnelle Harris, one of my favorite singers here in Louisville, says that when their church service really gets going, the steeple on top begins to wave back and forth.

Which worship is appropriate? What is really acceptable in the eyes of God?

I heard a man say that one of the biggest disappointments of his life came when he was a boy. He saw a tent in a field and he thought there was a circus inside. He sneaked in under the flap and discovered that he was in the middle of a revival meeting. But he said that an even bigger disappointment came as an adult, when he went to church expecting a revival and discovered that it was a circus!

The church service should not be a circus. We don't gather for entertainment. "The Lord is in his holy temple; let all the earth be silent before him" (Habakkuk 2:20). First Corinthians 14:40 says, "Everything should be done in a fitting and orderly way." But what is fitting? What is orderly? The Bible also tells us to sing and shout, clap your hands, make a joyful noise unto the Lord. When are we supposed to be silent and when are we supposed to clap our hands?

I think most of our attitudes today about worship are a lot more cultural than they are scriptural. We develop attitudes about worship from tradition, and then we search out Scriptures that agree with our position. Let's look at what God's Word has to say about appropriate worship.

Acts 20 describes the gathering of Christians in the city of Troas. "On the first day of the week we came together to break bread" (v. 7). William Barclay says that this is one of the first accounts of what Christian worship was like. These few short verses reveal much about what true worship is supposed to be.

Celebration

The phrase, "On the first day of the week," implies that this worship was a time of celebration. Christians worshiped on the first day of the week for the distinct purpose of celebrating Jesus' resurrection from the grave. The Jews had worshiped on Saturday, the Sabbath day. It was a day of rest. The fourth Commandment said, "Observe the Sabbath day by keeping it holy. Six days you shall labor and do all your work, but the seventh day is a Sabbath to the Lord your God." The Sabbath day acknowledged that God is the creator of the world.

But in the New Testament, the day of worship shifted from Saturday to Sunday. Jesus had risen from the grave on the first day of the week. The church was established on the first day of the week, the day of Pentecost. The New Testament church developed this habit of regularly worshiping on Sunday. Paul said, "On the first day of every week" each person should set aside part of his money (1 Corinthians 16:2). John said, "On the Lord's Day I was in the Spirit" (Revelation 1:10). The Lord's day seemed to be the new designation of Sunday, the day of worship for the Christian.

Seventh-Day Adventists, Jehovah's Witnesses, and others suggest that we still ought to worship on Saturdays, but they are disregarding the new covenant with Christ. "Therefore do not let anyone judge you by what you eat or drink, or with regard to a religious festival, a New Moon celebration or a Sabbath day. These are a shadow of the things that were to come; the reality, however, is found in Christ" (Colossians 2:16, 17).

In the Old Testament, the Jews worshiped on Saturday to remember a finished creation. In the New Testament, the Christian worships on Sunday to celebrate a finished redemption. Christ's resurrection from the grave finished our redemption from sin.

One woman said she felt guilty about worshiping because she always enjoys it. "I don't know whether I'm worshiping or whether I'm being entertained," she said. But the Christian worship service should be a celebration! Christ has risen from the grave! We have hope in death. We have forgiveness of sin. We have a meaning to life.

To me, one of the most touching moments ever on television came at the end of the 1980 Winter Olympic Games, in which the United States hockey team beat the Russians. That was an incredible feat. It was like a college team beating the world's best professional team. All during the hockey game the cameras focused on goalie Jim Craig, one of the heroes of the team, and on his father in the stands. Craig's mother had recently died, and he and his father had grown closer through the months of grief.

When the United States team won the victory, a tremendous celebration erupted out on the ice. Players clenched their fists in the air and celebrated and soaked it in as the people cheered. Flags waved and music played. Players embraced. All of a sudden the camera focused in on Jim Craig, skating alone up and down the ice, scanning the stands. You could read his lips: "Where's my dad? Where's my dad?" It was the happiest moment of his life, and he wanted to celebrate it with the one who was closest to him. The last scene showed Jim Craig and his father embracing.

Christians have much to celebrate in Christ's resurrection from the grave and God's continued goodness. It's appropriate that we regularly come to worship and celebrate the resurrection of Christ with our Father, who comes closer and closer to us as we grow in Him.

When we come to celebrate the resurrection, what is appropriate as an expression of praise and thanksgiving? All kinds of expressions are used to celebrate a victory in an athletic contest—some shake hands, some embrace, some weep, some laugh. All kinds of expressions are appropriate. Let the Bible set the boundaries.

I can see three types of acceptable praise in the Old Testament. The first we could call *vocal praise:* singing, shouting, speaking.

> Come, let us sing for joy to the Lord;
> > Let us shout aloud to the Rock of our salvation.
>
> Let us come before him with thanksgiving
> > and extol him with music and song.
> > > (Psalm 95:1)

The second we could term *audible praise:* making music with instruments or making noise with our hands.

> Clap your hands, all you nations;
> > shout to God with cries of joy.
>
> How awesome is the Lord Most High.
> > > (Psalm 47:1)

We teach our children when they're growing up to clap their hands when they sing, and then at some stage we tell them it's not appropriate any more.

> Praise him with the sounding of the trumpet,
>   praise him with the harp and lyre,
> praise him with tambourine and dancing,
>   praise him with the strings and flute,
> praise him with the clash of cymbals,
>   praise him with resounding cymbals.
> Let everything that has breath praise the Lord.
> (Psalm 150:3-6)

When Jesus entered Jerusalem a week before the cross, His followers lined the streets shouting, "Hosanna, Hosanna!" The Pharisees were angry. They asked that Jesus tell His disciples to be quiet. Jesus said, "I tell you, if they keep quiet, the stones will cry out" (Luke 19:40). The Lord is pleased with the audible and the vocal praise of His people.

The third expression of His praise we could term *body language*. "Come, let us bow down in worship, let us kneel before the Lord our Maker" (Psalm 95:6). "I will praise you as long as I live, and in your name I will lift up my hands" (Psalm 63:4). When a little child comes and lifts up his hands to his parents, that's not emotional. He is saying, "Lift me up!" or, "You're bigger than I am."

First Timothy 2:8 says, "I want men everywhere to lift up holy hands in prayer." This verse can be interpreted literally or figuratively, but the raising of hands was very much a part of worship in Old Testament times.

> Let the people of Zion be glad in their King.
> Let them praise his name with dancing
> and make music to him with tambourine and harp.
> (Psalm 149:2, 3)

When the Ark of the Covenant was brought back into Jerusalem after it had been captured, King David led the parade and worshiped God by dancing in front of the Ark of the Covenant.

I'm not advocating that we greatly alter our worship service. I'm not suggesting that we have an interpretive dance and begin to wave our hands when we sing. Jesus said, "Be careful not to do your 'acts of righteousness' before men, to be seen by them" (Matthew 6:1). Your best prayers are usually those prayers that you offer at home by yourself; I think that we often do our best worship in private too. Public worship does need certain restraints, lest it become a display of who is the most righteous.

I *am* advocating that we recognize and appreciate the differences in public worship. We should not be critical of churches that are more formal or churches that are more expressive. We should feel comfortable with clapping and we should know when to be quiet. We should know how to support a singing group if they raise their hands when they sing, or a teenage singing group if they have choreography when they perform.

All those expressions ought to be done decently and in order, and there is a danger of going too far. Still, I like Billy Sunday's suggestion: "I'd rather restrain a fanatic than resurrect a corpse any day!"

Reverence

Worship also should be a time of reverence. The first Christians' purpose in coming together was to observe the Lord's Supper. That was a time of reverence. When Jesus instituted the Communion, He said, "As often as you do this, do it in remembrance of me." He didn't say how often to do it, but the early Christians apparently did it every Sunday. "On the first day of the week we came together to break bread" (Acts 20:7). Early historians verify that it was an every-Sunday occurrence.

That's why we have Communion every Sunday. It's a good precedent to follow. We know that in weekly observance there is the danger of Communion becoming too commonplace, but we think the benefits far outweigh the dangers.

Once a week is not too often to be intimate with the One you love.

The observance of the Lord's Supper is a time for reverence. It is a time to be still and know God. You cannot think about the cross without a sense of awe. Jesus said, "This is my body, given for you.... This cup is the new covenant in my blood, which is poured out for you" (Luke 22:19, 20). Not a bone of His body was broken, the Bible says, but His skin was pierced. The briar pierced His brow, and the blood flowed. Fists punched and bruised His face, and the blood flowed. The whip lacerated His back, and the blood flowed. Nails pierced His hands and feet, and the blood gushed. The spear was thrust deep into His side. Blood and water flowed together from that wound.

> See, from his head, his hands, his feet,
>   sorrow and blood flow mingled down.
> Did ere such love or sorrow meet
>   or thorns compose so rich a crown?

Instruction

The preaching of the Word of God was prominent in the early church. "It pleased God by the foolishness of preaching to save them that believe" (1 Corinthians 1:21, KJV) The world regards the preaching of the Bible to be foolish. The lecture method is the least efficient means of communication. Many people regard preaching as an antiquated practice that ought to be replaced with something modern like a multimedia presentation. But God uses the weak things of the world to shame the strong (1 Corinthians 1:28).

The world may regard preaching as foolish, but God uses it in a special way to convert the lost. "Everyone who calls on the name of the Lord will be saved. How, then, can they call on the one they have not believed in? And how can they believe in the one of whom they have not heard? And how can they hear without someone preaching to them?" (Romans 10:13, 14). God works in a special, mystical way through the preaching of His Word. It may seem foolish to the world, but God uses preaching to edify the Christian.

Paul wrote, "Preach the Word; be prepared in season and out of season; correct, rebuke, and encourage—with great patience and careful instruction" (2 Timothy 4:2). Something about the preaching of God's Word becomes like meat and potatoes to our souls. It may have seemed ridiculous to the people of Troas, but the Christians stayed up all night long just to hear Paul preach the Word of God. They were fed, they were edified, and they were excited about what they were receiving.

But an unusual event happened while Paul preached. Sometimes the strangest things happen in church. Paul preached on and on, and a young man named Eutychus fell asleep and fell out the window (they were on the third story). If we had seats like that in the modern church, we would probably have to open up a morgue in the basement as people went to sleep!

I feel sorry for Eutychus. He was a young man, the room was crowded, the air was stuffy, the smoke from the lamps filled the room, and he just couldn't keep his eyes open as Paul preached on and on. Have you ever been to a church and you started falling asleep, even though you didn't want to? I have. You pinch yourself and try to stay alert, but it's a terrible battle.

I don't get upset when people sleep in church. When they start to snore, that's a little much. But sleeping has been a kind of tradition in my family. My father is a great Christian man, an elder in the church. When I was young, he worked two jobs, and anytime he would sit down and be quiet, he would go to sleep. He went to sleep a lot in church. But we could never talk about it, because he thought that sleeping in church was a sign of a lack of spirituality. He was very sensitive about it.

One Sunday morning he had slept through almost the entire service. My younger brother, who didn't know this, was sitting next to him in the car as we were going home.

I whispered, "Hey, John, ask Dad how he liked the sermon."

John asked, "Dad, how did you like the sermon?"

My father is usually a gentle man, but he punched my brother's shoulder. My brother hasn't forgiven me to this day!

I have been known to sleep in church too. One Sunday afternoon I was working in the office after an exhausting weekend. At six o'clock I was so tired I didn't even know if I could preach in the evening service, which began at seven. I lay down on the floor. I realized that I was dozing off, but I thought, "That's okay. I'll hear the people coming in, or my wife or somebody who cares will come in and wake me up when it's time."

The next thing I knew, I awakened and looked at my watch and it was 7:35! I was supposed to be preaching! I went into the bathroom and washed my face and came walking into the church service like I had just been counseling somebody. The song leader had been dragging the song service out for so long that he just quit and motioned for me to come up. I didn't know whether it was announcement time or preaching time. I meant to ask, "Where are we in the service?" but what I said was, "Where am I?"

He said, "Announcements, announcements."

I could not think of a single announcement. I started rambling. Finally I said, "Folks, I've got to be honest with you. I was sleeping in the office and I just woke up."

Things were not exactly done "decently and in order" for the rest of the evening, but the next day when I came to my office there was a sign on the door that read, "Do Not Disturb." When I opened the door and went in, I discovered all the furniture was gone. It had been replaced by a cot, on which there was a little teddy bear sucking its thumb. I felt like the preacher who dreamed that he was preaching and then he woke up and he was!

Charles Swindoll tells about some funny things that happen when people go to sleep in church. People bump their heads on the pew in front of them. People drool on their Bibles. People remain seated when others stand, or drop their hymnals. I heard that once, in a country church, a wife nudged her husband to awaken him and he stood up and had the benediction right in the middle of the sermon!

When Eutychus fell out of the window, the congregation raced downstairs and picked him up, and discovered that he had died. But Paul said, "Don't be alarmed." Paul had miraculous power and he raised that young man from the dead. Then they went back upstairs and ate. After that Paul began preaching again; he preached until dawn. I imagine the most attentive listener was Eutychus!

Worship should be a time when we receive instruction, a time when we are fed from the Word of God. If you're hungry and you sit down to a meal of oyster crackers and Kool-Aid, you are going to get up frustrated, still hungry. If you come to church and we don't deal with the Bible, if all we talk about are social problems or current events, and if you're not fed, you go home hungry. Jesus said, "Man does not live on bread alone, but on every word that comes from the mouth of God" (Matthew 4:4).

If you're going to be instructed, that means you ought to *come rested*. If you stay out too late on Saturday night and you're exhausted on Sunday morning, you're not really giving God your best. I think the most important discipline is not getting up early, but getting to bed on time.

Another way to get more instruction on Sunday is to *take notes* during the sermon. That doesn't help everybody; some people are distracted by taking notes. But for many of us, jotting down an idea or two as it is spoken helps us to follow the sermon and slows down our minds so we don't go off on tangents. It's not that the sermon ought to be preserved forever, but taking notes can help us to follow the main ideas. Jotting down Scripture references helps us to look them up later.

One other thing we can do to receive better instruction in a more meaningful way is to *pray*. Before the message, pray that what is said will be of special benefit to you. It has been said that "Prayerless pews make powerless pulpits." It's a lot tougher to be critical if you're praying for the speaker. You become more sympathetic and attentive as a listener.

Two words described the manner in which Eutychus left, and the same words ought to describe how we leave a worship service. "The people took the young man home alive and were greatly comforted" (Acts 20:12). We go home alive *and comforted*. Alive because we've celebrated the resurrection of Jesus Christ from the dead. We've reverently gathered around His table to thank Him for His death, and since we're fed from His Word, we've been strengthened. *Comforted* because we've got our values in their proper order again. We've got our priorities in perspective. We know that God is still on the throne. Regardless of what problems we face today or next week, God has promised, "I will never leave you or forsake you" (Joshua 1:5).

Distinctives of Christian Love

Acts 20:17-38

ONE OF MY favorite stories is about a rigid seminary student who fell in love with a beautiful girl. He wanted desperately to kiss her, but his sensitive conscience would not permit him to succumb to his desires. Every night he would walk her to the dormitory, look at her longingly, and just shake hands.

He searched the Scriptures to try to come up with some justification for kissing her. He was delighted when he found the verse in Romans that says, "Greet one another with a holy kiss." But he didn't want to misinterpret the verse, so he took it to his hermeneutics professor who informed him that it referred to a church setting and not a dating situation at all.

Disappointed, yet true to his conscience, he walked his girl to the dormitory that night, looked at her longingly and thrust out his hand. She grabbed him by the collar and backed him against the wall and planted a kiss on him that lasted ten seconds. He came sputtering up for air, saying, "Chapter and verse, chapter and verse!" She grabbed him to kiss him again and said, "Do unto others as you would have them do unto you!"

The Bible has a great deal to say about Christian love and

its proper expression in the church. It is the single most important virtue in the fellowship of believers. But the world also has a great deal to say about love. All kinds of theories are advanced by the experts of this age. But the love offered by Jesus Christ is different from the kinds of love that are usually practiced in the world.

Acts 20 describes a brief reunion Paul had with the leaders of the Ephesian church. Paul was concluding his third missionary journey. He was going back to Jerusalem anticipating that he would be imprisoned and probably killed. On the way back he stopped at a port called Miletus, and the elders from the nearby church of Ephesus came to bid him farewell.

This is one of the most emotion-charged accounts in the book of Acts. It reveals the kind of compassion that existed between Paul and the leaders of the church at Ephesus. In our study of Paul as the champion of truth, we sometimes forget that he was also a loving man. Paul cared about the people he had won to Christ, and they cared about him. That's evident in this scene, which overflows with deep love. Jesus said, "All men will know that you are my disciples if you love one another" (John 13:35). A unique kind of compassion exists within the fellowship of believers.

It Is Rooted in God

The love the world tries to manufacture is strictly a human effort. Humanism, which is a major religion of our society, teaches that man is capable of saving himself, that man can create a loving, peaceful environment on his own. Humanism believes that if we just work hard enough, we will be able to live together in love. Think of all the songs that have promoted that idea over the last couple of decades. "What the world needs now is love, sweet love," "If I had a hammer, I'd hammer out love between my brothers and my sisters, all over this land." "We are the world, we are the children, we are the ones to make a brighter day so let's start giving." Bumper stickers urge us to hug our children and love one another. Billboards promote Brotherhood Week.

Politicians put pressure on foreign nations to honor human rights.

All of those efforts are noble and they are needed, but they are not very successful. Crime, child abuse, prejudice, divorce, terrorism, and war testify that those appeals for love on a human level are not working. The reason is that man is uprooted from the source of love, who is God. "Dear friends, let us love one another, for love comes from God. Everyone who loves has been born of God and knows God. Whoever does not love does not know God, because God is love" (1 John 4:7, 8). We're not going to have a brotherhood of man until we acknowledge the fatherhood of God. That's what Jesus was talking about when He said that the first great commandment is to love God with all your heart; the second is to love your neighbor as yourself. We're not going to get the horizontal relationship straight until we have the vertical relationship, until we are rooted in love for God.

Paul Arnold had been an all-city halfback in Louisville years ago; he's a very athletic-looking person. I'll never forget when he came forward in church and said, "I want to give my life to Jesus." Two months later he asked to see me in the office. He brought with him a beautiful woman whom he introduced as his former wife, Moira. He said, "We had a lot going for us, but our life was outside of Christ. We have a four-year-old daughter. Now Moira wants to give her life to the Lord, too. We would like to be remarried."

"That's right," Moira said, "and I want to be baptized at our wedding ceremony, because I know my family is going to be there. I want that to be a testimony to them that our faith has brought us together."

A few days later I performed their remarriage with their four-year-old daughter standing between them. At the end of the marriage ceremony Moira was baptized. (I decided to do it that way so we wouldn't have a wet-haired bride!) Later when they came forward in church they said, "We wouldn't be together if it were not for Jesus Christ."

The Lord gives us a new capacity to love. It is not easy, but the potential is there. That's true of every level of relationship, not just marital love. The love that existed between Paul and the leaders of this Ephesian church was rooted in Christ. The reasons for this love can be found in Acts 20:18-24.

Paul *lived a consistent life* among them. "You know how I lived the whole time I was with you.... I served the Lord with great humility and with tears, although I was severely tested by the plots of the Jews" (vv. 18, 19). Love is based on respect; nothing will undermine love like the discovery of hypocrisy. Paul was authentic to the core. He said, "My life has been consistent."

He *proclaimed a faithful message.* "You know that I have not hesitated to preach anything that would be helpful to you but have taught you publicly and from house to house. I have declared to both Jews and Greeks that they must turn to God in repentance and have faith in our Lord Jesus" (vv. 20, 21). Paul had made a commitment that he was going to say whatever God wanted him to say without fear—even if it was not popular. People don't like to be told that they need to repent, but Paul was faithful to his message and they respected and loved him for that.

Paul also *had the courage to obey.* "Now, compelled by the Spirit, I am going to Jerusalem, not knowing what will happen to me there.... The Holy Spirit warns me that prison and hardships are facing me. However, I consider my life worth nothing to me, if only I may finish the race and complete the task the Lord Jesus has given me" (vv. 22-24). Here's a man who loves the Lord with all his heart. He's going to obey God even if it means death. His love for God was greater than his instinct for self-preservation. Since he was committed to the Lord, and the Ephesian leaders were also committed to the Lord, the love that bound them together was rooted in God. We sing,

> Blest be the tie that binds
>   our hearts in *Christian* love.
> The fellowship of kindred minds
>   is like to that above.

It Develops With Time

So often the love of the world diminishes with time, but Christian love intensifies with time.

The world considers love to be an instantaneous emotion. To the world, love is a feeling created by the right chemistry or physical attraction. To the world, you instantly fall in love or you helplessly fall out of love. Like falling off a bicycle, it's involuntary. For years the popular songs have suggested that. "Some enchanted evening, across the crowded room, you will meet a stranger" (and oh boy, the electricity flows). Elvis Presley sang, "I Can't Help Falling in Love With You." The Righteous Brothers sang, "You've Lost That Lovin Feeling." The worst was a song the rock group The Doors sang awhile back, "Hello, I Love You, Won't You Tell Me Your Name?" Somebody told me that on "Hill Street Blues," one of the policeman met a woman, and after they were together for a little over an hour, they left by saying, "I love you."

There is such a thing as instant infatuation. If The chemistry is right or there's physical attractiveness, the electricity flows. But infatuation does not last. It is always temporary. In fact, studies show that marriages that begin with intensive infatuation usually have a harder struggle when reality sets in.

I read an article a while back called *The Seven Stages of a Married Cold*. It showed a husband's reaction each of the first seven years of marriage when his wife gets sick.

The first year he says: "Sugar Dumplin', I'm worried about my baby girl. You've got a bad sniffle. There's no telling about these things with all the strep going around, so I'm putting you in the hospital this afternoon for a general check-up and a good rest. I know the food is lousy there so I'm bringing in food from a caterer. I've got it all arranged with the floor superintendent."

The second year: "Listen, Darling, I don't like the sound of that cough. I've called the doctor and he's coming right over. Go to bed like a good girl and rest."

The third year: "Maybe you better lie down, Honey. Nothing like a little rest when you feel lousy. You got any canned soup?"

The fourth year: "Now look, Dear, be sensible. After you feed the kids and get the dishes done and the floor finished, you'd better lie down."

The fifth year: "Why don't you take a couple of aspirin?"

The sixth year: "Well, if you'd just gargle or something instead of just sitting around barking like a seal all evening . . ."

The seventh year: "For Pete's sake, stop sneezing. You trying to give me pneumonia or something?"

Genuine love in Christ should deepen with the passing of time. It's not just a feeling. It is a commitment of the will; it is a deliberate giving of myself to the other person. It is a growth process. It withstands pressures like the flu and financial stress and wrinkles and disagreements.

Ray and Dottie Barnett had been married for over 43 years. They had an ideal marriage. They both insisted they had never exchanged a harsh word. Their love deepened with time. Several months ago, Ray died at about two o'clock in the morning at a local hospital. After he died, Dottie sat in the room with him and I heard her say, "You know, tonight will be the first time in 43 years and 7 months that I haven't heard him say, 'Goodnight, Darling. I love you.' We always said that before we went to sleep. In fact, when he was overseas in the service, we had a pact with each other that we would say that out loud before we went to bed at night."

That got to me! I went home at three o'clock in the morning and woke up my wife, and said, "Good night, Judy. I love you."

She said, "What's the matter with you?"

Love ought to deepen with the passing of time. That is true of every kind of loving relationship, not just married love. Paul loved these people of Ephesus because they had spent time together. He spent three years in Ephesus. He began by teaching these people in the synagogue. When they got kicked out of the synagogue, the Christians went to a lecture hall and there Paul taught them about God's love every day. Then there was a riot in the city against the Christians. The local citizens felt threatened by them. Paul wanted to preach to them, but his friends said, "No, don't preach." No wonder they loved each other—they had spent time together; they had gone through hardships; they had shared in the teaching of God's Word. Their love had deepened with the passing of time.

Tony Campolo said, "As you grow older as a Christian, the traits you find attractive in other Christians ought to mature, too. For example, I knew I was getting older when I went to a wedding ceremony and the mother of the bride was more attractive to me than the bride!" I know what he's talking about. I watched a rerun the other day of "Leave It To Beaver" and I thought Mrs. Cleaver was attractive! I had never noticed that before. Someone suggested that if I watch "The Beverly Hillbillies." and Granny starts looking good to me, it's time to quit preaching! Campolo said if you're 40 years of age and you're still attracted to an 18-year-old girl, that's immature, that's shallow. As time passes, our appreciation of people and our love ought to mature and deepen.

It Has Character

The world's concept of love is kind of syrupy. It's a nondiscerning emotion; it's nondiscriminatory. The world has a naive concept that love never confronts evil. It just tolerates everybody and everything that goes on. For example, loving parents would never spank a child; the loving parent just loves the child and hopes the child will respond properly. The liberal politician continues to yield; it's the loving thing to do, he says, to be kind to Qadaffi and Castro and the Communists and lay down our arms and assume they will respond in love. The naive Christian is disturbed if there is ever a confrontation against evil. Somehow it doesn't seem loving to confront.

But Christian love has character. It has the courage to stand up for that which is right and oppose that which is wrong. "Love must be sincere. Hate what is evil; cling to what is good" (Romans 12:9). You cannot love your child without hating leukemia. You cannot love God without hating the things that threaten the children of God.

Nobody was more loving than Jesus. He had gentleness and compassion and yet He confronted the Pharisees, calling them "blind guides" to their faces, calling them "hypocrites" and "whitewashed tombs." He went into the temple and cleansed the temple of the moneychangers. To somebody who has a shallow concept of love, that seems unloving, but love practices discernment. Discernment is the ability to detect and identify truth. Discernment is skill in separating good from evil. Love hates evil and clings to that which is good.

That's what Paul is saying to these Ephesian leaders. He says, "Keep watch over yourselves and all the flock of which the Holy Spirit has made you overseers. Be shepherds of the church of God" (Acts 20:28).

A shepherd loves his sheep. The shepherd guides the sheep and knows them by name. He feeds and he waters, but the shepherd also protects the sheep. He doesn't just let them wander wherever they want to go; he takes the crooked end of his staff and he draws them back into the fold because there's danger in the wilderness alone. The shepherd knows there are predators. He takes the blunt end of his staff and he knocks the wolves away. Paul told the Ephesian elders, "After I leave, savage wolves will come in among you and will not spare the flock. Even from your own number men will arise and distort the truth in order to draw away disciples after them" (vv. 29, 30).

So, if you love the flock like a shepherd loves the sheep, don't be gullible. There are power-hungry, popularity-starved, insecure people who will do anything to get a following, and they'll come right from your own church. They'll come right from your own Christian schools. They'll come right from your own seminaries. Be on your guard against them. In an effort to try to impress people with their intelligence, they'll distort the truth. False teachers don't identify themselves. A false teacher doesn't come up to you and say, "Hi, I'm a heretic, can I lead you astray?" The wolf comes in sheep's clothing. The Bible says that Satan can masquerade as an angel of light. False teachers will call themselves Christians. They will appear to be good people. they will quote the Bible. Therefore, love has to be discerning. Love has to have character. Love has to be able to separate good from evil.

A couple of decades ago, two professors of a Christian seminary began to distort the truth and deviate from basic Bible teaching. The administration and the trustees were hesitant to confront that. Confrontation didn't seem very loving, so they waited, hoping the situation would correct itself. They tolerated it so long those two professors had led a number of young men astray. Paul told Timothy that false teaching is like gangrene; it doesn't get better. Finally, when there had to be surgery, it created real havoc. Several young men with tremendous potential to preach are not preaching today—are not even in the church today—because love lacked the character to confront, and it resulted in ruined lives. Cling to that which is good and hate that which is evil; that's Christian love.

It Is Self-Effacing

The world's concept of love is self-centered. "I love you because you turn me on. I love you for what you do for me. You make me feel good. But when you no longer do those things for me, then I'll no longer love you, and I'm sorry; it's over."

I can remember in high school watching some linemen at halftime of a football game. Those big macho guys would take an orange and just suck it until the pulp was dry, then discard the rind in the garbage pail and lick their lips and say, "Man, I love oranges." I saw those same guys whisper the magic words, "I love you," to some girls in our high school and manipulate them in the same way. When the feeling was no longer there, the girls were discarded too. It was really themselves that those boys loved the most.

But Christian love should be different. It is self-sacrificing. Paul said, "I have not coveted anyone's silver or gold or clothing. You yourselves know that these hands of mine have supplied my own needs and the needs of my companions. In everything I did, I showed you that by this kind of hard work we must help the weak, remembering the words the Lord Jesus himself said: 'It is more blessed to give than to receive'" (Acts 20:33-35). Paul was important. He could have thrown his weight around. He could have demanded that people give a bigger offering to support him. That wasn't Paul. He worked with his own hands so that he wouldn't be a burden to them.

If you are in a position of authority, whether it's big or little, you will always be tempted to manipulate people. You can use your influence for your own personal advantage. But Christian love *sacrifices* self for the other. It doesn't have to be in big dramatic ways. Love is often tested in quiet, behind-the-scenes ways in which you just give of yourself.

When I get up in the morning and go down to shower, there might be only two towels in the closet. One is a thin, frayed towel and the other is a big, fluffy towel, and I know that my son is going to shower right after me. Which towel do I use? Nobody will know, and I'm the dad!

I noticed my wife the other day pouring the drinks when we were going to have pizza. She had one liter of coke that was full and one with about a glassful in the bottom that had been standing for days. I knew it was flat. I hoped it wouldn't be my glass. I watched her out of the corner of my eye as she poured it. She quietly sat it by her own plate. That's love. It is self-effacing. First Corinthians 13:5 says simply, "Love . . . is not self-seeking."

It Is Demonstrative

Three times this Scripture passage speaks of Paul's tears. "I served the Lord with great humility and with tears" (Acts 20:19); "I never stopped warning each of you day and night with tears" (v. 31); "They all wept" (v. 37). Tears are an open expression of a compassionate heart. Some by nature weep easily, others not so often.

> Record my lament;
>> list my tears on your scroll—
>> are they not in your record?
>>> (Psalm 56:8)

God takes note of unselfconscious, passionate tears.

One of the great drawbacks of our sophisticated society is a reluctance to show tears. We're too removed to care that deeply. Men feel that's a sign of weakness. Women who wish to show strength don't want to weep in public, either. We honor those who practice restraint. Dirty Harry, James Bond, and Rambo don't cry a whole lot. When Senator Ed Muskie was running for President, he wept in public one day when his wife was criticized. I don't think it was coincidental that his popularity began to decline after that.

The Christian is different. We're not afraid to show compassion; we're willing to weep. Nobody was stronger than Jesus Christ, yet He wept. Jeremiah was used by God greatly in the Old Testament, yet he was called "the weeping prophet." Sometimes he was so broken over people's sins that he couldn't speak; he just wept. It seems strange that God would use a man like that in Israel's most critical hour unless you value tears the way God does. Paul wept, and then he embraced the Ephesian elders and they kissed. This would be the last time they were going to see Paul. They embraced.

Our society is becoming more and more expressive in a physical sense. Thirty years ago you would seldom see people in public embracing or weeping, but now we're rediscovering the value of physical touch. The church ought to be a place where, in an appropriate way, we can touch—a warm handshake, an arm about the shoulder, an embrace, or the words, "I love you. I care about you."

The Ephesians not only expressed their love for each other, they expressed their love for God. They wept, they kissed, and they knelt and prayed together. It's one thing to demonstrate your love for people, but a little tougher to demonstrate your love for God. That gets into the innermost part of your heart. It calls for an absence of pride. That's hard on your ego. To sing enthusiastically or to kneel to show your love for God is not easy. But we are constantly reminded that without God, we are nothing.

Everybody was crushed when the space shuttle *Challenger*, carrying seven astronauts, exploded one minute off the launch pad. We all felt that grief in the pit in our stomach. Yet thousands died in Mexico City in an earthquake; hundreds die in plane crashes, and yet these deaths do not produce that kind of national grief. Maybe it's because it was so public. We witnessed it live, dramatically, on television. Or maybe it's because we identified with those people. We saw them interviewed and we saw pictures of their families. The schoolteacher on board was, in a way, representing the rest of us going into space. We hurt when she died.

But I wonder if part of the reason we mourned is because that tragedy reminded us of our own fallibility. We admire the whole space program because it shows our greatest technology and our greatest expertise. We can send an unmanned satellite to take pictures of a faraway planet and send them back to earth. Yet with all our computer science and all of our technology, we still fail. We're still mortal. We're still insignificant compared with the God who hung the stars in space.

How desperately we need Him. How much we need to be rooted deep in His love. How much we really need to have a love that deepens with the passing of time, that can discern between right and wrong and stand for that which is right, that sacrifices and gives of itself. Only He can give us that kind of love.

When God's Will Is Perplexing

Acts 21:1-23:11

BOB BENSON HAD been scheduled to be the speaker for a women's retreat at the church I serve, but he was not able to come. We were disappointed because Bob is a skilled author and a humorous, heartwarming speaker. Those who had heard Bob speak were anxious for him to come and share with us. Thirteen years before, Bob Benson developed throat cancer. He was told then that he didn't have long to live, but God gave him some additional years. Over the next 13 years he had written books and touched thousands of lives. But the cancer had resurfaced. A few months later, he died.

Bob Benson was in his mid-50's; he had much more to contribute. That's another reminder that God's will is hard to understand at times. We are told repeatedly in the Bible that if we surrender to Jesus Christ, God directs our lives. "In all your ways acknowledge him, and he will make your paths straight" (Proverbs 3:6). Yet many times events occur for which there is no logical or human explanation.

If I were in charge of the universe, I would have good people like Bob Benson live to be 100 and bad people die at 50. If I were in charge of the universe, every Sunday would be perfect weather, every Christian would be healthy, and every passage of Scripture would be easy to understand and complete with a three-point outline in the margin. But God's ways are not our ways. His thoughts are not our thoughts. "Our God is in heaven; he does whatever pleases him" (Psalm 115:3). God is in charge of the universe and we're not, and that is a good thing because we would certainly mess it up.

God's heavenly plan at times makes no earthly sense. It is important that we understand that, because if we don't, we will be confused, bitter, angry, and defiant at times in our Christian life. The Bible says we have to walk by faith and not by sight, because there are times that God's plan makes no earthly sense.

That's certainly true when we come to Paul's last missionary journey. If we were writing the Scripture for the apostle Paul, we would have his third journey end with a ticker-tape parade in Jerusalem. Christians would line the streets and applaud his efforts. There would be a big article about Paul in the Jerusalem Journal and the mayor would dedicate a plaque in his honor. A street would be named for him. He would live happily ever after—a "missionary emeritus" or something. But that's not what happened at all. At the end of his missionary journey, his life seems to fall apart.

Paul's Difficult Experiences

As Paul made his way back toward Jerusalem, he was repeatedly warned that danger lurked there. When his ship landed at Tyre, the Christians there warned Paul not to go on to Jerusalem. When his ship docked at Caesarea, and Paul was ready to go inland to Jerusalem, a prophet named Agabus came from Jerusalem to meet him. Agabus performed an object lesson, tying his own hands and feet with Paul's belt. He said, "The Holy Spirit says, 'In this way the Jews of Jerusalem will bind the owner of this belt and will hand him over to the Gentiles" (Acts 21:11). The people pleaded with Paul not to go.

The Holy Spirit warned Paul repeatedly that danger awaited him in Jerusalem. Why did he go? Some people suggest that Paul was stubborn and went against the will of the Spirit, and he had to pay for it with four years in prison. But I don't think the Holy Spirit was trying to dissuade Paul from going. He was just trying to prepare Paul for the danger that awaited him there.

Somebody might say to you, "I'm so excited. I have fallen in love and I'm going to get married. I can't wait—it's going to be so great!" And you say, "May I talk with you a minute? Let me tell you there are going to be problems." You are not trying to dissuade him from getting married. You just want him to go into it realistically.

The Holy Spirit was preparing Paul and his followers for what was going to happen in Jerusalem. He wasn't saying, "Don't go." But Paul's friends heard the message and misinterpreted the conclusion. They loved Paul and wanted to protect him from any harm. At times we have to ignore the counsel of well-meaning Christian friends and do what we know the Lord wants us to do. Paul asked them, "Why are you weeping and breaking my heart? I am ready not only to be bound, but also to die in Jerusalem for the name of the Lord Jesus" (v. 13). "When he would not be dissuaded," Luke wrote, "we gave up and said, 'The Lord's will be done'" (v. 14).

Martin Luther had a close associate who tried to warn him not to go to the Diet of Worms and debate the authorities there because his life would be in danger. Luther responded by saying, "Though devils be as many as tiles on the roof, yet thither will I go." In spite of danger and resistance, he said, "Here I stand. I can do no other." There comes a time in life when you have to stand for your convictions regardless of the consequences.

The first thing Paul had to do when he arrived in Jerusalem was to arrange a compromise with the Jewish Christians in order to avoid controversy. He reported on his missionary journey in detail and they rejoiced, but then they told Paul he was presenting a problem for them. They said, "You see, brother, how many thousands of Jews have believed, and all of them are zealous for the law" (v. 20). These people became Christians, but they were still practicing circumcision, and abstaining from certain meats. They didn't fully understand grace and freedom. The Jewish Christians were uncertain about Paul. "They have been informed that you teach all the Jews who live among the Gentiles to turn away from Moses, telling them not to circumcise their children or live according to our customs" (v. 21).

That rumor was not entirely true. Paul did tell the Gentile Christians they didn't have to become Jewish, but he never told the Jewish Christians to abandon their customs altogether. In fact, Paul had had Timothy circumcised just to appease the Jewish Christians. But some rumors have just enough truth in them to be believable, and some emotional, impulsive people are ready to believe anything they hear.

I heard of a woman who spread the rumor throughout her church that the preacher had a drinking problem. The preacher traced the rumor to its source and asked the woman how in the world she had come to that conclusion. She said, "Well, I saw your car parked in front of the saloon one day." He explained to her that it was the only parking place on the street when he was going to the drug store three blocks down. But just to teach her a lesson, that night he parked his car in front of her house and left it there all night long!

The Bible makes it clear what we are supposed to do with a rumor when it surfaces. "If your brother sins against you, go and show him his fault, just between the two of you" (Matthew 18:15). Don't get on the telephone and tell someone else about the problem. You go to that person and say, "Let's talk this over." Until you can do that, just keep quiet.

This false rumor about Paul, that he was teaching against the law of Moses, posed a potential divisive problem in the church. The leaders proposed a compromise to appease the legalistic brothers. They told Paul, "Do what we tell you. There are four men with us who have made a vow. Take these men, join in their purification rites and pay their expenses, so that they can have their heads shaved. Then everybody will know there is no truth in these reports about you, but that you yourself are living in obedience to the law" (Acts 21:23, 24).

To make a vow in that day was like a New Year's resolution, only it was more binding. The person who made the vow promised he would not eat meat, drink wine, or cut his hair until the vow was fulfilled. The last week of the vow would be spent entirely in the temple, offering animal sacrifices to God. At the end of the vow he would cut his hair off and burn it on the altar as a sign that the vow was complete. It could become expensive to buy all those animal sacrifices and to be off work for a week, so it was considered a pious deed for a wealthy person to finance somebody else's vow. The Christians in Jerusalem said, "Paul, if you would finance the vows of these four men and spend time with them in the temple, then the people will know that there is no truth to this rumor that you completely disregard Jewish customs."

That probably went against Paul's grain, but he did it to keep the peace. He once wrote, "I have become all things to all men so that by all possible means I might save some" (1 Corinthians 9:22). A mature Christian has to learn to compromise in matters of opinion. If you are rigid, if you demand that you get your way all the time, you can create havoc. We are all called upon to do some things and to say some things (in matters of opinion) that we would prefer not to do or say. At a Sunday-school class party, a Hawaiian luau, I had to don a grass skirt and do the hula. I didn't especially like having to do that. I don't have a great deal of rhythm. I don't remember reading about that in my ordination papers, either, but I did it to keep peace in the class and in my family.

Paul was flexible. He wasn't rigid. He agreed to participate in these vows to appease the legalistic brethren. Barclay wrote, "There can be no doubt that the matter was distasteful to Paul. For him the relevancy of things like that was gone, but it was a sign of a truly great man that he can subordinate all wishes and views for the sake of the church." Sometimes compromise is not a sign of weakness, but of strength.

But as often happens, the attempted compromise backfired. While Paul was in the temple, he was attacked by the hostile Jewish people. "Some Jews from the province of Asia saw Paul at the temple. They stirred up the whole crowd and seized him, shouting, 'Men of Israel, help us! [You want to get attention in a crowd? Just yell, "Help!"] This is the man who teaches all men everywhere against our people and our law and this place. And besides, he has brought Greeks into the temple area and defiled this holy place!" (Acts 21:27, 28). Nobody was allowed to bring Gentiles into the court of the Jews. To do that was punishable by death. The Jews had seen Paul circulating in the city with Gentiles and they just assumed he had brought the Gentiles into the court of the Jews. That was not true, but a servant is no greater than his master, and Jesus had been falsely accused, too. "The whole city was aroused, and the people came running from all directions" (v. 30).

Mob violence is a terrible thing. A mob usually sinks to the level of its lowest participant. People at a close basketball game will do things they would never do anywhere else. They will stand and shout obscenities. I have heard preachers yell, "Kill the ref!" I think I've yelled that myself! A man in the stands at a televised game threw a cigarette lighter down onto the floor. If that person were in the stands by himself, he would never do that. People will do things in a mob they would not do otherwise.

This mob seized Paul and dragged him from the temple. They were too pious to kill him in the temple, so they dragged him outside. "While they were trying to kill him, news reached the commander of the Roman troops that the whole city of Jerusalem was in an uproar" (v. 31). Rome would not tolerate a riot—not by the person who instigated it, not by the commander who permitted it. So at once he took some of his soldiers and they ran down into the crowd flashing their swords, and there at the core was the apostle Paul nearly beaten to death. They arrested him and chained him, just as Agabus the prophet had predicted.

The officer asked the crowd, "What has this man done?" Some shouted one thing, some shouted another. Since he could not get an intelligent, coherent statement from the crowd, he dragged Paul off. "The violence of the mob was so great he had to be carried by the soldiers" (v. 35). Can you imagine that? They couldn't even escort him out. They had to put him on their shoulders and carry him out. "The crowd that followed kept shouting, 'Away with him!'" (v. 36) They came to the stairway that led up to the barracks, where Paul made an incredible request. He said, "Please let me speak to the people." (v. 39).

Can you believe that? Here's an angry crowd crying for his blood. He's been beaten within an inch of his life, spared by Roman soldiers who are carrying him up the steps. He looks down and sees this big crowd and he thinks, "Boy, what a chance to preach! Can I speak to these people?" The Roman officer was so astonished that he gave his permission.

Paul had confidence in the logic of the gospel. He had love for the Jewish people. He believed if he could just get them to listen, he could persuade them because he understood them. He motioned for the crowd to be quiet. Someone said you should always look a mob right in the eye. Paul did. He had that kind of courage. William Barclay said, "Nothing in all the New Testament shows the force of Paul's personality as the silence he commanded with a gesture to the mob who wanted to lynch him."

At that moment the power of God flowed through Paul as he spoke to these people, who were anxious for his blood. He gave them his testimony. If you are ever called upon to talk to someone who is hostile toward the gospel, just tell them the difference that Christ has made in your life. That's an irrevocable argument. He forgives your sins, gives you hope, gives you fellowship in the church.

The man born blind, whom Jesus healed, didn't know if Jesus was a prophet, but he said, "One thing I do know I was blind but now I see!" (John 9:25) You can't argue with that!

Paul said, "Brothers and fathers, listen now to my defense." He told them how he was once zealous for the law just like they were. But then when he was on his way to Damascus to persecute the Christians there, Jesus Christ of

Nazareth appeared to him. He had to admit that he had been wrong, and he yielded his life to Christ. But then the Lord told him not to stay in Jerusalem, because his message would not be accepted there. The Lord told him, "Go; I will send you far away to the Gentiles." The Bible says, "The crowd listened to Paul until he said this. Then they raised their voices and shouted, 'Rid the earth of him! He's not fit to live!'" (Acts 22:21, 22).

Emotion often takes precedence over reason. When people are stirred up they hardly ever want to listen to logic, no matter how well it's presented. When they shouted for the blood of Paul, he must have been perplexed. He must have wondered, "Why don't they listen to reason?" The commander ordered that Paul be taken into the barracks. He directed that Paul be flogged and questioned in order to find out why the people were so hostile.

To be scourged was not a pleasant experience. That had already happened to Paul. They used a leather whip studded with bits of stone and metal, which would slice open a man's exposed back. The scourging was not to punish Paul, but to extract a confession. Just when Paul was about to be beaten, however, he interrupted the soldier and stood up for his rights. "As they stretched him out to flog him, Paul said to the centurion standing there, 'Is it legal for you to flog a Roman citizen who hasn't even been found guilty?'" (v. 25). Roman law said a Roman citizen was never to be scourged; that was inhumane punishment. That mistake was punishable by death. When the soldier learned that Paul was a Roman citizen, he dropped the whip and went to the commander, who verified that Paul was a Roman citizen. They removed his chains, though Paul remained in prison.

Paul was not a wimp. He didn't let people just run over him. Henry Jacobson wrote, "Martyrdom is of value only when it can't be avoided with integrity." Paul was not ready to throw his life away meaninglessly. He stood his ground and avoided a scourging, though he remained in prison.

"The following night the Lord stood near Paul and said, 'Take courage! As you have testified about me in Jerusalem, so you must also testify in Rome'" (Acts 23:11). All of these circumstances made no common sense. It seemed his life was falling apart, but the Lord said "Paul, I have you right where I want you. You always wanted to go to Rome—I am going to see that you go to Rome. You're going at government expense, as a prisoner." As a result, Paul went right into the homes of governors and into the courtrooms. His message went right into Caesar's household itself. But God's heavenly plan, on the surface, made no earthly sense.

Three Lessons

God's will is often difficult to understand, so be obedient. There was no way Paul could understand what was happening to him. He just had to be faithful. There will be times in your life when God's will is not explainable and you've just got to hang on and be obedient.

A little boy had an uncle who was an agnostic. One day on the farm the uncle was trying to undermine the boy's faith. He said, "Look here in the garden at those pumpkins, those big old pumpkins on tiny little vines. Now look at this big old oak tree with such little acorns. It seems to me if God knew what He was doing when He was creating the world, He would have put the pumpkins on the oak tree and the little acorns on a little vine."

Just then an acorn fell out of the tree and hit the uncle on the head. The little boy said, "I'm sure glad that wasn't a pumpkin, aren't you?"

God knew what He was doing when He created the world. God knows what He is doing when He fashions your life, too. Some circumstances in your life may not be what you want. Maybe you are single and you wish you were married. Maybe you are trying desperately to keep your marriage together, but your mate is drifting away. Maybe you've had a mate who has died. Maybe you have financial pressures. You've tried to obey God's will but you are frustrated. It is important that you keep on obeying. Don't quit going to church; don't become bitter in spirit; don't become sour and negative in attitude. Don't lose your moral values. Just obey, because God's will is, at times, difficult to understand.

God's will might involve controversy—be courageous. Paul found himself at the center of conflict, even though he was doing exactly what God wanted him to do. He couldn't avoid it. There might be times, because of your faith, that you create controversy. Some of you go to church every Sunday without your mate. That creates problems in your homes about how often you come, how much you are involved, how much you talk about it, how much money you give, and whom you want to socialize with. You try to compromise with your mate, but you still have controversy. Jesus said He didn't always bring peace; sometimes He brings a sword. Even households will be divided because of Him.

Sometimes it's difficult for you to know when to take a stand and when not to. Maybe a member of your family has drifted away from his marriage. He moves in with somebody with whom he is not married, and then he invites the whole family to come over for the holidays. If you don't go the family is going to be angry at you, and if you do go it looks to your children as if you endorse that relationship. No matter what you do, you feel like you are wrong.

We need to remember the words of the psalmist: "The Lord is my light and my salvation—whom shall I fear?" (Psalm 27:1). You can be doing the will of God and still be right in the center of controversy. You can't avoid it.

God's will always ends in blessings—be confident. Paul did go to prison, but in prison he wrote the letters that became a part of the Bible. He made contacts that he would have never made otherwise. Romans 8:28 promises, "In all things God works for the good of those who love him, who have been called according to his purpose." If you just hold on, in the end God blesses.

Cleve and Jan Stone prayed that God would bless their marriage with a child. They prayed and prayed, but no child came, and that was perplexing. Finally they prayed that God would enable them to adopt a child. That kept being delayed and delayed, and that was perplexing. Then they were notified that a child was going to be born in three weeks and that child would be theirs, but one week before that child was to be born—even though they had been thanking God for His answered prayer—the parents reversed their decision and decided to keep the baby.

Then a 3-year-old boy became available. Not everyone wants a 3-year-old boy; almost everybody wants a little baby. But Cleve and Jan Stone adopted that 3-year-old boy. One week after the adoption procedures were complete, Jan learned that she was expecting a baby. Somebody said, "Are you going to give the other child back?" They said, "Oh no! We're thankful for God's timing, because He wants us to have this 3-year-old boy, too. We think that's why He delayed so long."

Maybe it doesn't happen that dramatically, but if we hang on and courageously stand for what we believe to be right, in the end God blesses—though not always in this world. I have talked to people who have prayed for God's blessings and they have been barren their entire life. It may be in eternity, but in the end God works through those things for His glory and for our good.

William Cowper was filled with despair. One bleak morning he decided to end it all by drinking poison, but he didn't drink enough and he survived. A few days later he hired a coach to take him to the Thames River where he was going to jump off a bridge and end it all, but something restrained him. A few days later he took a knife and fell on it, but the blade broke and he survived. A few days after that he tried to hang himself. He was found unconscious and he again survived.

He finally decided that he wasn't supposed to commit suicide. In his despair, William Cowper picked up a Bible. He read through the book of Romans and there he discovered grace and the forgiveness of God. He discovered Romans 8:28, "In all things God works for the good of those who love him," and he submitted his life to the Sovereign of the universe. He became a Christian. Though his life after that was rewarding, it was filled with storms.

Toward the end of his life he summarized his experience with God by writing these words:

> God moves in a mysterious way,
>   His wonders to perform.
> He plants his footprints in the sea
>   and rides upon the storm.
> Deep in unfathomable minds
>   of never failing skill,
> He treasures up his bright designs
>   and works his sovereign will.

"Our God is in heaven; he does whatever pleases him" (Psalm 115:3). It is important that we be submissive in attitude and spirit, knowing that He works for the good of those who love Him.

Responding to Anger

Acts 22:30–23:35

IN HIGH SCHOOL I was involved in an unusual football game. Some of the opposing players were biting our ball carriers! Whenever there was a gang tackle, someone on the bottom of the pile would just "chomp down" on the arm of one of our players. When you get bit on the arm, your natural reaction is to withdraw your arm for protection. But when that happened the referee saw the jerking of the arms of our players and assessed our team a 15-yard penalty for unsportsmanlike conduct. At halftime our coach marched a couple of players to the referee to show him the teeth marks on their arms. After the game, some of our guys wanted to go to the doctor for a tetanus shot!

How do you react when other people "bite" you? An adage in sports says that it's the second man who gets caught. Often in a basketball game if someone is deliberately shoved, he will shove back, but he's the one who is seen and assessed the foul. Coaches attempt to train their players not to retaliate, in hopes that the real culprit will be spotted and penalized.

That same principle holds true in everyday life. We are all going to be the victims of anger on occasion. In some arena of life it is inevitable that you will be treated unfairly. If you are a leader, whether it's in the home, school, church, or business, your reaction is going to be much more noticeable than the offense against you. How you respond will reveal a great deal about your character and your qualifications for leading.

Dr. James Dobson wrote, "Having been in the church all my life, I've observed that Christians are often in more danger when they are right in a conflict than when they are clearly wrong. In other words, a person is more likely to become bitter and deeply hostile when someone has cheated him or taken advantage of him than the offender himself." E. Stanley Jones agreed, stating that "A Christian is more likely to sin by his reactions than his actions." Maybe that's one of the reasons that Jesus told us to turn the other cheek and walk the second mile. He knew the devastation anger can cause in an innocent victim.

In Acts 23, Paul stands before the Jewish Sanhedrin. He is a victim of vicious hostility. The Sanhedrin was supposed to be the spiritual governing body of the Jewish nation. Paul was brought before this group because he was accused of desecrating the Jewish temple. The air was tense. Nerves were raw. A life-and-death matter would be decided here.

Paul began by stating his innocence. He said, "I have fulfilled my duty to God in all good conscience to this day" (v. 1). At that Ananias, the high priest, the head of the Sanhedrin, ordered that Paul be slapped in the face. At this point it doesn't take a mental giant to realize it's going to be tough to get a fair trial.

Paul's reactions throughout this event teach us some lessons about our proper response to anger.

Hostility

Paul's initial reaction was one of hostility. "Then Paul said to him, 'God will strike you, you whitewashed wall!'" (v. 3) That's a pretty strong statement. To call a man a whitewashed wall was a cutting insult in that day. One of the worst things a Jew could do was to touch a dead body. That rendered him unclean for religious ceremony. When a person was buried in a cave or a tomb, people would whitewash the outside of the grave as a warning to passersby that there was death inside—stay away.

Jesus called the Pharisees "whitewashed tombs, which look beautiful on the outside but on the inside are full of dead men's bones and everything unclean" (Matthew 23:27). When Paul called the priest a whitewashed wall, he was saying, "You look good on the outside, but you're a phony inside. You're spiritually dead. You're a disgrace to your office."

Josephus, a first-century historian, indicates that probably Paul was right. Ananias had a terrible reputation. He was a greedy man who used violence to get his own way. He was eventually charged with complicity by Rome. He was supposed to be a spiritual leader, but he was a disgrace to his office.

Paul's response, though it was hostile, was understandable. He was under a lot of pressure. Many Jewish Christians had deserted him, thinking he was too tolerant of the Gentiles. In the temple he had been attacked by the Jews and nearly beaten to death. Now he stood on trial for his life, and the judge ordered him struck. No wonder he lashed out in hostility. Who wouldn't?

But another man under similar circumstances responded with much less hostility. Jesus also once stood trial before the Sanhedrin. He had been deserted by His friends. He had been scourged and abused by His enemies. The high priest questioned Jesus about His disciples and His teaching.

"I have spoken openly to the world," Jesus replied. "I always taught in synagogues or at the temple, where all the Jews come together. I said nothing in secret. Why question me? Ask those who heard me. Surely they know what I said."

When Jesus said this, one of the officials nearby struck him in the face. "Is that any way to answer the high priest?" he demanded.

Jesus' response to this treatment is more compassionate than Paul's. "If I said something wrong," Jesus replied, "testify as to what is wrong. But if I spoke the truth, why did you strike me?" (John 18:20-23)

Paul was a great man, but he wasn't Jesus. Under similar circumstances, the Lord Jesus spoke less harshly. But Paul was angry, and initially he responded with hostility.

There are several ways we can retaliate when somebody is angry with us. One is *physical attack*. Hit me in the face, and I'm going to smack you back. Stick your finger in my chest, I'll stick my finger in your chest. Many husbands who abuse their wives justify themselves by saying, "Well, she just kept hitting me. Who wouldn't respond?"

More frequently, though, we respond with *verbal abuse*. Paul didn't hit the high priest; he just sliced him up with his tongue. Some people have a special gift for sarcasm. They hold in reserve all kinds of poison darts and it's hard to restrain themselves because they're so good at it.

George Bernard Shaw once sent a sarcastic note to Winston Churchill, inviting him to the opening of one of his plays. At the end of the note he added, "Bring a friend if you've got one."

Churchill responded, "I'm sorry, but I can't come to the opening night of your play. I'll come to the second show if there is one."

"A gentle answer turns away wrath, but a harsh word stirs up anger" (Proverbs 15:1). We know how to cut people down with sarcasm. But you can stir up anger with harsh, biting, sarcastic words.

Another popular reaction today is *emotional withdrawal*. This is a potent weapon for people who have little confidence in their verbal skills or who hate confrontation. They'll punish you by withdrawing their friendship; they'll make you pay by not speaking to you. This is a favorite ploy of husbands and wives.

"What's wrong with you?"
"Nothing."
"You're awfully quiet."
"I've got nothing to say."
"Are you sure there's nothing wrong?"

"If there's something wrong, I'll tell you."

That doesn't accomplish anything positive! We're really not sure how much damage we inflict by that approach; it has to continue on for a long time before we're sure that justice has been served. But it seems so much more pious just to be quiet than to physically or verbally abuse someone. It's like the woman who shot and killed her husband with a bow and arrow so she wouldn't wake the children! Somehow, doing it silently is supposed to be more kind.

One other popular means of retaliation today is *peer recruitment*. If you hurt me, I'm going to hurt you by turning as many people against you as I can. When husbands and wives separate they often start recruiting friends into their camps.

We have many clever ways to react in hostility toward those who are angry with us. Some soldiers in Korea had a Korean houseboy in their apartment. They kept playing pranks on him. They nailed his shoes to the floor, smeared grease on the doorknobs, and put a bucket of water over the door so that when he came in he got doused with water. But the houseboy was always compliant and he never retaliated. Eventually, they felt guilty and apologized.

He said, "You mean, no more shoes nailed to floor?"

"No, we're not going to do that any more."

"No more grease on doorknob?"

"No, we're not going to do that any more."

"No more water over door?"

"No. No more."

"Okay," he said. "No more spitting in soup."

We have all kinds of clever ways to retaliate.

Apology

"Those who were standing near Paul said, 'You dare to insult God's high priest?'" Paul immediately apologized. He said, "I did not realize that he was the high priest" (Acts 23:4, 5). Some people suggest that Paul was being sarcastic, saying, "I can't believe a man who would talk like that could be the high priest." But I think his apology was genuine. To me it suggests that Paul had poor eyesight.

Elsewhere Paul wrote that he had "a thorn in the flesh" that he had asked God three times to remove, but God said no. He had a physical infirmity that kept him humble. It would be humbling not to be able to see very well and to have to depend on other people all the time. When Paul concluded his letter to the Galatians, he wrote a portion of the letter himself instead of dictating it to a secretary. He said, "See what large letters I use as I write to you with my own hand!" (Galatians 6:11)

In Paul's younger years he had aspired to be a member of the Sanhedrin. He would have recognized the protocol of dealing with the high priest. I think that when he heard a voice say, "Strike him in the mouth," he didn't realize it was the high priest. When he realized what he had done, he apologized, quoting Scripture—"Do not speak evil about the ruler of your people" (Acts 23:5).

Even though Paul did not respect the man who held the office, he had a responsibility to respect the office itself. It's still that way today. God ordained parents to rule the home, judges and governors and presidents to rule the nations, and leaders to rule the church. You may not always agree with everything those leaders do, and you might not respect the life of everyone who is a leader, but as a Christian you still must have a spirit of submission to their leadership. "Obey your leaders and submit to their authority. They keep watch over you as men who must give an account. Obey them so that their work will be a joy, not a burden, for that would be of no advantage to you" (Hebrews 13:17).

The idea of having a submissive spirit towards leadership goes against our pride and against the defiant spirit of this age, but then again, the Christian represents a counterculture. He is to respect those in authority. Paul didn't respect the man holding the office, but he respected the office, so he apologized for what he had said.

It's hard to admit it when you're wrong. In one episode of *Happy Days* years ago, The Fonz had to admit that he was wrong. It was difficult for him, because it shattered his image of always being cool and having it all together. He just couldn't get the words out of his mouth. He said, "I was wrr—I was wrr—wrong."

Do those words get stuck in your throat sometimes? If you are a proud person, you can go to your grave protecting your dignity, and all the while never be restored to a right relationship. Some of you are alienated from former friends, but your pride keeps you from saying, "I was wrong. I'm sorry."

Paul's apology shows us that you don't have to be 100% in the wrong to need to apologize. Paul was just 1% wrong, but he said he was wrong. Whatever your part in the alienation is, you need to apologize for that part without qualification. It takes a big person to go ahead and say, "I was wrong, I'm sorry," without wording it in such a way that demands a reciprocal apology by the other person.

We're clever in doing that. We say, "Well, I'll admit that *some* of it was my fault." (Will you respond by saying that some of it was your fault?) Or we say, "I'll admit that my reaction to what *you did* was not right." Or better still, "I've been praying about this matter, and I think I need to confess that some of it is my fault." (In other words, "If you had prayed about it like I did, you would have come to me a long time ago.") It takes a big person to be able to apologize without a qualifier. Paul said, "I shouldn't have done that," and he stopped.

The tone of an apology is important. When someone angrily says, "Well, *forgive* me!" that hardly reflects a repentant spirit. Jesus said, "If you are offering your gift at the altar and there remember that your brother has something against you, leave your gift there in front of the altar. First go and be reconciled to your brother; then come and offer your gift" (Matthew 5:23, 24). In God's process of worship and forgiveness, He wants us to confess openly our sins, not just to Him but also to the person we have wronged. That takes humility and courage, but we benefit from this practice because we no longer feel guilt or that barrier between us and the other person.

As the prodigal son marched home in humility, he rehearsed his apology: "Father, I have sinned against heaven and against you. I am no longer worthy to be called your son; make me like one of your hired men" (Luke 15:18, 19). He was so broken in spirit and so sincere in apology that the father interrupted the confession. It wasn't necessary.

I have to admit that at times I have reversed this process in my home after a harsh confrontation with one of my boys. I feel badly about it later. A couple of times I have gone into their room when they're pretending to be asleep. I sat down on the edge of the bed and said, "Son, your dad was wrong, and I want you to know I'm sorry."

Each time they said, "That's okay, Dad." I wanted them to say, "I was wrong, too," but they just say, "That's okay, Dad." But the embrace that follows and the reconciliation is worth whatever pride I had to swallow.

Cliff Barrows said, "There are twelve words that hold a relationship together. They are "I was wrong," "I am sorry," "Please forgive me," and "I love you." Is there somebody to whom you need to speak these words soon?

Avoidance

An apology, regardless of how sincere it is, does not automatically resolve conflict. These people still hated him. They still wanted to kill him. They were not ready to apologize for their wrongdoing. Paul had to find some way to avoid the situation altogether, so he tried a clever maneuver. "Paul, knowing that some of them were Sadducees [that's the liberal party, who didn't believe in the supernatural] and the others Pharisees [that's the conservative party, who believed in life after death], called out in the Sanhedrin, 'My brothers, I am a Pharisee, the son of a Pharisee. I stand on trial because of my hope in the resurrection of the dead'" (Acts 23:6). That would be like standing up in the U.S. Senate and saying, "I'm a Republican. I'm really on trial today because I oppose big government." Paul deliberately tried to divide the court and get a mistrial so he could get out of there.

He was successful. "When he said this, a dispute broke

out between the Pharisees and the Sadducees, and the assembly was divided.... There was a great uproar.... The dispute became so violent that the commander was afraid Paul would be torn to pieces by them. He ordered the troops to go down and take him away from them by force and bring him into the barracks" (vv. 7-10).

The next day, Paul's nephew came and told him about a plot to kill him. Forty men had plotted to assassinate Paul. They had vowed not to eat until Paul was dead. They were going to request that he be brought back to the Sanhedrin, lie in wait along the way, and kill him before he got there.

Paul told his nephew to take the message to the Roman commander immediately. When the commander was informed of the plot, he ordered that 470 soldiers escort Paul to the city of Caesarea under cover of darkness that night. They put him on a horse and rode him out of Jerusalem at nine o'clock. At Caesarea they hoped he would get a fair trial.

We can't usually leave the city when we have a confrontation with people, but there are other ways to avoid angry conflict. The first is the easiest: *Overlook the offense.*

"A man's wisdom gives him patience; it is to his glory to overlook an offense" (Proverbs 19:11). A wise man doesn't let his feelings get hurt easily. A wise person is patient with a thoughtless world. Shallow people wear their feelings on their sleeve and make a federal case out of nothing. There is as much suffering caused in this world by those who take an offense as by those who give it.

A man told me about going to visit his mother after his father died. Often she would say to him, "Maurice, you don't love me very much, do you?"

"Why do you say that, Mom?" he'd ask.

"You hardly ever come to visit me," she would say.

It would have been easy, he said, to take offense at that and begin to banter back and forth with his mother, but instead he'd say, "Mom, you're really lonely, aren't you? You miss Dad, don't you?" It is a wise person who learns to overlook an offense.

Somebody said, "Maturity is moving from a thin skin and a hard heart to a soft heart and a tough skin." Don't wear your feelings on your sleeve, because if you get offended easily you react in hostility. You can paint yourself into a corner where you can't get out. It's been said, "Anger gets you in trouble and pride keeps you there." I've been sorry for things I've said impulsively, but I've hardly ever been sorry for my silence. Overlook the offense.

Second, there are times you need to *back off from the relationship*. Paul recognized that there was no way out of this problem, so he just got out of town. There are some conflicts we can't resolve with an apology and we just need to remove ourselves from the confrontation.

Joyce Landorf, in her book, *Irregular People,* suggests that we all have some people with whom we have constant personality clashes. No matter how hard we try, we just can't please them. We don't get along.

Now what do you do if you've made every effort and apologized and tried to be nice, but the person still is alienated from you? You can walk on eggshells around that person and baby them and be phony-nice to them, but I think you're better off, once you've done what you could, to continue to be polite but seek a close relationship elsewhere. That's not always easy to do. There's a little limerick that says, "He who has a thousand friends has not a friend to spare, but he who has one enemy meets him everywhere." As kindly and effectively as possible, back off the relationship. Romans 12:18 says, "If it is possible, as far as it depends on you, live at peace with everyone." But it may not always be possible, and it may not always depend on you.

James Garfield was elected President in 1880. Six months after that he was shot in the back with a revolver. He was taken to a doctor, who tried to probe the bullet hole with his little finger to find the bullet. He couldn't find it, so he took out a silver-tipped probe and went in a little more deeply to find that piece of metal. But he still couldn't find it. Garfield never lost consciousness. He was taken to Washington, D.C., where teams of doctors kept probing to find the bullet, but they couldn't find it. Alexander Graham Bell was called in out of desperation. He probed the wound looking for the bullet, but he also failed.

Garfield kept getting weaker and weaker. He survived through July and August, but in September he died. He did not die of the bullet wound. He died of the infection. The constant probing of that wound, intended to help him, really resulted in Garfield's destruction.

Some emotional wounds are like that, too. The best way to handle an emotional wound is to identify the source and correct it. But some wounds are so complex and go so deep that you can't get at the source. You're better off just letting them heal during the course of time.

The third way to avoid hostility is to *express kindness to the offender.* "Do not repay anyone evil for evil," it says in the book of Romans. "Be careful to do what is right in the eyes of everybody.... Do not take revenge, my friends, but leave room for God's wrath, for it is written: 'It is mine to avenge; I will repay,' says the Lord. On the contrary: 'If your enemy is hungry, feed him; if he is thirsty, give him something to drink. In doing this, you will heap burning coals on his head'" (Romans 12:17, 19, 20).

That doesn't mean you're going to get even because he's going to burn. In that day, if you didn't have a fire you would go next door to your neighbor and borrow some of his coals. He would put the coal in a clay jar, which you would carry home on your head. If your neighbor heaped burning coals in the jar, that was an act of kindness.

"Do not be overcome by evil, but overcome evil with good" (Romans 12:21). The best way to respond to the anger leveled against you is by finding some way to express kindness to the person who has offended you. If you do, some may say, "That's a sign of weakness; that's admitting defeat." But just the opposite is true—it's a sign of strength of character, an ultimate victory in Jesus Christ.

Tony Campolo says that he watched the newsreel of Martin Luther King and his followers going across a bridge during the march on Selma, Alabama. The camera focused on the National Guardsmen and the police on the other side of that bridge, armed with their helmets and their clubs and their guns. There was no question who was going to win the confrontation. Martin Luther King and his followers knelt on the bridge. As the militia came to arrest them, some of them lost control and began to wield their clubs and spill blood. But King and his followers did not retaliate. Campolo said, "When I saw that, I knew that Martin Luther King had won."

You say, "He won? He was arrested and beaten up!" But he won the support and sympathy of the American people. He proved that love is still stronger than hate, forgiveness is better than retaliation, and the meek still do inherit the earth.

Many of our problems could be resolved if we had the courage to emulate the example of Jesus. Men lashed out unfairly in anger against Him. They beat Him and crucified Him. He could have retaliated; with one word He could have called 10,000 angels to come and blast this planet into oblivion in seconds. But He responded in kindness, saying, "Father, forgive them; for they know not what they do" (Luke 23:34, KJV).

He offers that same forgiveness to you and me today, regardless of what we have done. We need to apologize, confess, and repent. When we do, He doesn't make us pay. He says, "I bury your sins in the deepest sea and I remember them no more." But He does ask that we become a special people, that we forgive others the way He has forgiven us.

Courage to Stand Alone

Acts 24:1-21

MY FRIEND LEE Skaags served on the local Human Rights Commission when it wrestled with the question of human rights for homosexuals. Should homosexuals be permitted to teach in our schools, adopt children, operate day care centers, and have every other privilege of a free society? That question would have been easy to answer 25 years ago, but traditional values are rapidly eroding.

Lee took a stand in the 15-member commission that homosexuals *should not* be granted equal rights. He argued first that there was a health threat. AIDS is a serious epidemic whose source is homosexuality. We need to think about quarantine rather than exposure. He also presented the moral reason. Certain choices of behavior result in the forfeiting of human rights because they are a threat to the well-being of others. If a person chooses to be a drunk, he may lose his right to drive an automobile. A responsible society has to protect its citizens from potentially dangerous people. Homosexuals pose a threat both to the health and the moral standards of our community.

Third, he presented a biblical objection. "If a man lies with a man as one lies with a woman, both of them have done what is detestable" (Leviticus 20:13). In the Old Testament that sin carried the death penalty. In 1 Corinthians 6:9, 10 we are warned that the unrepentant homosexual will not inherit the kingdom of God.

Although his position was based on sound Christian and moral principles, Lee Skaags stood almost alone on that committee (which included a priest and a former school board member). He was singled out by the media as almost the only conservative voice on the commission. His suggestions were jeered and ridiculed by most in the audience.

The Importance of Standing Alone

Lee's experience underscores the important truth that the Christian occasionally has to stand alone. As our society becomes increasingly pagan, we will frequently be called upon to take stands that are not popular with the world around us. Jesus Christ said, "If the world hates you, keep in mind that it hated me first. If you belonged to the world, it would love you as its own. As it is, you do not belong to the world, but I have chosen you out of the world. That is why the world hates you." Jesus went on to say, "No servant is greater than his master. If they persecuted me, they will persecute you also" (John 15:18-20).

An article in the December 9, 1985 issue of *U.S. News and World Report*, entitled "Morality Test," documented the rapidly declining moral values of our culture. The first line said, "Many Americans today are stretching the boundaries of traditional morality." For example, 1,000 Americans were asked, "Is it wrong for a man and a woman to have sexual relations before marriage?" Only 20% of those in the 18-29 age bracket thought that was wrong. Twenty percent! Fifty-two percent of the younger Americans said that they might vote for a homosexual if one were running for President of the United States. The survey showed a permissive attitude prevailing in almost every moral issue.

We Christian people are to live distinctive lives regardless of how pagan our society is. For us, right and wrong are not determined by popular vote but by the God of Heaven, who never changes. He urges us not to be conformed to this world. He reminds us that "Heaven and earth will pass away, but my words will never pass away" (Mark 13:31).

Anytime you go against the tide of popular opinion, it takes courage. It is not easy to stand alone. Peer pressure can be awesome. No one wants to be thought of as peculiar. But courage is the inner conviction that stands for truth, regardless of the threats. Moses demonstrated that when he stood alone before that pompous Pharoah and refused to be intimidated saying, "Let my people go." David had it when he grabbed a slingshot and headed across the valley of Elah to fight Goliath alone. Elijah showed it when he stood against 400 prophets of Baal alone. Daniel demonstrated it when he alone refused to bow down to the idol of Darius, even at the risk of being thrown into a den of lions. Esther demonstrated it when she stood by herself to plead for her people, saying, "If I perish, I perish."

It is important that we Christians muster the courage to stand alone today when it's necessary. It may not be as dramatic as standing before a commission or before Pharoah. Standing alone, for you, may be as simple as saying, "No, I'm not going to go to that movie," when five or six of your peers look at you like you're some kind of nerd. It may mean speaking up in a classroom and saying, "I believe that God created the world," when the rest of the class sneers and smirks. It may mean speaking up at work and saying, "I won't sign that paper saying I've approved of it when I really haven't investigated it yet," and having your superior get irritated. It may mean standing alone in a business meeting and saying, "I don't approve of the ethics of this," knowing that dozens of investors are going to be irritated with you because you pose a threat to their profits. It may mean just sharing your faith in a group of people who aren't very sympathetic. It may mean saying to some out-of-town guests in your home, "We're going to go to church in the morning. Would you like to come along?" when you know they never go. It may mean saying to your drama teacher, "I'm sorry, I can't participate in this play," or to your coach, "I can't practice on Sunday morning. I've got to go to church."

I don't know why the space shuttle *Challenger* crashed, but Rockwell International, where some of the parts are manufactured, recently reported that 25% of the workers there work under the influence of drugs or alcohol. That's true in almost any plant. Another article reported that some scientists warned the temperature was too low when the liftoff took place. From the beginning of the project until the end, not enough people had the courage to speak out and say, "Let's stop this," or "Let's abort the takeoff," because the ball was already rolling. The President was going to speak that night. To abort the takeoff would have cost time, money, and prestige and no one would have known if they were right. But moral cowardice always leads to disaster. It is in the little everyday issues along the way that character is molded and families are solidified and nations are built. It is important to develop the courage to stand alone.

An Example of Standing Alone

Paul stood on trial before a Roman governor named Felix. He would later write, "At my first defense, no one came to my support, but everyone deserted me" (2 Timothy 4:16). Paul stood in this courtroom all by himself. What an intimidating circumstance this was!

Felix was not the kind of man you would want to be your judge. He had begun life as a slave, but because of the political influence of his brother he had been freed. Through pulling the right strings he became the first slave ever to become governor of a Roman province. But he was a ruthless governor. Tacitus, the Roman historian, said that Felix exercised the prerogatives of a king with a spirit of a slave. He had been married three times to three different princesses, and the woman he was living with now, Drusilla, he had seduced from the king of Edressa.

The Jews hated Felix and Felix hated the Jews. Once when there had been an uprising in Judea, he had dispatched his army and killed thousands of Jews. They robbed and pillaged the houses of the wealthiest people in Jerusalem. The

Jews were so irritated that they reported him to Rome for brutality. Felix was, in a sense, on probation by his superiors. William Barclay says that "Felix was a powerful, unscrupulous leader capable of hiring thugs to murder his closest supporters."

The Jews who were accusing Paul had hired an articulate lawyer by the name of Tertullus. We don't know much about Tertullus, but he was the very best they could find. He began his speech with exaggerated praise of the governor. He said, "We have enjoyed a long period of peace under you [that was not true; it had been just a few years since a horrendous uprising], and your foresight has brought about reforms in this nation [history doesn't record any significant contribution by Felix]. Everywhere and in every way, most excellent Felix, we acknowledge this with profound gratitude [Isn't this nauseating?] But in order not to weary you further, I would request that you be kind enough to hear us briefly" (Acts 24:2-4).

"Whoever flatters his neighbor is spreading a net for his feet" (Proverbs 29:5). Tertullus was spreading a net for Felix. He laid it on pretty thick.

Then Tertullus gave three serious (but false) charges against Paul. The first is *treason against Rome*. "We have found this man to be a troublemaker, stirring up riots among the Jews all over the world" (Acts 24:5). You have to admit, there was trouble everywhere Paul went on his missionary journeys. He didn't instigate it, but the people who opposed Christianity created riots. This was a serious charge; Rome would not tolerate disobedience. But it must have seemed odd to Felix that the Jews would arrest a man for being a troublemaker against Rome when they would usually support anybody opposing the imperial government.

The second charge was that Paul was a *leader of an illegal religion*. "He is a ringleader of the Nazarene sect" (v. 5). Rome permitted recognized religions to function in their provinces. Judaism was a legal religion. But Tertullus branded Christianity an illegal sect, implying Paul should be punished. Rome had to take this charge seriously.

Third, Tertullus accused Paul of *defiling the temple.* He said Paul "even tried to desecrate the temple; so we seized him" (v. 6). This charge was completely false, but Roman law did give the Jews permission for the death penalty if somebody defiled the temple.

All of these charges were half-truths. They were twisted facts, but they sounded pretty good when Tertullus, this articulate lawyer, presented them. Then the situation got even more intimidating. "The Jews joined in the accusation, asserting that these things were true" (v. 9).

I once had about 20 people angry with me. They would come to church every Sunday and sit in a section in front together and cross their arms and try to glare me down. When I would say something, they would whisper out of the sides of their mouths, and I didn't know what they were talking about. I would try to say something funny and they wouldn't even smile. I wanted to hide behind the pulpit. By the end of the sermon you could barely see my eyes. They made a basket case out of me. But here is Paul in a courtroom with an unscrupulous judge, a lying lawyer, and a completely hostile crowd all by himself, and then the governor motioned for him to speak. If that had been me, I wouldn't know what to say.

If I were producing a movie and casting the character to portray the apostle Paul, I would pick Peter Falk, the actor who played Columbo. He was a short, stoop-shouldered guy. You almost felt sorry for him until he started talking. Then all of a sudden you realized this person was really sharp. In contrast to the flattery of Tertullus, Paul gave a truthful introduction. "I know that for a number of years you have been a judge over this nation; so I gladly make my defense" (v. 10).

Dr. Lewis Foster, a respected professor from the Cincinnati Bible Seminary, was in the audience for about the third sermon I ever preached. I was very anxious to know what he was going to say about my sermon. He came up to me afterward and said, "Bob, I'll remember that sermon a long time." Isn't that good? We were taught in school as preacher boys, "Sometimes people will bring an ugly baby to you, but don't be crude and say it's ugly. Don't undermine your integrity either. Just say, 'Now that's a baby!'" Paul stood before Felix and said, "Felix, you're a judge." He didn't say, "You're a good judge," he said, "You've been a judge a long time." He didn't undermine his integrity with flattery. "I'll gladly make my defense," he said, and one by one he answered the accusations clearly, courageously, and graciously.

First, he had been accused of stirring up crowds and causing civil disobedience. "You can easily verify that no more than twelve days ago I went up to Jerusalem to worship" (v. 11). Since he had been in Caesarea for five days, he was only in Jerusalem seven days, hardly enough time to start a revolution. "My accusers did not find me arguing with anyone at the temple, or stirring up a crowd in the synagogues or anywhere else in the city. And they cannot prove to you the charges they are now making against me" (vv. 12, 13).

Second, he was accused of being a part of the "Nazarene sect," an illegal religion. "I admit that I worship the God of our fathers, as a follower of the Way, which they call a sect. I believe everything that agrees with the Law and that is written in the Prophets, and I have the same hope in God as these men" (vv. 14, 15). Paul believed that the Messiah had come and had proved His identity by rising from the dead. His hope in the resurrection of both the wicked and the righteous was founded on Jesus Christ. That was not a sect, but the culmination of Judaism.

Third, Paul was accused of defiling the temple. "I was ceremonially clean when they found me in the temple courts" (v. 18), he said. He had come to bring gifts to the poor and his offering. There was no crowd with him, no Gentiles, no disturbance—until some Jews from Asia came and made trouble. Paul admitted that he did create a disturbance in the Sanhedrin, when he called out, "It is concerning the resurrection of the dead that I am on trial before you today" (v. 21).

All alone in this hostile crowd, Paul just calmly and courageously refuted every charge against him. There are two reasons Paul had this kind of courage, and these are the two sources of courage in our lives today.

First, he had a *clear conscience*. If you're going to take a stand for what is morally right, you'd better live morally right. "I strive always to keep my conscience clear before God and man," he said (v. 16). If you consistently violate your conscience, guilt will undermine your courage. Guilt will take the conviction from your voice and the sincerity from your eye and you will not be courageous or believable. Samuel Johnson said, "Shame arises from the fear of men, courage from the fear of God."

The second reason Paul had this kind of courage was that he was *aware of God's presence*. "At my first defense, no one came to my support," he wrote, but he added, "the Lord stood at my side and gave me strength, so that through me the message might be fully proclaimed" (2 Timothy 4:16, 17). Paul knew, when he stood in that courtroom alone, that God stood by his side. Paul plus God made a majority, regardless of how many people were against him. In Romans 8:31 he wrote, "If God is for us, who can be against us?"

John Knox, the reformer, was noted for his undaunted courage. He once had an audience with Mary, Queen of Scots, who was noted for her moods of murderous temper. Just before the interview, one of the advisors said, "Don't go in. She's in a terrible mood today." Knox just brushed off the advice. "Why should I fear five minutes with the queen?" he said. "I've just come from three hours with the King!" If you're sure the King of the universe stands by your side because of your clear conscience and His promise, you need fear no man. Psalm 46 says God is "an ever present help in trouble. Therefore we will not fear."

Contrast Paul's courage with the cowardly evasion of Felix, the governor. Felix was afraid because he did not have a clear conscience. He had brutalized the Jews in the past, and he didn't want to get in trouble with them again. But he didn't want to convict Paul because he would be going against Roman justice; that could get him in trouble, too. So he adjourned the proceedings, saying he would make a decision at a later time.

A few days later Felix "sent for Paul and listened to him as he spoke about faith in Christ Jesus" (v. 24). Paul came back in to talk to Felix and his wife, Drusilla (actually his live-in mistress). If you were Paul and you had a private audience with the man who held your life in the balance and he was living unmarried with a woman (his third such relationship), what would you talk about?

A guest preacher was nudged on the platform by the preacher of the church. "Don't preach against drinking today," he said. "There's a guy in the audience who likes to drink, and he's a big giver." A little later the preacher nudged the guest speaker again. "Don't preach against adultery. One of our deacons has a daughter who has run off with somebody." A little bit later he nudged him again and said, "Don't preach about stewardship. There's a millionaire here who really gets offended if you talk about money." Finally the guest preacher asked, "What *can* I preach about?" The preacher looked around and said, "Give it to the Pharisees! There's not a Jew in the house!"

If you were Paul, what would you preach about? "As Paul discoursed on righteousness, self-control and the judgment to come, Felix was afraid" (v. 25). Paul went straight to the heart of the matter. What a contrast between the courage of Paul standing alone and Felix, who stood with the majority but trembled. Felix interrupted Paul, saying, "That's enough for now! You may leave. When I find it convenient, I will send for you" (v. 25). The one who fears God need fear nothing else. On the other hand, the one who does not fear God needs to fear everything.

Two Lessons About Standing Alone

When you're standing for the truth, be courageous. When the world attempts to intimidate you, have the courage to stand for the truth, even if you stand alone. "My dear brothers, stand firm. Let nothing move you" (1 Corinthians 15:58). You and I are going to be called upon again and again to stand for Christian principles in a society where they are eroding away.

I've observed that these principles are clear at a distance, but they get out of focus when they're up close. If somebody you didn't know wrote and asked you, "My college-age daughter is living with a man to whom she is not married. She wants to come home for the summer and bring the man with her to live in our house. Should I allow it?" The principle would be very clear. You would write back, "No, don't do that. It would be endorsing that relationship. That sets a bad example, to your family and others, of what Christianity is all about. Even if she won't come home, don't let her do that." The principle would be clear at a distance. But if it were your daughter, suddenly the principle wouldn't seem so clear.

We need to have the courage to stand for a principle even when it involves people who are close to us. The truth has to take precedence, sometimes even over relationships.

When you stand for truth against the tide of popular opinion, there will always be those who say, "You're just wasting your time. The ball is rolling; you can't stop it. Everybody's doing it." I'm reminded of the legend about the man who went through the streets of Sodom warning people of God's judgment. People mocked and ridiculed him, and they said, "Why are you bothering everybody? You're not going to change people." The man answered, "Well, maybe I won't change them, but if I keep on shouting, maybe I can keep them from changing me." When you have to stand for the truth, be courageous.

When you stand alone, do so with grace. Do it gracefully. William Barclay wrote, "One thought that impresses me about Paul is that he speaks in his own defense with force, with vigor, and sometimes with a flash of indignation, but there never emerges accents of self-pity or bitterness, which would have been so natural in a man whose finest actions had been so cruelly and deliberately misunderstood." If we have to stand alone, even if we're standing for the right, we often get defensive and angry. Our voice raises an octave, and our countenance tightens up. We lose all sense of grace.

I heard about a man who got up to sing in church for the first time, and he sang terribly. He didn't hit a note. After he was finished, nobody knew what to say to him. It was an awkward moment, and one man of the church went to him and said, "Son, you sang to the best of your ability today. You shouldn't feel bad about that. But whoever asked you to sing ought to be shot!"

Often when we try to tell the truth, we have a hard time doing it gracefully. It takes a special measure of maturity to stand alone and maintain our composure, gentleness, and patience.

About 15 years ago I saw Billy Graham being interviewed on a television talk show. The audience was made up of rebellious, hostile college students who were challenging his moral values. They were angry and they would interrupt Dr. Graham. When he would say something that sounded traditional, you could hear the audience snicker and groan. I wanted so much for Billy Graham to interrupt back when they interrupted him, but he just patiently waited. I wanted him to raise his voice and be forceful back when they were forceful. But he didn't, and today I can't tell you what the argument was about, but I still remember his spirit. People will quickly forget your argument, but they will long remember your attitude.

Leonardo da Vinci once said, "He who truly knows has no occasion to shout." Truth carries its own force. You don't preach the love of God with a clenched fist.

We need to become more and more like Jesus Christ. John 1 says, "In the beginning was the Word, and the Word was with God, and the Word was God.... The Word became flesh and lived for a while among us. We have seen his glory ... full of grace and truth" (John 1:1, 14). When you have to stand for the truth, be courageous, but be full of grace.

A Profile of Procrastination

Acts 24:22-27

AFTER THE LOUISVILLE vs. Kentucky basketball game, I had a wedding just outside Lexington. I was not in the greatest of moods, because I'm a University of Louisville basketball fan and U.K. won. When the bride came down the aisle, even before the music stopped, she smiled at me and said, "Go Big Blue!" I didn't think that was so funny! It's tough to complete a wedding when the preacher walks out at the beginning!

We don't hesitate to let our loyalty be known when it comes to athletics. But when it comes to a more crucial matter like our relationship to Christ, why is it that we want to remain anonymous for so long?

Paul had been arrested and charged with defiling the temple in Jerusalem. His enemies said he had brought a Gentile into the court of the Israelites. They plotted to assassinate him in the Jerusalem jail, so the Romans took almost 500 soldiers and escorted Paul out of town to Caesarea, where they thought he could get a fair trial.

Felix, the judge, knew that Paul was innocent and should be released, yet he did not want to antagonize the hostile Jews. So he procrastinated. Torn between duty and expediency, Felix postponed his decision. "When Lysias the commander comes, I will decide your case," he said (Acts 24:22). Two years later, he still hadn't decided.

During those two years Felix postponed an even more crucial decision. He and his wife Drusilla had listened to Paul preach about Christianity. When Paul talked about righteous self-control and judgment, Felix was convicted, but he refused to make a commitment. Once he interrupted and said, "That's enough for now! You may leave. When I find it convenient, I will send for you" (v. 25). That procrastination may have cost Felix eternity. After two years he fades off the scene of the Bible and out of history. We never hear from him again.

The Importance of Deliberation

Important decisions should not be made impulsively. Felix was a judge in a critical case. A man's life was at stake. He needed to take time to deliberate. It was proper for him to listen to both sides of the argument. Impulsive decisions could lead to tragic mistakes. When Moses saw an Egyptian taskmaster brutally treating one of the Hebrew slaves, Moses impetuously killed the Egyptian. That cost him forty years of tending sheep in the wilderness.

Most of us have made impulsive decisions that we would later regret. Maybe you have a grotesque tattoo somewhere on your body. Maybe you have some worthless stock or a deed for some swamp land in Florida. You wonder how in the world you could have done such a dumb thing.

Important decisions should involve deliberations. That's certainly true in the Christian life. Paul did not ask Felix to make an emotional, uninformed decision about Christ. Felix was well acquainted with Christianity (v. 22). The Christians had permeated every culture with the gospel. Felix knew what it was about.

Jesus had made it clear that He wanted people to weigh their decision before becoming one of His disciples. When a man came to Jesus and said, "Lord, I will follow you wherever you go," you would have expected Jesus to say, "Great! Come on." But Jesus said, "Foxes have holes and birds of the air have nests, but the Son of Man has no place to lay his head" (Luke 9:57, 58). In other words, think about what you are getting into. It is an austere life. Are you willing to pay the price?

On another occasion Jesus said more about counting the cost. "Suppose one of you wants to build a tower. Will he not first sit down and estimate the cost to see if he has enough money to complete it? For if he lays the foundation and is not able to finish it, everyone who sees it will ridicule him, saying, 'This fellow began to build and was not able to finish'" (Luke 14:28-30).

Every time I read this Scripture passage, I think of the castle between Versailles, Kentucky, and Lexington, that has been under construction for twenty years. People say the builder began to build, but he didn't count the cost. Jesus is saying, "before you become a Christian, understand it is going to cost you. It is a lifestyle. It is a commitment of your time and of your money and of your desires. Don't make it impulsively."

I've known people who have come forward on the first Sunday they attended a church service and became great Christians and good church members. But that is the exception. Usually the people who respond too quickly are like seed that is planted in shallow soil. It grows up quickly, but it fades under the heat of summer because it lacks enough roots. A lifelong spiritual commitment merits a period of time for thought, prayer, and counsel.

The Danger of Procrastination

The tragedy of Felix was not one of deliberation but procrastination. He delayed the time to act. Paul's trial was over and the facts were in. It was time to say "guilty" or "not guilty." But Felix couldn't pull the trigger. He procrastinated the same way in regard to Jesus Christ. "I'll do it some more convenient time," he said. When Paul discoursed on righteousness, self-control and judgment, Felix was afraid. The King James Version says, "He trembled." Fear often keeps us indecisive.

I think of three kinds of fear. First there is fear of *failure*. Maybe the marriage won't work. Maybe the economy will take a nosedive. Maybe the church will split. Maybe temptations will drag me down and people will ridicule me. Some people do nothing at all because they are afraid of failure. They are like the man in Jesus' parable of the talents who buried his talent in the ground because he was afraid. He did nothing.

We're also afraid of *change*. Maybe we're not very satisfied with life the way it is now, but at least it is dependable. Security is important. It can be threatening to make a decision to change. Many people remain in unsatisfactory jobs, inadequate housing, bad habits, and dead churches. They complain about it, but they are secure in their complaints and they don't change.

The most prominent fear is fear of *sacrifice*. This may mean the fear of having to be unselfish in the future or just the fear of effort. I think that was the problem with Felix. Drusilla was his third wife. That was another area of his life where he couldn't make up his mind. Josephus said she was a woman he had stolen from King Azizus. Felix was a self-indulgent man. When Paul talked to him about self-control, he just couldn't bring himself to sacrifice some of his own pleasure. Procrastination is usually motivated by a fear of sacrifice. I might have to sacrifice effort or pleasure or time or money, and I'm not sure I want to extend myself that way in the future.

A young man had dated the same woman for seven years. Finally he asked her to marry him. But two days before the wedding he phoned her and said, "I'm going to call it off. I need more time to think it over." You might say, "Better two days before than two days afterward!" But the time to make that decision is long in advance. The girl was crushed and humiliated, gifts had to be returned, and over two thousand dollars had already been spent. Fear of failure, fear of effort, and fear of commitment make people back off.

I think more problems are created by procrastination than by wrong decisions. Most of the time you can recover from wrong decisions. You can admit you blew it and pull into reverse and make the correction. But indecision can immobilize us. It wastes time and saps incentive. It creates a false sense of security, negates influence, and makes right choices even harder.

Think of how procrastination humiliated our country during the Vietnam war. Half the country said, "We don't belong over there, let's get out." The other half said, "If we are going to fight a war, let's win it." But our leaders couldn't make a choice. As a result, it cost us 50,000 lives and who knows how many hundred thousands of scars.

Indecision is devastating to a marriage. If one partner in a marriage is always looking back, wondering, "Did I marry the right person?" or looking ahead, saying, "Can I find somebody more exciting?" that marriage is in trouble. Only when you say, "This is the person to whom I'm going to be married the rest of my life," is the marriage on solid ground.

Indecision cripples a business. If those at the top of your company cannot make tough decisions about advancement or personnel or cutbacks, that business won't accomplish anything.

I think indecision probably sends more people to Hell than materialism and Communism and atheism combined. The devil didn't tell Felix there was no Heaven. He didn't tell him there was no Hell. He just told him there was no hurry.

The Necessity of Decision

"Once to every man and nation comes the moment to decide," says one song. There comes a time when you have deliberated enough and it is time to bite the bullet and make a choice, one way or the other. To delay only makes the choice more difficult and eventually less meaningful. Maybe you miss the opportunity altogether. When you say, "I want to think about it some more," what you really mean is just the opposite—"I really don't want to think about it any more."

William Barclay tells about Agesilaus, a Spartan king who

assembled his men and prepared to go into battle. He sent word to a neighboring king asking for his help in the hour of peril, and the other king sent word back saying, "We'll consider it." Agesilaus replied, "Tell him, while he is considering it, we are going to march."

One consistent characteristic of people who are accomplishers in life is that they are decisive. It is not that they never make mistakes. But they make decisions and go on.

When Cortez landed on American soil, he burned his ships so that his men wouldn't have to think about going back.

Andrew Jackson said, "Take time to deliberate. But when the time for action comes, stop thinking and go on."

Winston Churchill said, "Between victory and defeat there are many decisions, but disaster is doing nothing at all."

J. L. Kraft, who built a multimillion dollar business in the cheese and dairy industry, was asked the secret of his leadership. He said, "When I have an important decision to make I weigh all the facts, I pray about it before I go to bed, and when I wake up, the first thing that comes to my mind I do. And I never look back. That system has worked well enough for me to believe that God is able to use it."

Decisive people get things accomplished. They inspire confidence. They take advantage of opportunities. I'll never forget Jim Pierson quoting the old philosopher who said, "If you have to swallow a frog, don't look at it very long. And if you have more than one frog to swallow, swallow the big one first. If you have decisions to make, make the tough one first and go on."

That's especially relevant when it comes to our relationship to God. You need to count the cost. You need to know what you're getting into. You need to deliberate. But there comes a moment to decide. Elijah asked the people, "How long will you waver between two opinions? If the Lord is God, follow him; but if Baal is God, follow him" (1 Kings 18:21). For goodness sake, make up your mind and get off the fence.

If we are going to do something, there is no better time to start than right now. In 1945 when Robert Lewis flew in that plane that dropped the atom bomb on Hiroshima, Lewis looked back on that mushroom cloud that was ascending from the earth and he knew in his mind the kind of devastation he had left behind. He spoke just six words. He said, "My God, what have we done?"

When I stand before God someday and He looks back over my lifetime and the devastation that occurred since the time I was born to the time I die—a million abortions a year, homosexuality being endorsed, pornography running rampant, people indulging in every kind of materialistic and hedonistic pleasure—I'm scared that He is going to ask me, "Russell, what in the world were you doing?"

I don't want to have to say, "I was thinking about it." I want to be able to say, "Lord, I tried. I put forth some effort. I made some decisions. I tried to help build a church. I tried to stand for Jesus Christ. I tried to stem the tide of evil. I took a stand for truth."

Don't you?

Let's do something. Something big. Even if it is risky. Something right, something positive. But let's do it now.

A Reasonable Faith

Acts 25, 26

PAUL HAD BEEN in prison for two years, accused of disturbing the peace in Jerusalem. Felix, the governor who had detained him, had now been replaced by Festus, a governor with a better reputation. The Jews badgered Festus to have a retrial of the apostle Paul because they desperately wanted to execute him. Paul, knowing that it would be impossible for him to get a fair trial in Jerusalem, exercised his right as a Roman citizen and appealed his case directly to Caesar himself. Festus had no recourse but to send Paul to Rome, but he still had a problem—he didn't know what crime to charge Paul with for such an important trial.

Just then Festus received a welcome visit from King Agrippa, a Jewish ruler presiding over a small area of northern Palestine around Galilee. Festus told Agrippa about his difficulty with Paul, and Agrippa, who was evidently intrigued by Christianity, told him, "I would like to hear this man myself."

A Dramatic Setting

"The next day Agrippa and Bernice [his mistress and also his sister] came with great pomp and entered the audience room" (Acts 25:23).

Imagine the scene. Agrippa came dressed in his purple robe and his gold crown. Bernice was wearing all of her jewelry and all of those status symbols so important to insecure people. Festus, the governor, donned his scarlet robe, and with the drum roll he entered with his bodyguard and all of the colorful legionnaires. The Bible says they came in "with the high ranking officers and the leading men of the city" (v. 23). That place was jammed with everybody who was anybody. All the VIPs were there.

Then at the command of Festus, Paul was brought in. In walked this little, unimpressive Jewish tentmaker with his hands tied. Tradition says that Paul was short, bald-headed, and bandy-legged. Regardless of his physical appearance, Paul had so much charisma that immediately when he walked into a room, every eye focused on him. Paul was filled with the Spirit of God, and he had that kind of power and presence.

Jesus once told His disciples, "On my account you will be brought before governors and kings as witnesses to them and to the Gentiles. But when they arrest you, do not worry about what to say or how to say it. At that time you will be given what to say, for it will not be you speaking, but the Spirit of your Father speaking through you" (Matthew 10:18-20). Paul was not intimidated by his audience. This was at least the sixth such trial he had been through in the last two years. Paul gave a brilliant defense; he just gave his personal testimony. If you give people an argument, they can give you a counter-argument, but if you give them a personal testimony, it's irrefutable. They can believe it or disbelieve it, but they can't argue with it.

Paul told his audience how he had once been a zealous Jew who hated and persecuted the Christians, sometimes even putting them to death. But one day as he made his way to Damascus to arrest more Christians, a bright light from Heaven knocked him to the ground. He looked up and asked, "Who are you, Lord?" and the answer came, "I am Jesus, whom you are persecuting" (Acts 26:15).

Jesus told Paul that He was going to send him throughout

the world to open people's eyes and turn them from darkness to light. And Paul said, "King Agrippa, I was not disobedient to the vision from heaven.... I have had God's help to this very day, and so I stand here and testify to small and great alike. I am saying nothing beyond what the prophets and Moses said would happen—that the Christ would suffer and, as the first to rise from the dead, would proclaim light to his own people and to the Gentiles" (Acts 26:19, 22, 23).

"At this point Festus interrupted. 'You are out of your mind, Paul!' he shouted. 'Your great learning is driving you insane'" (v. 24). Somebody once gave me this definition of shouting: "Shouting is the attempt of a limited mind to express itself."

If you believe in the message of the Bible, some people are going to tell you that you have lost your mind. They will say, "You mean you believe in the creation story? You believe in Noah and the flood? You believe in the resurrection of Jesus from the dead? You believe that someday He is coming back to this earth? You've got to be crazy! No intelligent person believes *that* any more."

If your faith begins to affect your daily life, people will think you've gone off the deep end. They will say to you, "It's okay if you go to church occasionally and if you're nice to people. But when you go to church all the time, when you begin to sacrifice a tenth of your income to support it, when you sacrifice worldly pleasure, and when Christianity begins to affect the way you think and feel and behave every day, you've really flipped out. You've lost your mind!"

A recent *Cagney and Lacey* television program dealt with abortion. Cagney and Lacey, the policewomen, were assigned to oversee an anti-abortion demonstration. Then the abortion clinic was bombed, and one of the pro-life activists was responsible. The person who bombed the abortion clinic turned out to be a woman who was "inspired" by the Bible. The guilty woman was described like this: "She's a serious wacko. Always has been. Always into causes, demonstrations. It's all that Bible stuff."

The message from the media is pretty clear. If you take the

Bible seriously, if you take Christianity to heart, you're going to end up being a wacko. You're going to bomb abortion clinics or something. You're an extremist. Like Festus said, all that learning is driving you insane.

But Paul's response was calm and confident. "I am not insane, most excellent Festus," Paul replied. "What I am saying is true and reasonable" (v. 25). Being a dedicated believer in Jesus Christ is the most sane and rational way of life. It's the nonbeliever, the non-committed person who really isn't thinking clearly. Paul could (and we can) be so confident for several reasons.

It's True

First, Christianity is historically valid. "What I am saying is true," Paul said. Skeptics suggest that Christianity is "anti-intellectual." Mark Twain once said, "Faith is believing what you know ain't so." A lot of people think that science deals with facts, and Christianity deals not with facts but with ethics. But Paul said, "The king is familiar with these things.... I am convinced that none of this has escaped his notice, because it was not done in a corner" (v. 26).

The facts about Jesus were a matter of public record. They are historically true. He lived at a definite point on the globe—Palestine. He died on a real cross. His resurrection from the dead was a literal event. It's not something we imagined in our minds.

Several years ago an unusual meeting took place at Harvard University. Hundreds of students gathered to hear an address by Professor J. M. D. Anderson, Dean of the Faculty of Law of the University of London. Anderson's brilliant address surveyed the evidence of Jesus' resurrection from the viewpoint of a lawyer. He smashed many of the theories that have tried to explain away the resurrection. He closed his address by listing a number of historical facts that would have to be explained some other way if the resurrection didn't happen.

"If there were no resurrection," he asked, "how do you

explain that the Christian Church could be traced back to the first century, when the New Testament says its founder was raised from the dead? Is there any other theory that fits those facts? How do you explain the success of the early church? How did the apostles make thousands of converts in Jerusalem by preaching about the resurrection, when any one of those people could have taken a short walk to the tomb to prove that it wasn't true?"

What changed the apostles? What changed Peter from a man who denied three times that he even knew Jesus to a man who, after the resurrection, openly defied the priests concerning the resurrection? What changed James, the brother of Jesus, who didn't even believe that Jesus was the Messiah, to the place where, after the resurrection, he became a leader in the New Testament church? What changed Paul from a persecutor to an apostle?

None of these things were done in a corner, Paul said. The documents are there to examine. The evidence is there for you to consider. If you cannot accept the historicity of the resurrection, what explanation do you have?

In his defense, Paul asked two questions we need to consider. The first was a *philosophical question.* "Why should any of you consider it incredible that God raises the dead?" (Acts 26:8) You have to believe that either you're here by creation or by accident. If you're here by creation, the God who made life and the God who created the universe can do anything. He is certainly capable of raising people from the dead. If you are here by accident, then you have to believe in a series of coincidences so incredible, it's a lot tougher to believe in them than to believe in the resurrection.

National Public Radio recently reported on a new theory of our origin called "Directed Pan Spermia." The theory of origin called "Pan Spermia" suggested that our planet was hit by sperms that were floating through the universe. When they hit earth, they found fertile soil because of the water that was here. But the new theory, called "Directed Pan Spermia," suggests that aliens sent space ships to earth that contained life seeds.

Can you believe that? You know, if some of these intellectuals ever go crazy, we won't be able to tell the difference! If people are falling for that kind of stuff, then why is it so incredible to believe that the God who created this world can raise people from the dead?

The second question is a *biblical question*. "Do you believe the prophets?" Paul asked. How are you going to explain the Old Testament predictions about the coming of Jesus if Christianity is not factual?

We can't, with all of our sophisticated equipment, predict the weather tomorrow. We can't predict the outcome of the ball game this afternoon. But the Bible accurately predicted over sixty specific events about Jesus hundreds of years before He was born.

The Old Testament predicted He would be born in Bethlehem of a virgin, that He would grow up in Nazareth, that He would come out of Egypt, that He would be betrayed by a friend for thirty pieces of silver, that He would be executed on a cross between thieves, that His side would be pierced, that He would be buried in a borrowed tomb, that people would cast lots for His garments, and that He would rise from the dead. Since the discovery of the Dead Sea Scrolls forty years ago, and with the carbon-14 method of dating, we know that these scrolls containing these specific predictions go back several hundred years before Jesus was born. Compare the predictions with historical facts, and you have to acknowledge that Christianity is historically valid.

Dr. Peter Stoner was the Chairman of the Department of Astronomy and Mathematics and Engineering at Pasadena City College. He worked with more than 600 of his students for several years applying the principles of probability to Bible prophecy. They took eight prophecies from the Old Testament concerning Jesus, and they estimated that the chances of one man's life fulfilling all eight, simply by chance, were one in ten to the thirty-second power (that's one in ten with thirty-one zeroes behind it)! That's why when we see Christ fulfilling those Old Testament predictions, it's just further confirmation that the Bible is true.

Peter said, "We did not follow cleverly invented stories when we told you about the power and coming of our Lord Jesus Christ, but we were eyewitnesses of his majesty" (2 Peter 1:16). Paul said, "The king is familiar with these things ... none of this has escaped his notice, because it was not done in a corner" (Acts 26:26).

It Works

Christianity is reasonable because it can be pragmatically applied. Paul zeroed in on Agrippa. The room was packed. He looked Agrippa right in the eye and said, "King Agrippa, do you believe the prophets? I know you do" (v. 27). Agrippa was on the spot. Everyone was looking at him, and he tried to escape through sarcasm. He said to Paul, "Do you think that in such a short time you can persuade me to be a Christian?" (v. 28). That's the way people do it. They say, "Are you trying to convert me or something? It's going to take somebody a lot smarter than you to convert me!"

Paul responded, "I pray God that not only you but all who are listening to me today may become what I am, except for these chains" (v. 29).

One of the acid tests of belief is its effectiveness. Does it work in practical daily life? A tourist in Chicago was appalled when his cab driver drove right through a red light. "Hey, that light was red," he said.

"Don't worry about it," said the cab driver. "My brother does it all the time."

They came to a second red light, and the cab driver cruised right on through. "That's dangerous," the man said. "You're going to get us killed!"

The driver said, "No, don't worry about it. My brother does it all the time."

Then they came to a green light, and the driver stopped. "That light is green," the man said.

"I know," said the driver, "but you never know when my brother might be coming through!"

Skeptics have tried to explain Christianity away as a delusion, as some kind of psychological quirk. But the bottom line is, it works. The transforming power of Jesus Christ has left positive influences on people's lives for centuries.

In an article, *The Resurrection of Jesus Christ, The Matter of Public Record*, Leighton Ford tells of a vicious gang leader in Harlem who became a preacher. He tells of a savage Indian chief in South America who butchered missionaries, but who later became a leader in the church of his tribe. He tells about a prizewinning biochemist at the University of Minnesota who was converted at the age of 50, and then greatly influenced his colleagues by the courageous way in which he faced down cancer.

I think of the son of Madeline Murray O'Hair, Bill Murray, who was converted to Christianity at age 33. He wrote the *Baltimore Sun* apologizing for the fact that he had allowed his mother to use him in removing prayer and Bible reading from schools. He has written a book called *My Life Without God*, in which he tells about what positive changes occurred in his life since he's come to know the Lord.

I think of a man who had a terrible drinking problem. He had been a kind person, but he had come under the grip of alcoholism and he couldn't overcome it. But one day he prayed, "Lord Jesus, if I'm going to overcome this problem, I've got to have Your help." He took every bottle he had in his house and poured it down the drain. He never touched another drop of liquor.

There are thousands of testimonies like that. Many of us who have grown up in the church do not have that kind of dramatic testimony, but we are thankful that the Lord has prevented some of those problems from scarring our lives. Hundreds and thousands of people have had dramatic changes in their lives that cannot be explained psychologically. Christianity is evident in their lives in a practical way. It has worked. Psalm 34:8 says, "Taste and see that the Lord is good."

It's Needed

Some skeptical people suggest that only weak people need the Lord. "If you're handicapped you need a crutch. If you're poor, you need welfare. If you're emotionally unstable, you need religion."

Some people feel that if you're young, intelligent, wealthy, and confident, you don't need the church and you don't need the Lord. But Paul was young, brilliant, ambitious, and wealthy, and God struck him to the ground. Agrippa was powerful, famous, and indulgent. Paul looked at him and said, "I pray God that not only you but all who are listening to me today may become what I am."

When Jesus appeared to Paul on the Damascus road and said to Paul, "I want you to be my messenger," He knew how badly people needed to hear that message. All people, regardless of how young or old, rich or famous they may be, need the Lord.

They need Him *for direction in life*. He told Paul, "I am sending you to open their eyes and turn them from darkness to light" (Acts 26:17, 18).

A little boy delighted his atheist uncle when he said his dog had just given birth to atheistic puppies. When the uncle came to visit a week later, he said, "I want to see those puppies." When the boy showed him, he said, "What kind of dogs are those again?"

The little boy said, "Those are Christian puppies."

"I thought you said they were atheist puppies," the uncle said.

The boy responded with a smile, "That's before they got their eyes open!"

The nonbeliever has his eyes closed to spiritual truths. All he's interested in are things he can touch himself—possessions, pleasure, power, and prestige. He gives himself to those things. But at the same time he is spiritually blind, because those things are all that matter to him.

I saw a plaque the other day that read, "I don't know what I want, so why am I killing myself to get it?" That's descriptive of many people in our world. They don't know what they want. They're killing themselves working to accumulate things or indulging themselves in pleasure, but it's not satisfying.

But when Jesus Christ comes, He opens our eyes. He gives us a light. We know who we are and where we're going; we have a purpose in life. The Word of God is a lamp for our feet and a light for our path. Jesus gives direction. We all need that.

We need Him *to conquer evil.* Jesus also sent Paul to turn people "from the power of Satan to God" (v. 18). Satan has awesome power. Sin is addictive. The drunk in the city slum and the indulgent youth in the suburbs both need the Lord desperately to overcome temptation.

Michael Ray Richardson was an outstanding basketball player in the NBA, but he was kicked out of the league for two years because he failed three straight drug tests. Here's a man who was making in the vicinity of $300,000 a year, but he could not resist the evil of cocaine.

Only Jesus Christ can give us the power to overcome the temptations of the world. Paul said, "I am not ashamed of the gospel, because it is the power of God for the salvation of everyone who believes" (Romans 1:16).

We need Him *to grant us the cleansing of guilt.* Paul was sent "so that they may receive forgiveness of sins" (Acts 26:18).

Albert Speer was recently interviewed on *Good Morning, America.* "Speer, the Hitler confidant whose technological genius was credited with keeping Nazi factories humming throughout World War II, in another era might have been one of the world's industrial giants," Charles Colson writes. "The only one of twenty-four war criminals tried in Nuremburg to admit his guilt, Speer spent twenty years in Spandau prison.

"Interviewer David Hartman referred to a passage in one of Speer's earlier writings: 'You have said the guilt can never be forgiven, or shouldn't be. Do you still feel that way?'

"I will never forget the look of pathos on Speer's face as he responded: 'I served a sentence of twenty years, and I could say "I'm a free man, my conscience has been cleared by serving the whole time as punishment." But I can't do that. I still carry the burden of what happened to millions of people during Hitler's lifetime, and I can't get rid of it. This new book is part of my atoning, of clearing my conscience.'

"Hartman pressed the point. 'You really don't think you'll be able to clear it totally?' Speer shook his head, 'I don't think it will be possible.'"

A few weeks later Albert Speer died. How desperately he needed to hear the words of Scripture, "Though your sins are as scarlet, they shall be as white as snow" (Isaiah 1:18). How desperately he needed to learn the words of that stanza of "Rock of Ages":

Could my zeal no respite know,
Could my tears forever flow,
All for sin could not atone;
Thou must save, and thou alone.

Nothing in my hand I bring,
Simply to Thy cross I cling.

No one here has been responsible for murdering millions of people, but you may have things in your background from which you cannot find release from guilt. You cannot atone for those things. You cannot erase them from your memory. But,

What can wash away your sins?
Nothing but the blood of Jesus.

We all need Him for cleansing.

We need Him *to have hope in death*. Jesus sent Paul so that people could have "a place among those who are sanctified by faith in me" (Acts 26:18). To be sanctified means to be set apart for a distinct purpose. Every Christian is set apart for the distinct purpose of living eternally with God.

I don't care how rich you are, how young you are, how attractive or brilliant you are—one day you're going to die, and you will desperately need Jesus Christ. He is the only one in history who has ever died and risen from the grave.

He is the only one who can legitimately say to you, "I am the resurrection and the life. He who believes in me will live, even though he dies" (John 11:25). Everybody—everybody—needs that promise.

A wise old man asked his nephew what he was going to do with his life. The young man said, "I'm going to get my college education."

"That's good," the old man said. "What then?"

"Well, then I'd like to settle into a career."

"Good—what then?"

"Then I'd like to get married and have a family."

"What then?"

"Well, to be honest about it, I'd like to make a lot of money."

"What then?"

"Well, then I guess I'd like to retire, I think at a young age, and travel with my family and enjoy life."

"What then?"

"Well . . . I guess one day I'll get old and die."

"What then?"

The young man could not respond. He had made no provision for life beyond the grave.

The world may shout, "You're out of your mind!" but the Bible says, "The fool says in his heart, 'There is no God'" (Psalm 14:1). How can you resist the message of Christianity when it is so true? So effective? So needed? You see, if it is true that God created you (and it is), if it is true that you have sinned and alienated yourself from God (and it is), if it is true that God in His love came down and died on a cross to reconcile you to himself (and it is), if it is true that He arose from the grave to prove He's the Son of God, and you can do it too (and it is), if it is true that He said, "Whoever believes and is baptized will be saved" (and it is—Mark 16:16), then the only reasonable response is to give yourself totally to Jesus Christ right now.

Confidence That Inspires

Acts 27:13-26

"DO NOT THINK of yourself more highly than you ought, but rather think of yourself with sober judgment, in accordance with the measure of faith God has given you" (Romans 12:3).

God wants us to have a realistic appraisal of our own ability. We are not to be arrogant people. We are not to have an inflated view of our own importance. We are not to have an exaggerated concept of our gifts so that we volunteer to do things we are not capable of doing. But on the other hand, we are not to be plagued by feelings of inferiority either. God says, "Think of yourself with sober judgment, in accordance with the measure of faith God has given you."

I think a lot more Christian people suffer from low self-esteem than suffer from arrogance. We get our feelings hurt easily. The slightest offense can take us down to the pit. It wouldn't be that way if we had confidence. We are also easily intimidated by people. We dread having to stand up in front of people, and we'd be horrified if we had to get up and speak to a group of people.

Our lack of self-confidence can be seen in the way we are dissatisfied with our appearance. I was sitting in the lounge of a hospital right by the elevator, where there were several mirrors. I watched as people came and waited for the elevator and looked at themselves in the mirror. Almost no one was satisfied with the way they looked. Everybody had to readjust their clothing or straighten out their hair or smooth out the wrinkles. I didn't see one person who looked in the mirror and smiled and said, "You good-looking devil, you." We don't like the way we look. We are self-conscious about it. Maybe it's because the media has placed such an image of perfection before us that we realize we can't measure up to Christy Brinkley or Tom Selleck. We feel self-conscious and inadequate.

That's one of the reasons *Peanuts* has been a favorite comic strip of so many people over the years. We identify with Charlie Brown, who is plagued by feelings of inadequacy. One day Charlie Brown was explaining his problem to his friend Linus. He said, "You see, Linus, it goes all the way back to the beginning. The moment I was born and set foot on the stage of life they took one look at me and said, 'Not fit for the part.'"

A lot of people go through life feeling they are not fit for the part. But self-confidence is absolutely essential for a successful Christian life. You cannot be joyful or reach your highest potential as a Christian unless you believe that God has placed you here for a purpose and you know what that purpose is. A musician who is self-conscious will not inspire others; a public speaker who is overly nervous makes the audience uncomfortable; a golfer who doesn't believe in his own ability will not sink many crucial putts; an overly timid driver is as dangerous as a careless one. Can you imagine an airline pilot coming over the intercom with a quiver in his voice, saying, "I hope we'll be able to land this baby in Atlanta. Cross your fingers." I want one who says with confidence, "Don't worry about the turbulence, everything is okay. We will be landing soon."

If you are a leader in any field, it is essential that you have a proper degree of self-confidence. Whether you are a schoolteacher, a doctor, a foreman, the president of a company, or just a leader of a small group—people will not follow you if you don't believe in yourself. Many parents get themselves into trouble because they communicate feelings of inadequacy to their children, who in turn lose respect. We need confidence in ourselves to instill confidence in others.

Lee Iacocca, an outstanding leader of the Ford Motor Company and later the president of Chrysler Corporation, exudes confidence. In his television ads he says with authority, "If you can find a better car, buy it." His confidence inspires people to purchase. In his book he says many executives fail not because of a lack of intelligence, but a lack of confidence. "Often decisions have to be made when only 95% of the information is in. If you don't have enough confidence to make the decision, and wait until the 5% additional information is in, too much time has transpired," he says. "The difference is in the confidence to take charge, to make decisions and go ahead."

Confidence is essential for success in the Christian life too. "God did not give us a spirit of timidity, but a spirit of power, of love and of self-discipline" (2 Timothy 1:7). To me there are three enemies of self confidence. First there is *guilt*. When Adam and Eve sinned they felt guilty, lost their self-esteem, and hid from God. Sin makes us feel inadequate and unloved. For example, if you are lazy over a period of time, you begin to feel guilty and your confidence takes a nosedive.

The second enemy of self confidence is *failure*. I know people who have held respected positions in the community who functioned well, for years, but then made one serious mistake. Suddenly they lost all self-confidence. They say, "I should have never become a teacher," or, "I should have never taken this position—I don't have what it takes."

The third enemy of confidence is a *sense of rejection*. If somebody we respect ignores us or criticizes us, then we lose our self-esteem. I talk with preachers who get dozens of compliments every Sunday, but they wallow in low self-esteem because of one critic. Divorced people often lack confidence because they feel rejected; the person who should have loved them the most doesn't want them. Sometimes single people struggle with low self-esteem. They think, "If I were more lovable, somebody would want to marry me."

An Example of Confidence

Paul was able to inspire other people because he had confidence in himself that was rooted in his trust in God. In the eyes of the world, Paul might have been considered a failure. He wasn't impressive physically, he had little money, he had been rejected by people, he was single, he was a prisoner. Yet he had a positive, realistic evaluation of who he was and what God wanted him to do. People followed him. He wasn't intimidated by them. He began his voyage to Rome as a prisoner and he wound up in charge of the ship. A man can't do that unless he has tremendous self-confidence.

When they left port on this journey to Rome, Paul urged the ship's captain not to sail any further than Crete. In the Mediterranean Sea, sailing after September 1 was considered dangerous, and after November 1 it was impossible. The winter storms and cloudy skies made navigation difficult and dangerous. It was now October. The journey had been slow. The ship had harbored in a little town called Fair Havens. The soldiers and sailors on board this ship wanted to go about 40 miles further to Phoenix for the winter, because it had a better harbor to protect the ship and it was a larger city with more activity.

The captain called a meeting of the leaders of the ship. Evidently Paul was included. The navigator, the captain, the owner, the centurion and Paul discussed whether they ought to advance. It may seem strange that Paul, the prisoner, was included, but that shows you leadership is not as much a designated role as it is a confident personality. Paul was an experienced sailor (he had been shipwrecked three times). People respected his knowledge of sailing, so he was included in this meeting. Paul warned them, "Men, I can see that our voyage is going to be disastrous and bring great loss to ship and cargo, and to our own lives also" (Acts 27:10). He was not afraid to tell people what he thought even if it wasn't what they wanted to hear. "But the centurion, instead of listening to what Paul said, followed the advice of the pilot and of the owner of the ship" (v. 11). You can get yourself in trouble a lot if you listen to the experts of the age and don't listen to the voice of God. When a deceiving gentle wind began to blow, they thought surely they could make it 40 miles, so they set sail.

Disaster struck. A sudden, violent storm came whipping down from the island, and this boat—probably about 140 feet long—began to bob up and down, thrashed by the waves. They couldn't head to shore because there was no harbor and they would be dashed to pieces on the rocks, so they let the wind blow them farther out to sea, hoping that the storm would subside. But the wind intensified to gale force. Day after day it kept blowing, and the ship began to take in water. To lighten it they threw the cargo overboard. They lowered ropes under the ship and tied it up like a package, hoping it wouldn't fall apart. "When neither sun nor stars appeared for many days and the storm continued raging, we finally gave up all hope of being saved" (v. 20). They didn't know where they were. They thought they might be dashed against the rocks and drowned.

Only once have I been on board a big ship at sea. A couple of years ago I was a speaker on a Christian cruise ship in the Caribbean. That ship was probably ten times the size of the one Paul was on. We left port at midnight and I went right to sleep, but I woke at 6:30 in the morning, and I was surprised to feel this big ship rocking back and forth. I looked at the DO NOT DISTURB sign going back and forth, back and forth, hanging from the doorknob. I thought, "First day out and we're in the middle of a storm." I got up and walked up to the deck to find that the sun was shining and the sea was calm. So I dashed back down to the cabin. "Judy, you have to get up," I told my wife. "It's beautiful up there." She got up for three minutes and headed right back to bed for a day and a half with seasickness. I cannot imagine what it would be like to be on a small boat in the middle of a storm of gale force winds for 14 days.

After 13 days of this terrible agony, Paul spoke some needed words of encouragement. "You should have taken my advice," he said (v. 21). I think he was just reminding them of his credentials to speak. "Keep up your courage, because not one of you will be lost; only the ship will be destroyed. Last night an angel of the God whose I am and whom I serve stood beside me and said, 'Do not be afraid, Paul. You must stand trial before Caesar; and God has graciously given you the lives of all who sail with you.' So keep up your courage, men, for I have faith in God that it will happen just as he told me" (vv. 22-25).

The source of our courage is faith in God. If you believe that God is at work in your life, then you don't have anything to fear. "The Lord is my light and my salvation—whom shall I fear?" the psalmist said (Psalm 27:1). When I was a preschool child, my mother told me the story of Jesus and the disciples in the little boat on the Sea of Galilee in the middle of a storm. Jesus was asleep, and the disciples were fearful the boat was going to capsize, so they awakened Him saying, "Jesus, help us. Don't you care if we die?" And Jesus stood up and calmed the storm. I remember saying, "Mother, weren't those disciples silly? Jesus was with them in the boat and God wasn't going to let Jesus die. They didn't need to be afraid."

My mother took advantage of that opportunity and said, "That's right, Bob, and you remember that Jesus is always with you. You don't need to be afraid in a storm, either." I have never forgotten that lesson, though I have not always applied it.

Paul had confidence to confront those who were going contrary to God's will. "On the fourteenth night we were still being driven across the Adriatic Sea, when about midnight the sailors sensed they were approaching land. They took soundings and found that the water was a hundred and twenty feet deep. A short time later they took soundings again and found it was ninety feet deep. Fearing that we would be dashed against the rocks, they dropped four anchors from the stern and prayed for daylight" (vv. 27-29).

There are no atheists in foxholes, and there are few unbelievers on a ship (or a plane, for that matter) in a storm.

In the middle of the night the sailors panicked and decided to abandon ship by the lifeboat. They pretended to be lowering an anchor from the bow, but actually they were going to leave the ship and let everyone else stay behind. (I once saw a sign on board a ship that read, "Upon the orders, 'Abandon Ship,' women and children will go first. Follow me. Your Captain.") Paul saw what they were doing and confronted the situation. He told the centurion, "Unless these men stay with the ship, you cannot be saved" (v. 31), so the soldiers chopped the ropes and let the lifeboat splash into the sea. You can imagine the kind of heated exchange that took place between the soldiers and the sailors at that point. I'll guarantee that the apostle Paul was not a very popular person with those sailors, but he didn't care. He had the confidence to confront.

Everybody on board was near panic, so Paul completely took over the ship by both word and example. Just before dawn he urged them all to eat. They hadn't eaten in 14 days. "I urge you to take some food. You need it to survive. Not one of you will lose a single hair from his head" (v. 34). Paul was practical; he didn't say, "God's going to take care of us—we don't have to do anything." He said, "Look, God is going to take care of us; let's do everything we can to help Him. Eat so that you can get some strength."

"After he said this, he took some bread and gave thanks to God in front of them all" (v. 35). In the middle of the storm, surrounded by heathen soldiers, Paul said, "Let's pray together." He was using this opportunity to turn the attention of these people to the God he served.

Then Paul ate in front of them, and "they were all encouraged and ate some food themselves" (v. 36). Nothing inspires other people like a positive example. There's no greater opportunity for you to give a testimony about your faith in the Lord than when you are in some storm, whether it's disease, tragedy, financial problems, a death in your family, or marital difficulty. Your problem puts the spotlight right on you. That is the time for you to have courage in the Lord. Your testimony at such times can be more effective than during years of ordinary living. Paul had a calm spirit in the midst of turmoil.

As he predicted, everyone survived. "When daylight came, they did not recognize the land, but they saw a bay with a sandy beach, where they decided to run the ship aground.... They hoisted the foresail to the wind and made for the beach. But the ship struck a sandbar and ran aground. The bow stuck fast and would not move, and the stern was broken to pieces by the pounding of the surf" (vv. 39-41). At this critical point, the soldiers planned to kill all the prisoners, because if the prisoners escaped they would lose their own lives. But the centurion wanted to spare Paul's life. He ordered everyone who could swim to jump overboard and swim to shore, and those who couldn't swim to grab hold of a plank or a piece of the ship and make their way the best they could. In this way everyone reached land safely.

Paul's confidence wasn't pretense. His predictions came true. He wasn't faking a vision from God. What he said came to pass, and everyone was spared because of God's providence and because of Paul's confidence.

Developing Self-Confidence as Christians

If you are going to develop self-confidence, *repent of your self-centeredness*. When God appeared to Moses in the burning bush and said, "I want you to go lead the children of Israel out of Egypt," Moses felt inadequate. He said, "Not me, Lord, get somebody else. I can't do it. I am not a good speaker; they won't listen to me." The Bible didn't say God was pleased with Moses' humility. It says that the wrath of God was kindled against Moses because of his lack of faith. A sense of inadequacy is not humility. It is a lack of faith. Moses did not care so much about the million slaves in Egypt as he did about preserving his own life.

Don't rationalize inferiority as humility. Don't excuse

yourself by saying, "That's just the way I am. I can't change." Inferiority is self-centeredness. It is egotism. It means, "I care mostly about me." But God is in the business of changing people. He gave Moses confidence by giving him miraculous power. He brought about humility in Paul with a thorn in the flesh. He changed them and He can change us, if we will repent of our self-centeredness.

One wonderful young woman was so shy she never talked to anybody. She said, "When I graduated from high school I don't think three people knew my name. But when I went off to college," she said, "I realized I could not go the rest of my life intimidated by people. I had to learn to talk to people." She befriended somebody who had self-confidence, and that association was a great help. She forced herself to talk. She developed her personality and leadership ability and she became the president of a small college. Now she is working with the University of Louisville in a leadership capacity. She has a vibrant personality. She has been influential in bringing dozens of people to her church. God can change us if we will repent and begin to let Him work in our lives.

Second, *accept yourself as God made you.* So many people wallow in low self-esteem because they don't like their appearance. They're too short, or they're bald, or they're too fat, or they've got a big nose, or they've got wrinkles, or they're skinny, or they're not as talented musically or athletically as somebody else. God is our designer. He made us for specific purposes just as we are. Isaiah 44:2 says that God formed us from our mother's womb. If there are some things about our appearance we can improve upon, we ought to go to work on those things. But otherwise, accept what you are as God's design for you. He knew what He was doing. He has you looking like that for a specific purpose, believe it or not.

Tim Hansel tells us about Mark Speckman, a man born without any hands. Rather than feeling inadequate and sorry for himself all of his life, he just used his handicap in a positive way. He has a great sense of humor and self-confidence. Hansel said he and Speckman were shopping in a supermarket when two little boys came and looked at him.

"Mister, what happened to your hands?" they asked.

Speckman looked down at the ends of his arms and gasped, "I don't know! I must have lost them in the cereal boxes!" He began to pull out cereal boxes, and those little boys began to pull cereal boxes out all over the floor looking for his hands. Then Speckman said, "I know—I just washed my hands in the restroom!" He and the two little boys dashed to the restroom looking for Mark's hands.

Mark Speckman was once a college all-American football player. He said he used to love it when the referees called him for holding. He'd go up to the referee and hold out his arms and say, "What was that call?" The referee would say, "It wasn't my call, son—somebody else."

There may be something about your body or your appearance that you are not crazy about, but God made you for a specific purpose. Paul was not impressive physically. He had a physical handicap, but he didn't let it intimidate him. He still had confidence.

Third, *concentrate on your gifts.* "Do not think of yourself more highly than you ought, but rather think of yourself with sober judgment, in accordance with the measure of faith God has given you" (Romans 12:3). God has given each of us different gifts. We are not all brilliant; we are not all musically inclined; we are not all athletically gifted; we are not all leaders; we are not all teachers; but God has given every one of us at least one gift. The secret of confidence is focusing on that gift, developing it, and rejoicing in the gifts He has given other people.

A little boy made his way to the ball park with a ball and bat. As he went he kept saying, "I'm the greatest hitter in the world. I'm the greatest hitter in the world." He got to the empty ball park, threw the ball into the air, swung the bat, and missed. Strike one.

He said, "I'm the greatest hitter in the world." He threw the ball up a second time, swung, and missed. Strike two.

"Only takes one," he said. "I'm the greatest hitter in the

world." He threw the ball a third time and missed again.

There was a long pause.

He said, "I'm the greatest pitcher in the world. I just struck out the greatest hitter!"

We all have different gifts. You need to find out what your gift is and be confident in that and rejoice in it.

Finally, and most important, *forget yourself in service to others*. Paul wasn't concerned about what people thought about him. He was concerned about what God thought about him. Quit worrying so much about what people think, find some people you can help, and find out what God wants you to do. If you worry too much about what people think of you, you'd probably be disappointed to find out how *seldom* they did.

I read an article the other day about Ron Harper, the all-American basketball player at Miami of Ohio. He was so insecure as a child that he had a terrible stuttering problem. He excelled in basketball, but he hated to be asked questions by the media because it was so embarrassing. He decided to work on it. Just recently he befriended a third-grade boy in his community who has a terrible stuttering problem. He visits that grade schooler two or three times a week and tries to help him overcome his problem. The little boy idolizes Ron Harper, and by helping him, Ron Harper has helped himself. He has become quite articulate. The media loves to interview him because of his sincerity and the growth that he has demonstrated. By helping somebody else, he helped himself.

Jesus said, "Whoever finds his life will lose it, and whoever loses his life for my sake will find it" (Matthew 10:39).

Paul could be confident because he believed in God and he knew that God believed in him. God believes in you, too. While you were yet a sinner He valued you so highly that Christ came to die for you. How can you lack confidence when your heavenly Father is the owner of the universe? You ought to be able to say with Paul, "I can do everything through him who gives me strength" (Philippians 4:13).

Faithful Unto Death

Acts 28:1-10

SOCIOLOGIST DANIEL YANKELOVICH has written an interesting commentary on our times in a recent book called *New Rules*. It's not a Christian book, but the conclusions that are drawn about our society's lack of commitment are right on target. He says that those under 40 have been trained in a philosophy of self-fulfillment, consciousness-raising and self-actualization to the point where young people in particular are lacking in commitment. The number one major in almost all of our universities today is "undesignated." The favorite phrase of today's college student is, "I'm leaving all my options open." The general attitude today is "I will be faithful as long as my needs are being met, but when I'm not fulfilled, I'll get out."

Yankelovich says the lack of perseverance stems from the lack of absolutes in our culture. Since all values are self-determined, what matters most is how I feel at the moment. Our generation is inclined to drop anything once it becomes unpleasant or avoid any responsibility that hints at a long-term commitment. Yankelovich makes this assessment: "As long as you try to keep all of your options open, you'll never be happy. Failure to commit one's self to a life task, or to a relationship, or to a lifestyle is a dead end."

I think he is right. Our generation is weak on follow-through. Old fashioned words like commitment, loyalty, duty, perseverance, and discipline have faded away. They've been replaced by phrases like burnout, mid-life crisis, runaway wife, finding myself, gearing down. Dieting is a discipline, so when it gets tough, we quit. Finishing school is a hassle, so we bail out. Sticking with the job becomes unpleasant, so we start looking elsewhere. Going to church regularly gets to be a drag, so we just go when it's convenient. Daily Bible reading and prayer really require discipline, so we quit after a few days. Working through conflicts in marriage is rough, so we start looking elsewhere.

A man named Glen Wolfe holds the record for being married the most times. He's been married 25 times. The longest was five years and the shortest was 27 days. Someone asked him, "Why bother? Why don't you just move in with some of these women?"

He said, "Oh, no, that would be a sin!"

In almost every facet of living there is evidence of a lack of faithfulness.

Jesus Christ calls us as His followers to be distinctive people. He said, "If anyone would come after me, he must deny himself and take up his cross and follow me" (Matthew 16:24). He said, "No one who puts his hand to the plow and looks back is fit for service in the kingdom of God" (Luke 9:62). He also said we are to be faithful unto death, so that we'll receive a crown of life. Though we've all quit tasks at times that we should not have, we need to think again and again about the importance of sticking with the project until it's done.

Cavitt Robert said, "Maturity is the ability to stay with a resolution long after the mood in which the resolution was made has left." We need to talk about "hanging in there" when the excitement and fun fade into discipline, routine, and courage. "Let us not become weary in doing good, for at the proper time we will reap a harvest if we do not give up" (Galatians 6:9).

In this matter of faithfulness the apostle Paul again serves as a good example for us. We have come to the last chapter in Paul's life. He was 60 or 62 years of age at this point. He had the right, if anybody ever did, to say, "Boy, I'm going to gear down in the final years of my life." Listen to Paul's assessment of what he has gone through. It's almost exhausting just to read this: "I have worked much harder, been in prison more frequently, been flogged more severely, and been exposed to death again and again. Five times I received from the Jews the forty lashes minus one. Three times I was beaten with rods, once I was stoned, three times I was shipwrecked, I spent a night and a day in the open sea, I have been constantly on the move. I have been in danger from rivers, in danger from bandits, in danger from my own countrymen, in danger from Gentiles. . . . I have labored and toiled and have often gone without sleep; I have known hunger and thirst and have often gone without food; I have been cold and naked. Besides everything else, I face daily the pressure of my concern for all the churches" (2 Corinthians 11:23-28).

If anybody ever had the right to say, "It's time to turn the reins over to a younger person. Just let me fade away for the final years of my life," Paul had that right. But Paul was faithful and enthusiastic right up to the end.

Patiently Serving

Paul and the other passengers had been shipwrecked on an island called Malta. The two incidents recorded here demonstrate that Paul was still patiently ministering to people.

When the natives built a fire, Paul gathered a pile of brushwood to help them. Paul didn't have to do that. He was cold and wet and the natives were building the fire for the shipwrecked people. But Paul was one of those individuals who had to be active. Paul could sit and talk with kings, but he could also gather some wood for the fire. He was like Jesus, who said, "The Son of Man did not come to be served, but to serve" (Matthew 20:28).

George Washington once saw a corporal yelling at two other soldiers down in a creek bed trying to lift out a log. Washington, on his horse, stopped and asked what was wrong. The corporal said, "I can't get those men to get that log out of there." Washington got off his horse, went down into the creek bed, put his shoulder to the log, and helped push it out. The corporal stood there with his mouth open as Washington rode off, but he never forgot the lesson. Truly great leaders never get so important that they can't get their hands dirty.

"Paul gathered a pile of brushwood and, as he put it on the fire, a viper, driven out by the heat, fastened itself on his hand" (Acts 28:3). I don't know the difference between a poisonous snake and non-poisonous snake, so I am no respecter of snakes. I despise them all! I would not have wanted to be in Paul's shoes at this point.

The natives, realizing that Paul was a prisoner, jumped to a conclusion. "This man must be a murderer; for though he escaped from the sea, Justice has not allowed him to live" (v. 4). There are always people who are ready to blame any problem on sin. "The reason you're having your trouble is that God is judging you," they will say.

One woman just hated taped background music in church. I guess all of us would prefer a live orchestra, but that's not always possible. But this woman was just adamant about it. She complained and complained to the church's music director. Then one Sunday the tape recorder flubbed up. After church she made a beeline for the music director and said, "*Somebody* is trying to tell you something about taped music."

There will always be people saying, "God's causing this to happen as a judgment." The natives saw Paul bitten by a snake and they said, "He must be a murderer—Justice is not going to let him live." But Paul shook the snake off in the fire, and when he didn't die, they reversed their opinion and said he must be a god. The Lord used this incident to immediately focus the spotlight on Paul, so that the natives would respect him and listen to his message.

A second incident on the island has Paul serving again. He went to an estate that belonged to the chief of the island. The man's father was sick, so Paul healed him. Here again Paul served by healing.

When you heal people of emotional hurts, or you have nursed them when they are sick, it drains you emotionally. When a woman in the crowd touched the hem of Jesus' garment to be healed, Jesus stopped and said, "Who touched me?" Peter said, "Master, the people are crowding and pressing against you." Jesus said, "Someone touched me; I know that power has gone out from me" (Luke 8:45, 46). When Paul healed this man it took a certain amount of his attention and power. Verse 9 says "When this had happened, the rest of the sick on the island came and were cured." The reward for a good job is usually more responsibility. The news got out, and the sick flocked to Paul and Dr. Luke to be cured.

What really impresses me about Paul was not just that he was still serving on the island, but that he was serving in the middle of frustrating circumstances. All his life Paul had wanted to go to Rome. He got aboard a ship to go to Rome, but instead of going to Rome, he wound up on this little, out-of-the-way island. He had lost everything except the clothing on his back. The rest was at the bottom of the Mediterranean Sea. He had to stay on this insignificant island for three months. This was a perfect opportunity for Paul to get exasperated and throw up his hands and say, "I quit!" or, "I'm going to wait until something more important comes along." But a great servant-leader is willing to help people even when things don't go according to plan. Robert Schuller has a slogan—"Bloom where you are planted." Paul didn't want to be planted on Malta, but that's where he found himself for three months, so he went about ministering to people.

We all occasionally find ourselves in the middle of circumstances we did not ask for. We didn't plan for our mother-in-law to get sick and move in with us; we didn't plan for the business to transfer us to night work; we didn't plan to have to go to another school or move to another community. But rather than wallowing in self-pity, we need to bloom where we are planted, to minister where we are.

One night at the airport at St. Louis, I discovered that my flight home to Louisville had been cancelled. No other planes were flying to Louisville that late, so I had to rent a car and drive. I was exhausted. I had spoken three times the day before at the Missouri State Convention in the Ozarks, and then I had flown in a little plane from Columbia, Missouri to St. Louis only to discover that my flight home had been cancelled. So I went to a rent-a-car booth. The man said, "That will be $150."

"There must be a mistake," I said. "I didn't want to buy the car, I just want to drive it to Louisville."

He said, "There's a $100 deposit that you have to give whenever you are leaving it at another city."

Then I remembered to bloom where I'm planted. I said, "Thank you, I'd be delighted to pay $150." The clerk detected I was not very sincere!

One of the keys to faithfulness is the spirit of servanthood, even in the middle of circumstances you cannot control. Somebody said, "The shortest distance between two points is always under construction." If you don't learn to go with the flow sometimes, you'll quit.

Tim Timmons tells of a man who bought chemicals from Sears and Roebuck to kill the dandelions in his front yard. The dandelions continued to prosper, so he wrote a letter to the company. They sent him back more weed killer, more powerful that the first, but it didn't work either. He wrote another letter, they sent more chemicals. He sent a third letter, a fourth letter and a fifth letter, but nothing worked. The Vice President of Sears wrote him a letter and said, "Dear Sir: We have no more chemicals to send you. May I suggest that you learn to love dandelions."

You can't do anything about some circumstances. The only hope is a change of attitude. Learn to bloom where you are planted. Love the dandelions if necessary. Paul didn't want to be on Malta, but he looked for an opportunity to patiently minister to people. When spring arrived, Paul and the rest of the passengers headed toward Rome.

The Roman centurion put them on board an Alexandrian ship. Within a few days they arrived at a port in Italy called Puteoli. Paul had never been in this area, but a small pocket of Christians in Puteoli invited Paul to stay a week, and he did. Then from Puteoli, Paul and his team began to walk the Appian Way toward Rome.

When the Roman Christians heard that Paul was coming they walked 43 miles to meet him. "The brothers there had heard that we were coming, and they traveled as far as the Forum of Appius and the Three Taverns to meet us" (Acts 28:15). They were excited about his arrival. Paul was kind of a Christian celebrity like James Dobson or Billy Graham. The Greek word "they came out to meet Paul" was a word used for a city deputation going out to meet a general or a king.

When our church's Bible Bowl team won a national tournament last year, I flew back to Louisville with them. When we landed at Standiford Field, almost 200 people from the church came to greet them. They brought flowers and a banner that read "Congratulations to Southeast Christian Church—National Bible Bowl Champs."

Other people on board the plane said, "We didn't know there were celebrities on board!"

I said, "Oh yes, these are the National Bible Bowl champs from our church. I'm the preacher and that's my son." The Bible says we ought to pay honor to whom honor is due. We shouldn't put people on a pedestal, but it's entirely appropriate that we pay respect and say "Thank you" for an outstanding effort.

The Bible says, "At the sight of these men Paul thanked God and was encouraged" (v. 15). Paul was encouraged by these people. This meant something to him. He didn't slough it off saying, "Oh, these little peons have come out to greet me," or, "You all should have stayed in Rome and witnessed for the Lord." For two years he had been a prisoner. He had been treated like scum, he was exhausted from this hazardous journey, and he wondered if it was worth it all. When these Christians came out to meet him as a special person, that was encouraging to him, and he thanked God for them.

Paul ministered to many people, but he let people minister to him too. Some Christians do well in serving other people, but they're too proud to let anybody serve them. Some people are good at complimenting and encouraging others, but they don't receive compliments well.

When Jesus went to wash Simon Peter's feet, Peter said, "Oh no, Lord, don't wash my feet. You might wash the other disciples' feet, but not mine.

Jesus said, "Peter, if I don't wash your feet you have no part in me."

Peter said, "In that case, give me a bath!"

And Jesus said, "Just your feet."

The mature Christian should be a good receiver as well as a good giver. People sometimes need to give to you. They need to minister to you. If you don't let them do that, they're deprived of the opportunity to express love. If you love people, be encouraged by their kindness. It's a form of pride that refuses to let other people help you. It's love that says "Thank you, you mean a lot to me; you've encouraged me; I'm grateful that you care enough to do that."

I once approached a preacher and complimented him on his sermon. I said, "That was really a good sermon." He said, "You thought so? I thought it was terrible." I thought, "Well, I guess I don't know much about preaching. I thought it was pretty good."

I approached another guy later and said, "I thought that was a good sermon." He said, "Oh, thank you very much, Bob. I respect you a lot, and if you thought it was good, that's really encouraging." That made me feel better. In fact, the sermon seemed better than I first thought after I had talked about it.

Learn to accept other people's encouragement. We have to learn to receive as well as give. Jesus did. When Mary came and anointed His feet with valuable perfume, the disciples rebuked her for being wasteful and impulsive. Jesus told them to leave her alone, for she had anointed His body ahead of time for burial. Jesus didn't make her feel like a loser; He made her feel like a million dollars. To faithfully love people means that you let them love you. Paul did. The people came out to greet him and he was appreciative.

Faithfully Witnessing

Back on his second missionary journey Paul expressed the desire to go to Rome. He knew that Rome was the capital city, the hub of the Roman Empire. If he could capture Rome for Christ, the gospel would spread rapidly. Now he had arrived. He came as a prisoner, but he was not an ordinary prisoner. He wasn't thrown in the dungeon to be served to the wild beasts. Paul was a Roman citizen who had appealed his questionable court case to Rome. "Paul was allowed to live by himself, with a soldier to guard him" (v. 16). Verse 30 says he lived in a rented house. He was under house arrest.

Even then Paul didn't retire and say, "Well, I can't leave the house; I've just got to stay here and watch TV." He was free to have visitors and to say what he wanted to say, so it wasn't a terrible situation. Verse 17 says, "he called together the leaders of the Jews." Paul almost always went to the Jews first, and he made no exception here. He was still doing at the end of his ministry what he did in the beginning.

When the leaders came to his house, he gave them a summary of his case. The Jews told him they had not heard anything bad about him from Jerusalem, "But we want to hear what your views are, for we know that people everywhere are talking against this sect [Christianity]" (v. 22). So they arranged a meeting, and people came out in even larger numbers than before. "From morning to evening he explained and declared to them the kingdom of God" (v. 23). Paul preached and taught from morning to evening. He was an older man now, but still faithful in witnessing.

Some were convinced by what he said; others would not believe. The Bible doesn't say, "they *could* not believe," it says, "they *would* not believe." Whether you believe in Jesus Christ or not is a matter of choice. The evidence is credible; you either choose to believe or you choose to disbelieve. When the Jews refused to believe, Paul reminded them of an Old Testament passage that said some people would hear and not understand, see and not perceive.

"For two whole years Paul stayed there in his own rented house and welcomed all who came to see him. Boldly and without hindrance he preached the kingdom of God and taught about the Lord Jesus Christ" (vv. 30, 31). Paul is still being Paul regardless of the circumstances, regardless of his age, regardless of rejection, regardless of responsibility, regardless of his physical health. He was faithful unto death.

While in prison he wrote this to the Philippians: "Now I want you to know, brothers, that what has happened to me has really served to advance the gospel. As a result, it has become clear throughout the whole palace guard and to everyone else that I am in chains for Christ" (Philippians 1:12, 13). Paul wasn't witnessing only to the Jews who came to visit him and to the Christians; he was talking to those soldiers who were guarding him. Some of them became Christians. Some of Caesar's soldiers became believers in the Lord Jesus Christ.

Luke ends his account here, because Acts is not really a biography of Paul. It's the record of the advancement of the gospel from Jerusalem to Rome. Tradition has it that Paul was found not guilty and released, that he made some other tours, including Spain, and that Nero re-arrested Paul, threw him into a dungeon, and had him executed. Paul wrote 2 Timothy during an imprisonment in a dungeon, and this letter records some of his final words. "The time has come for my departure. I have fought the good fight, I have finished the race, I have kept the faith. Now there is in store for me the crown of righteousness, which the Lord, the righteous Judge, will award to me on that day—and not only to me, but also to all who have longed for his appearing" (2 Timothy 4:6-8). Paul was faithful to the Lord until his death. He was confident that he would receive the crown of life.

Remember just one lesson from this final chapter: *Don't give up until you go up.* There are many temptations in the Christian life to just quit altogether. Sometimes we make horrible mistakes and we allow those mistakes to discourage us. Sometimes circumstances come that discourage us, and we want to throw up our hands and say "I quit, it's not worth it." But be determined to be faithful in spite of circumstances and in spite of your past mistakes. The Greeks used to have a marathon race in which the runner carried a torch. The object of the race was not just to cross the finish line first, but to cross the finish line with the torch still burning. Let's be determined that we're going to cross the finish line with the torch of zeal still burning in our lives; zeal for the Lord Jesus Christ.

The headmaster of Harrow, the British prep school, once invited Winston Churchill to come and speak to his graduating students. Churchill was an alumnus of that school. The headmaster instructed his students to bring their pencils and note pads so that they could record what Britain's greatest man of the century would say. Churchill was given a flowery introduction. He stood before that graduating class and he spoke these words, his shortest speech. He said, "Young men, never give in. Never give in. Never, never, never." And he sat down.

Are you tempted to throw in the towel on a project or relationship or commitment that you know in your heart is right? May I challenge you, don't be weary in doing good, for in due season you will reap a harvest if you don't give up. Jesus Christ didn't give up on us. He was tempted, too, but He didn't keep all His options open. He went to the cross.

Never give in. Never, never, never.